THE CHANGING IRISH
PARTY SYSTEM

RECENT CHANGES IN EUROPEAN PARTY SYSTEMS

A research project sponsored by the European Consortium for Political Research

Project directors and editors

Hans Daalder, Leiden University
Peter Mair, University of Manchester
Mogens N. Pedersen, University of Odense
Rudolf Wildenmann, University of Mannheim

Volumes published

Hans Daalder and Peter Mair, eds, *Western European Party Systems: Continuity and Change*, London, Sage, 1983.

S. E. Finer, *The Changing British Party System (1945–1979)*, first edition, Washington DC, American Enterprise Institute, 1980; second edition, London, Frances Pinter (forthcoming).

Paolo Farneti, *The Italian Party System (1945–1980)*, London, Frances Pinter, 1985.

Hans Daalder (ed.), *Party Systems in Denmark, Austria, Switzerland, the Netherlands and Belgium*, London, Frances Pinter, 1987.

Peter Mair, *The Changing Irish Party System*, London, Frances Pinter, 1987.

Other volumes to be published by Frances Pinter:

The British Party System by Samuel E. Finer.

Additional volumes on *France* and *West Germany* are in preparation.

THE CHANGING IRISH PARTY SYSTEM
ORGANISATION, IDEOLOGY AND ELECTORAL COMPETITION

Peter Mair, Department of Government,

University of Manchester

A statesman is an easy man,
He tells his lies by rote;
A journalist makes up his lies
And takes you by the throat;
So stay at home and drink your beer
And let the neighbours vote

W. B. Yeats, 'The Old Stone Cross'

*(Permission by A. P. Watt Ltd. on behalf of
Michael B. Yeats and Macmillan
London Ltd.)*

 Pinter Publishers, London

First published in Great Britain in 1987, reprinted 1988 by
Pinter Publishers Limited
25 Floral Street, London WC2E 9DS

British Library Cataloguing in Publication Data

Mair, Peter
   The changing Irish party system: organisations,
   ideology and electoral competition.—
   (European party systems series).
   1. Political parties—Ireland
   I. Title   II. Series
   324.2417   JN1571
ISBN 0-86187-370-X
     0-86187-734-9 (PBK)

Typeset by Joshua Associates Limited, Oxford
Printed by SRP Ltd, Exeter.

For Jeanette and Johnny

CONTENTS

List of Tables and Figures   viii

Acknowledgements   xi

Introduction: the Problem of Party System Change   1

1. The Development of the Irish Party System
   The Irish Party System: A Historical Overview; The
   Freezing of Alternatives? Persistence, Change and the
   Relevance of Party Competition   12

2. Do Irish Parties Compete?
   Voters in Competition; Types of Irish Voter; Towards a
   More Competitive System?   61

3. How the Parties Organise
   Party Structures in General; Ancillary and Affiliate Organ-
   isations; Members and Branches; Finance and Staffing;
   Organisational Style; Revitalisation; Does Organisation
   Matter?   94

4. What Divides the Parties?
   Dimensions of Competition and Domains of Identification;
   An Overview of the Data; What the Parties Emphasise; The
   Dimensions of Competition; Dimensions of Competition
   and Coalition Formation; Conclusion   138

5. The Changing Irish Party System?
   The Constraints on Party Strategy; The 1987 Elections;
   Lessons from Ireland?   207

Bibliography   230

Index   241

LIST OF TABLES AND FIGURES

TABLES

1.1	Party share of electoral vote and number of Dáil seats, 1923–44	20
1.2	Party share of electoral vote, index of electoral fractionalisation, and index of volatility, 1948–87	30
1.3	Distribution of Dáil seats, index of legislative fractionalisation, and turnover of seats, 1948–87	32
1.4	Irish elections 1948–87: indices of proportionality for the three main parties	35
1.5	Patterns of government formation, 1948–87	37
1.6	Social class and party support, 1969	39
1.7	Social class and party support, 1977–87	41
1.8	Index of class voting, 1969–87	43
1.9	Voting percentages, 1927–33	49
1.10	Electoral mobilisation: party shares of electorate, 1927–33	49
2.1	Inter-party competitiveness of Irish constituencies, 1961–87	66
2.2	Electoral record of party dissidents, 1948–87	68
2.3	Constituency count in Sligo–Leitrim, February 1982	71
2.4	Aggregate electoral volatility by region, 1948–87	81
3.1	Individual membership figures for Fine Gael and Labour, 1974–86	104
3.2	Numbers of branches of Irish parties, 1948–86	105
3.3	Declared head office expenditure of Irish parties, 1974–85	107
3.4	Declared head office income of Irish parties, 1974–85	110
3.5	State financial aid to parties, 1 July 1985	113
3.6	Number of electors and Fianna Fáil voters by cumann and by region	117
4.1	Coding categories used in the analysis of Irish party programmes and mean percentage of references to each category, by party, 1961–82	148
4.2	What the parties emphasise: leading categories, 1961–82	158
4.3	What the parties emphasise: leading categories, 1948–57	160

4.4   Consensual issues, 1961–82   168
4.5   Factor analysis of the manifesto data, 1961–82   172
4.6   Mean scores of parties and level of polarisation   176
4.7   Inter-party distances, 1969 and 1973   200

FIGURES

2.1   The relationship between economic well-being and the
       electoral performance of incumbent parties, 1948–87   77
2.2   Index of intensity of party identification, 1978–85   79
2.3   Typology of Irish voters   85
4.1   Party movements along dimension 1, 1961–82   190
4.2   Mean party positions on dimensions 1 and 2   194
4.3   Mean party positions on dimensions 1 and 3   195
4.4   Mean party positions on dimensions 1 and 4   196
5.1   Party alignments, 1987   221

ACKNOWLEDGEMENTS

This study has been a long time—perhaps too long—in the making, and in the course of my research and writing I have incurred many debts to friends, colleagues, and to the Irish politicians who are the subject of my work. In particular, I would like to thank Brian Farrell, Tom Garvin and Maurice Manning of University College, Dublin, who first encouraged my research interests in Irish politics. Other academics, both in Ireland and elsewhere, also provided much intellectual stimulus and encouragement over the years, and I would like to thank in particular Stefano Bartolini, John Coakley, Karl Dittrich, Michael Gallagher, Galen Irwin, Michael Laver, Lars Norby Johansen, Dick Katz, Mogens Pedersen and Richard Rose. Ian Budge and David Robertson were the original devisors of the scheme for analysing election programmes, which forms a major party of this study, and my debt to them both is evident. The enormous intellectual debt owed to the work of Giovanni Sartori will also be evident to anyone who perseveres to the end of this study. Hans Daalder has always been a strong source of encouragement, and I wish to thank him most sincerely. I also owe an especial debt to Maria Maguire, for which no paltry acknowledgement can prove adequate.

This study grew out of a larger project on recent change in Western European party systems, directed by Hans Daalder, and I have benefited from the generous financial support offered to this project by the Volkswagen Foundation. I would also like to acknowledge the financial support of the Nuffield Foundation, which to date has funded research trips to Ireland on three occasions, and which has always proved both generous and accommodating.

The staff and leaderships of the Irish political parties have proved exceptionally helpful, and in particular I would like to thank Seamus Brennan and Frank Wall of Fianna Fáil, Dan Egan and Miriam Kearney of Fine Gael, and Seamus Scally and Marion Boushell of Labour. I would also like to thank Bob Hobby, who has always been an enthusiastic partner in our various joint expeditions into the hotbeds of Irish political campaigning, and John Mair, who was always willing to pick up the phone and recount details of the latest political chicaneries. In Florence, Peter Kenneally was always ready to offer a sceptical audience for some of the more tentative conclusions about Irish politics, while Leigh Hancher has proved a constant source of encouragement as well as acute criticism, both of which were essential in the final stages of writing. For this, many thanks.

They are all, of course, absolved of any responsibility for what follows.

Peter Mair, Manchester, March 1987

INTRODUCTION
THE PROBLEM OF PARTY SYSTEM CHANGE

In 1987, the Irish party system was suddenly thrown into disarray. A new party, the Progressive Democrats, which had been launched just 14 months before, polled almost 12 per cent of the vote in the February 1987 election and won 14 Dáil (i.e. parliamentary) seats. The traditional parties—Fianna Fáil, Fine Gael and Labour—which had come to monopolise both votes and seats since the 1960s, polled their lowest combined vote since 1948. Fianna Fáil (literally, the 'Soldiers of Destiny'), the largest of the three, recorded its lowest vote since 1961. Fine Gael (literally, the 'Family of Ireland'), the main challenger to Fianna Fáil for the past half-century, polled its lowest vote since 1957. And Labour, the Cinderella of the Irish party system, which was already virtually the smallest social democratic party in Western Europe, polled less than 7 per cent of the vote, recording its worst result since 1933. At long last, the Republic of Ireland had seemed to join the ranks of the volatile Western European party systems.

The contemporary literature on parties and party systems in Western Europe is bathed in an image of change, an image in which the erosion of traditional cleavages, the emergence of new values and new ideologies, and the increasing importance of new modes of interest intermediation are seen to herald a wholesale transformation of traditional patterns of politics. The wave of electoral volatility which first broke over the party systems of Western Europe in the late 1960s still shows little sign of ebbing, new parties have emerged to challenge the traditional hegemony of their once dominant older rivals, and change seems to be the order of the day: 'Virtually everywhere among the industrialised democracies', state Dalton *et al* (1985, p. 451), 'the old order is changing'.

Except in the Irish Republic—or so it had seemed prior to 1987. Within the rapidly changing universe of Western European politics, Ireland appeared to shine like a beacon of stability and steadfastness. While the post-war period has witnessed some considerable electoral volatility, this was more evident in the first post-war decades, when many other Western European party systems were characterised by a relative electoral stability, while the most recent wave of volatility which has destabilised many other neighbouring party systems appeared to have left Ireland relatively unscathed (Pedersen 1979; 1983). Indeed, stability and persistence were such that the same parties mobilised the vast bulk of electoral support in the early 1980s as did so half-a-century before. For example, over the two elections of February and November 1982, the traditionally dominant Fianna Fáil party recorded an average vote of 46 per cent; 50 years previously, in 1932, its vote was also 46 per cent. Fine Gael, the second largest party, averaged 38 per cent of the vote in 1982; in 1932 its predecessor, Cumann na nGaedheal, won 35 per cent. Labour, the third party in the system, averaged 9 per cent in 1982; in 1932 it won 8 per cent. In politics, as the Irish Tourist Board would have us believe of many other aspects of Irish life, it was as if time had stood still.

Yet in many respects, as I will attempt to make clear in this study, time has not stood still for Irish politics, with the change in 1987 being symptomatic of a more fundamental contingency of partisan support which, in turn, has belied the apparent continuities. In the first place, and most obviously, the apparent long-term stability has concealed a considerable degree of intermediate electoral fluctuation. In earlier decades new parties did emerge to challenge the traditional alignment, even if they finally fell by the wayside. The Labour Party in particular had seen its fortunes fluctuate, drifting from an essentially marginal role in the system to one where even some of its most pragmatic supporters believed it could challenge for an overall majority, and then drifting back to its present Cinderella status. Cumann na nGaedheal/Fine Gael had also seen its fortunes fluctuate, falling from its role as the first party of government in the newly independent Irish state to a position of near extinction in the late 1940s and, in the 1970s and 1980s, recovering to be the dominant partner in anti-Fianna Fáil coalition governments. Fianna Fáil, to be sure, has retained a reasonably consistent level of support through time, but given that Fianna Fáil is but one—albeit important—element in the party system, even this level of continuity should not be overestimated.

Second, notwithstanding *electoral* change or continuity, it will also be argued that there has in fact been a significant degree of change in terms of other dimensions of the party system, that is in terms of party strategy, party organisation, in the manner in which the parties compete, and in both the form and substance of their ideological appeals. In effect, the Irish parties have been obliged to run a great deal in order to end up in the same place—no easy task given the striking transformation of both economy and society (e.g. Litton 1982; Maguire

1985). Hence, even if a high level of aggregate electoral volatility is only apparent as recently as 1987, nevertheless this should not be taken to imply the absence of long-term party system change as such.

The image of change in Western European party systems is certainly seductive, particularly since the main factors which seem to underly this change can be identified with such apparent ease. The undeniable mutability of the class structure in contemporary Europe is thus seen as one crucial factor leading to the transformation of parties and party systems, and, since at least the early 1960s (e.g. Lipset 1964), scholars have identified the decline of the traditional working class and the increasing demographic and political importance of a new profes-sional middle class as critical elements in a process of long-term political change. More recently, and in a related vein, the emergence of a new 'post-materialist' generation and a sea-change in traditional value systems (e.g. Inglehart 1977) are seen as harbingers of a new complex of political interests which go far beyond the remit of the established political alternatives. Finally, the sheer capacity of parties to govern and to act as effective channels of political demands is also seen to be threatened, as the crisis of government overload (e.g. Rose 1980) and a new reliance on neo-corporatist modes of interest intermediation (e.g. Schmitter and Lehmbruch 1979) are seen to push parties to one side and to deem them irrelevant to key decision-making processes.

The immediate effects of these 'environmental' changes are also perceived to be readily identifiable, as are their implications. In other words, not only can one specify the processes which might be expected to lead to a transformation of Western European party systems, but one can also witness the most evident sign of this transformation, which is volatility and change at the aggregate electoral level. Thus, while 20 years ago Lipset and Rokkan (1967, p. 50) could assert that 'the party systems of the 1960s reflect, with few but significant changes, the cleavage structures of the 1920s', a more recent analysis which incorporated data on electoral volatility in the 1970s could argue that these 'significant exceptions ... are no longer few, but constitute a larger and growing part of all European party systems' (Pedersen 1983, p. 35). More specifically, while an empirical assessment of electoral trends between 1945 and 1969 concluded that 'the electoral strength of most parties in Western nations since the war had changed very little from election to election, from decade to decade, or within the lifespan of a generation' (Rose and Urwin 1970, p. 295), a more recent updating of this analysis to the end of the 1970s found that 'the period

since 1960 has been characterised by a substantial degree of change'
and concluded that 'European party systems cannot now be regarded
as inherently stable structures' (Maguire 1983, pp. 91, 92). Given such
clear cause—a transformation of the social and governmental environment, and such clear effect—increased aggregate electoral volatility—it
is not then surprising to find that expansive conclusions are drawn
about the transformation of traditional party systems.

But is evidence of aggregate electoral change a necessary or even
sufficient condition for party system change? More than 20 years ago
Otto Kirchheimer (1966) published a now classic essay on the subject
of party system change, entitled, appropriately, 'The Transformation of
the Western European Party Systems'. Yet while this essay has had an
immense impact on subsequent theorising about party system change,
and while it laid great stress on the ideological and organisational
transformation of parties, it is worth recalling, as Dittrich (1983) points
out, that it scarcely referred to that most popular of contemporary
indicators of alleged transformation, aggregate electoral change. Moreover, as Dittrich (1983, p. 264) also emphasises, even if the most generous interpretation takes Kirchheimer's assertion that catch-all parties
will succeed as a reference to the potential aggregate electoral growth of
such parties, his parallel assertion that other parties will imitate the style
of the catch-all parties implies that these other parties may also succeed
and, in the process, may replicate the original equilibrium in such a way
that the alleged transformation may be barely evident at the aggregate
electoral level. For Kirchheimer at any rate, the transformation of
Western European party systems involves something other than, or at
least something more than aggregate electoral change.

As Kirchheimer's analysis made clear, and as has been indicated
above, it is possible to conceive of a variety of dimensions of change
which are relevant to the study of party systems—ideological change,
organisational change, electoral change, and so on. Yet, to a large
extent, one finds in the contemporary literature that these different
dimensions are either conflated into a general sense of change or, more
commonly, one individual measure—usually aggregate electoral
change—is taken to be the surrogate of a potentially wider range of
dimensions. Thus *party-system* persistence or change is measured in
terms of *electoral* persistence or change, regardless of the extent of
variation or persistence in any other potential dimension(s).

Of necessity, the poor availability of data for effective cross-national
studies reinforces this emphasis on electoral change as an indicator of
party system change. As yet, we simply do not have sufficient system-

atic and cross-national data on, say, the ideological or organisational patterning of Western European politics, to effect measures of change on dimensions other than the electoral, although the data in Budge *et al.* (1987) do represent a significant advance in our understanding of change at the level of party appeals and party programmes. Yet while the absence of alternative data can to some extent account for the widespread emphasis on electoral change, there is less excuse for other assumptions and, in particular, for the simple and essentially unidimensional assumption that electoral change—and particularly aggregate electoral change—in itself means party system change, and the necessary correlate that aggregate electoral continuity means party system persistence.

Recalling Kirchheimer's emphases also raises another problem in the discussion of party system change, for Kirchheimer was quite unequivocal in his stress on the subjective force of the parties themselves in this transformative process. As against this, however, much of the contemporary literature views the parties as objects rather than as subjects, as creatures of a circumstance defined elsewhere, and as agents which at most may respond or adapt to external forces, but which rarely, if ever, determine the political constraints of those forces. Again, it is the seductive image of electoral change which facilitates this siting of parties at the receiving end of a causal change. Something has happened, i.e. electoral volatility has increased, and it is relatively easy to read back from that event and provide a host of explanatory factors, drawn from the social structure, the political culture or from the institutional arena. That the same explanatory factors may also be present in systems which are not characterised by such high levels of volatility is ignored, for the emphasis lies in explaining change rather than persistence, and in treating change on the electoral dimension as the only real indicator of party system change *per se*.

However, it must also be recognised that, in electoral terms, party systems may prove stable *despite* changes in the social structure, in the political culture or in the institutional arena, and that these same party systems may in fact be characterised by change in dimensions other than the electoral. In other words, there is no clear and unequivocal causal relationship between changes in the environment of the parties on the one hand and changes in the electoral performance of these parties on the other. Parties can resist environmental change or find themselves threatened by environmental change. They determine as well as being determined. Yet insofar as contemporary analyses of parties and party systems focus on electoral change rather than persistence, on electoral discontinuity rather than on stability, so also is there a tendency to emphasise the impact of the environment on the parties, rather than a willingness to accept that the parties themselves are possessed of a capacity to mould the political terms of reference of that environment. In other words, the focus on electoral change facilitates an emphasis on the sociology of politics, and a commensurate neglect of genuine political sociology (Sartori 1969).

Even the most cursory glance at the variation in the extent of party and party system change across Western Europe is sufficient to underline the importance of this problematic. To control for any imputed environmental cause or combination of causes of change is to find an immense amount of unexplained variance, even at the simple electoral level (see, for example, the country reports in Crewe and Denver 1985). Parties respond to their environments differently, they adapt differently, and in this sense they exert a varying capacity to *control* the impact of external change. In short, parties are not simply constrained or manipulated by circumstances, but both individually and through their mutual interaction they also constrain and manipulate their own environment (Sartori 1969; 1976).

It is relatively easy to identify the problems associated with an analysis of party-system change and stability (for earlier discussions of the problem, see Mair 1983; 1984). It is much more difficult to advance solutions and to propose more meaningful measures, and certainly it is not my intention to do so in this particular context. Rather, I simply wish to sound a note of caution, for to assert the existence of a process of systemic transformation when as yet we lack a systematic understanding of change at the ideological level or at the organisational level seems, at the very least, quite precipitate. Party systems cannot simply be described as *either* changing *or* persisting, but both change and persist at the same time, depending on the particular dimension of analysis. Moreover, it is also necessary to have a much clearer understanding of precisely those conditions under which party system change occurs, and those under which such change is resisted. If there is to be a meaningful theory of party system change, therefore, we need to build a much wider range of knowledge, and to go beyond simply electoral statistics in order to explore those other dimensions which have long been neglected in comparative party research.

Such a strategy can only begin with the systematic and in-depth study of individual party systems, for it is only by reducing the units of analysis to a minimum that we can begin to expand the range of actual properties or dimensions to be analysed. In this sense, the analysis of an individual party system facilitates a more *intensive* and specified research strategy than could be afforded by a more *extensive* and necessarily more abstract or unidimensional cross-national comparison (e.g. Sartori 1970).

It is in just such a spirit that this particular study of the Irish party system is being offered. Focusing as it does on the strategic, organisational, electoral and ideological dimensions of party competition, it is hoped that this study may be considered as a small contribution towards building a more refined analysis of the parameters of change and stability in Western European party systems in general. Moreover, in analysing the dynamics of the Irish party system, this particular study also focuses clearly and explicitly on the parties themselves—what they do, what they say, how they organise and how they compete—rather than on socio-structural or other environmental factors. In effect, the overriding assumption of this study is that the parties themselves matter, and that they are not simply the creatures of an external circumstance. And to the extent that working with this assumption can facilitate an understanding of the dynamics of the Irish party system, then this study can also be considered as underlining the importance of a genuine political sociology.

The Irish case is also offered as a useful corrective to the rather all-embracing notions of change which currently pervade the literature on parties and party systems (e.g., Dalton *et al* 1985), and offers a clear example of the difficulties involved in the analysis of party-system change. The difficulties themselves can be easily summarised: *Who* does the change concern—does it involve just one party, some of the parties, or all of the parties? *What* is the source of change—does it stem from the environment of the parties or from the party system? *When* does a party system change—at what point can one speak of discontinuity or transformation and at what point does one assert persistence and stability? Finally, and most crucially, *which* dimension of change is relevant—electoral change, change at the level of strategy, organisation, or ideology, or simply change in the mode or direction of competition? The Irish case does not offer unequivocal answers to these questions—no single case study could—but at least it does emphasise their importance.

Of course it can be argued that the Irish case offers virtually no lessons for the more general analysis of party system persistence and change in Western Europe, and that it should be dismissed as a deviant case. Certainly, this is its usual fate. At worst, Ireland is ignored by the comparative literature. At best, it is accorded to a residual category where few of the conventionally accepted theories apply. Irish politics is *sui generis*, concluded Whyte (1974, p. 648), and despite the relative volume of recent political science research in Ireland (see, in particular, Carty 1981; Gallagher 1985; see also Garvin 1974; Sinnott 1984), this conclusion still echoes through the contemporary literature. To adopt Hans Daalder's terms, Ireland remains a *terra incognita* on the map of comparative politics.

Part of the problem in locating the Irish case on the map of comparative politics is that neither of the two main parties seem to find ready parallels in neighbouring party systems. Neither Fianna Fáil nor Fine Gael seems easily classified in left–right terms, for example, nor are they easily slotted into the conventional political families in Western Europe—whether conservative or socialist, liberal or radical, Christian or agrarian. Even the most thorough analysts of Irish politics find it difficult to distinguish these two traditional rivals in any conventional sense. As noted below (Chapter 4), Carty (1981, p. 43) concludes that the two parties 'provide no real alternative to Irish voters on substantive issues', while Gallagher (1981, p. 279) concludes that both offer 'pragmatic images ... frequently not backed up by policies at all'. Labour, on the other hand, is readily understood in the comparative context as the rather soft-centred representative of the European social democratic tradition. But even here there are problems, for Ireland records the lowest socialist vote in Western Europe, and thus appears all the more deviant in a comparative context. The singularity of the Irish case is further underlined by the parties' lack of strong social roots and by their lack of association with any distinguishable social cleavage or social division. This is particularly true of Fianna Fáil and Fine Gael, which are characterised by strongly heterogeneous and catch-all electorates, with socio-structural divisions offering only a minimal capacity to predict voter choice (e.g. Rose 1974). To adopt another phrase from Whyte (1974), Ireland seems to have a politics without social bases, and as such stands at the margins of the more generalised European experience.

If that were not enough, the Irish puzzle is compounded by the long-term continuity of its political traditions, to which reference has already been made, with the apparent stability at electoral level being also reflected at governmental level. For example, in the 50 years and 17 elections which passed between its first attaining office in 1932 and its displacement by a Fine Gael–Labour coalition in 1982, Fianna Fáil had been defeated on only four occasions—in 1948, 1954, 1973 and 1981. Thus while other Western European party systems have been seen to undergo a major transformation, the Irish case could even be seen to reflect a strengthening of the traditional alternatives. Indeed, in the election of 1977, around the time when the hold of such traditionally dominant parties as the Christian Democrats in Italy or the Social Democrats in Scandinavia was seen to be under severe challenge, the traditionally dominant Irish party, Fianna Fáil, achieved a record Dáil majority.

Confronted by a politics which appears free of both social bases and commonplace ideological conflicts, and which also appeared to be inordinately stable, many analysts tended to seek for explanations in history and in notions of historical inertia. The lack of a social identity in politics is thus explained by the fact that the party system initially grew out of the constitutional cleavage concerning the pace at which the new state was to sever its links with Britain, whereas elsewhere in Europe social cleavages tended to be the basis for the initial mobilisation of mass politics. The subsequent stability can also be accounted for in the same fashion, in that the intensity of the constitutional conflict cemented political loyalties on both sides of the Fianna Fáil–Fine Gael divide, and left little room for the mobilisation of an alternative politics. Finally, history also explains the lack of conventional programmatic differences, in that Irish parties are still seen to divide around nationalist issues rather than around the more commonplace concerns and principles of parties elsewhere in Western Europe.

The crucial period was thus that of the 1920s and 1930s (e.g. Farrell 1970; Sinnott 1978), and since then little has changed. It is as if politics stopped more than half-a-century ago, as if the needle had suddenly jammed and the record had continued to repeat the same dull chorus through decades and through generations. Hence the puzzles are solved and the anomalies explained: Irish party politics are *sui generis*, for, as Whyte (1974, p. 648) goes on to suggest, 'the context from which they spring is *sui generis* also'.

An alternative, if related, explanation of Irish deviance argues that both the stability and lack of social identity derived, paradoxically, from an absence of real party politics. Voters are not concerned with political parties as such, but rather with candidates and personalities. Those seeking office do not mobilise on the basis of wide-ranging issues or ideologies—hence there is no difference between the parties—but instead on the basis of clientelism and brokerage. Political appeals in Ireland are thus not orientated to the collectivity, but rather to the individual, and it is not so much that the party represents a mass of voters, but rather that the individual party candidates perform services for individual citizens. Hence, while the party (as holding company, as it were) may remain stable, the real change and volatility can be seen in the rise and fall of individual candidate support. In short, Ireland is characterised by essentially *apolitical* politics. In a society far removed from the communist vision of Marx and Engels, politics had become simply 'the administration of things'.

This study intends to challenge these assumptions and to assert the relevance of the Irish case for comparative politics. Focusing primarily on Fianna Fáil, Fine Gael and Labour, I will argue that the party system has not been overly stable, either along the electoral dimension or along other dimensions; that voters are orientated to parties and choose between these parties on the basis of their policy appeals, their past record and their future promises; that the parties compete for these voters in fairly coherent ideological terms; and that the relative success of the individual parties is at least in part a function of their respective policy appeals, their organisational capacities and their electoral and governmental strategies. In short, I will argue that Irish politics is relatively normal and commonplace, and, as such, is likely to contain lessons for the wider comparative analysis of parties and party systems. Far from being deviant, the Irish case offers a real insight into more far-ranging questions about how party systems actually do persist and how they change.

In Chapter 1, I will review the origins of the party system and attempt to show that the political alternatives were not wholly frozen in the 1920s and 1930s, and that the undeniable evidence of electoral volatility and change suggests that the contemporary alignment derives at least as much from the strategies and independent intervention of the parties as it does from the sheer inertia of history. Chapter 2 looks at the party competition for votes, and argues that there is an increasingly available party electorate which belies any simple notion that the protagonists are uncompetitive, either in the sense that they can take their support for granted or in the sense that voters orientate only to candidates and not to parties. In Chapter 3, I will review the organisational structure and style of the three main parties, charting the recent growth of party Head Offices and the attempts at organisational revitalisation consequent on the need to be more competitive. Chapter 4 looks at what the parties compete about, analysing election programmes in order to assess their post-war policies and in an effort to define the issues and ideologies which divide them. Finally, Chapter 5 addresses the problem of the contingency of political appeals, and offers a basic synthesis of the dynamics of the Irish party system, particularly in the light of the 1987 outcome. Throughout the study I will employ different notions of comparative politics in an effort to show that the Irish case is readily interpretable in conventional terms, and that the organisational style, electoral strategies and ideological conflicts of post-war Irish politics should not be dismissed as simply bizarre. In short, I intend to show that Irish politics makes some sense in a comparative context and that, regardless of their essential lack of social identity, the parties mobilise and relate to their constituencies in much the same way that parties do throughout Western Europe.

There is also a secondary intention, which is to provide some relevant information in two largely neglected areas of party research in Ireland, that is party organisation and party policy. The origins and early development of the party system have already been reviewed in numerous publications, while voting behaviour in Ireland is also the subject of an increasing volume of valuable literature. As yet, however, little is known about how the parties organise, and scant attention is paid to their programmes and their policies. It is hoped that this study can now throw some badly needed light on these neglected topics. In addition, by focusing on the post-war period, and especially on developments since the late 1950s, I hope that this book will help to redress the historical balance and encourage other researchers to look beyond the early and formative years of the Irish party system. As I hope to show, a lot has happened since then, and an understanding of contemporary dynamics is at least as important as an understanding of the divisions of half-a-century ago.

Finally, and as noted above, it is hoped that this reasonably detailed focus on one particular party system will contribute to a broader understanding of the essentially multi-dimensional nature of party-system persistence and change. Precisely because party systems can be assessed along a number of different dimensions—organisational, ideological and electoral—it is in the end almost impossible to speak of transformation *per se*. Given the number of dimensions involved, party systems may persist as well as change, and as this study indicates, they may do so at one and the same time.

1

THE DEVELOPMENT OF THE IRISH PARTY SYSTEM

Irish party politics can be marked out in two important respects. First, by virtue of their apparent long-term continuity, and second, by virtue of their apparent singularity. While the Irish Republic is a relatively new state by Western European standards, the party system itself is old and, some would say, decaying. The parties which have dominated Irish politics over the past decades trace their origins back to the mobilisation of nationalist politics and to the consolidation of the Irish Free State in the early years of the century; indeed, according to Garvin (1981a), it is possible to trace their origins even further back in history to the struggles over land and nation in the nineteenth century. Moreover, despite massive social and economic change in the post-war period, these parties have also persisted to a degree which can only be envied by their more vulnerable counterparts in other Western European countries. Irish party politics is also quite singular in character, in that the initial alignment derived from a struggle over the extent to which the new state would sever its ties with the United Kingdom, and those classic conflicts which have defined the parameters of party systems throughout most of Western Europe—church versus state, workers versus owners, and so on—have always seemed of little relevance to the Irish case.

The combination of organisational continuity and a *sui generis* political conflict inevitably forces analyses of Irish politics back to the origins and early development of the party system; understanding the present is possible only when one also understands the past. And while the intention of this particular study is to focus on developments in the party system since World War II, it will also follow the pattern of other analyses and begin with a review of the origins and early years of mass politics in the immediate post-independence phase. The purpose of this review is threefold. First, such a review is necessary simply in order to introduce the political parties and to trace the broad sweep of their electoral development; second, it allows for a clearer understanding of the nature of the initial alignment; and third, it enables an assessment of the extent to which there actually has been a *genuine* continuity of both party and politics.

The Irish Party System: A Historical Overview

The three main parties in Ireland—Fianna Fáil, Fine Gael and Labour—were born in the twenty-year period surrounding the achievement and consolidation of Irish independence. Labour is the oldest of the three and, like its British counterpart, was formed as the political wing of an increasingly militant trade-union movement. The party was formally launched in 1912, developing into a genuine mass political organisation in 1922 (Mitchell 1974; Gallagher 1982). Fianna Fáil and Fine Gael were created from the ashes of Sinn Fein, a nationalist movement which had been founded in 1905, and which developed into a highly successful mass political organisation in 1917. Sinn Fein spearheaded the struggle for Irish independence, displacing the moderate Irish Parliamentary Party when it won the vast majority of seats in the 1918 Westminster election. The elected Sinn Fein MPs refused to sit in Westminster, and instead established a new Irish parliament in Dublin—the first Dáil—claiming a mandate to govern Ireland as an independent state (Farrell 1971). The success of the Sinn Fein campaign, together with the disruption caused by the Irish Republican Army—the military wing of Sinn Fein—led to the Anglo–Irish Treaty of 1921 which accorded the greater part of the island of Ireland the limited independence of dominion status within the Commonwealth. This resulted in the creation of the Irish Free State, comprising 26 of the 32 Irish counties, which was eventually to cut its remaining ties with the United Kingdom by 1937, and to be declared a Republic in 1949. The Treaty also made provision for six counties in the north-east of the island, that is Northern Ireland, to remain as part of the United Kingdom, albeit with a separate devolved parliament at Stormont, near Belfast.

Sinn Fein had campaigned for complete independence for the island as a whole, and the offer of dominion status, together with the decision to partition the island, was to provoke a split in the movement. One side urged acceptance of the Treaty provisions, arguing that further concessions could be won on a more gradual and piecemeal basis. The more radical wing urged rejection of the Treaty as an inadequate compromise, pledging continued loyalty to the original Sinn Fein demand for a wholly independent all-Ireland Republic. A Dáil vote narrowly favouring the moderate side led to a complete rupture in the movement and to a brief but bitter civil war which was waged from 1922 to 1923, with the division within the political leadership being paralleled by a similar division within the military wing, the IRA. The civil war ended with the defeat of the anti-Treaty faction.

This simple but fundamental division was to give rise to the two dominant parties in contemporary Ireland, Fianna Fáil and Fine Gael. Fianna Fáil is heir to the anti-Treaty faction of Sinn Fein, while Fine Gael is heir to the moderate pro-Treaty faction, which originally called itself Cumann na nGaedheal and which reorganised as Fine Gael in 1933.

Cumann na nGaedheal was the governing party in the new state between 1922 and 1932 and, while working within the confines of the Commonwealth, behaved very much as the government of a wholly independent state, stretching the conventional limitations of dominion status to an unprecedented degree (Harkness 1969; Mair 1978). The major opposition came from the old anti-Treaty faction, which retained the name Sinn Fein, and which refused to recognise the legitimacy of the Free State institutions. Since elected Sinn Fein TDs (TD = Teachta Dála = MP, also called Deputies) also refused to swear the oath of allegiance to the British crown which was incumbent on members of the Free State Dáil, they did not take their seats and did not participate in Dáil proceedings. Within the parliament, therefore, the only opposition to Cumann na nGaedheal came from the small Labour Party and other minor parties which, like Cumann na nGaedheal, had agreed to work within the confines imposed by the 1921 Treaty. Sinn Fein remained a wholly extra-parliamentary organisation.

In 1926 the then leader of Sinn Fein, Éamon de Valera, proposed an alternative strategy which would allow for a pragmatic recognition of the institutions of the Free State, and which would also allow Sinn Fein TDs to participate in the Dáil, but only if the oath of allegiance was abolished. The proposal was rejected at a special convention of the movement, following which de Valera resigned from the leadership and established a new party, Fianna Fáil, which rapidly displaced Sinn Fein as the major republican opposition to Cumann na nGaedheal. Sinn Fein thereafter became a minor force, virtually absenting itself from organised politics, and achieving an impact only through the increasingly clandestine activities of the IRA. In 1957 and 1961 Sinn Fein again contested elections as an abstentionist party, but with only a limited and very short-lived success. It was not until the 1980s that the party was to emerge once more as a major political force, and then only in Northern Ireland.

By the end of 1926, therefore, opposition to the Cumann na nGaedheal could be crudely classified into three separate categories. The first was the constitutional opposition, principally dominated by the small Labour Party, which effectively eschewed Treaty-related concerns and which confronted the government primarily in terms of its social and economic policy. The second was the minority and anti-system opposition of Sinn Fein, which refused to recognise the legitimacy of the new state and which was pledged to the creation of a 32-county republic. The third opposition was that of Fianna Fáil, which remained sympathetic to the traditional demands of Sinn Fein, and which refused to swear the oath of allegiance and to participate in the Dáil, but which also feared being isolated in the extra-parliamentary wilderness.

Within a year the situation was to change irrevocably. In 1927, following the assassination of a leading Cumann na nGaedheal Cabinet Minister, a Bill was enacted which made it mandatory for candidates at Dáil elections to pledge in advance their willingness to take their seats. A prior commitment to absentionism therefore implied total exclusion from the entire electoral process. Accordingly, in August 1927, de Valera led Fianna Fáil into the Dáil for the first time, swearing the oath of allegiance while at the same time declaring it to be a mere 'empty formality'. This shift in strategy, which marked the first major step forward in the legitimation of the Fianna Fáil opposition, was arguably the most crucial single event in creating the party system as it exists today.

In the shorter-term, however, the most immediate impact of Fianna Fáil's entry into the Dáil was to threaten defeat for Cumann na nGaedheal. Prior to August 1927, and as a result of the Sinn Fein–Fianna Fáil abstentionist strategy, Cumann na nGaedheal had had an easy and effective majority in the Dáil, despite holding only a minority of the total seats. The opposition benches had only been sparsely filled, and neither Labour nor the other minor parties which had followed the constitutional path were in a position to offer an alternative government. The legitimation of the Fianna Fáil opposition in 1927 now meant that for the first time there was a possibility of a constitutional— or at least 'slightly constitutional' (see, p. 18)—alternative.

During the period prior to August 1927, Labour had provided the major constitutional opposition in the Dáil. Labour had not contested the crucial Westminster election of 1918, arguing that its participation would have distracted attention from the overriding issue of the day— the question of national independence. The first election involving Labour was therefore the essentially non-competitive 'Pact' election of 1922 (see Gallagher 1979), in which both wings of Sinn Fein sought to effect a compromise list of candidates in order to defuse their burgeoning conflict. Labour won 17 seats (from a total of 153) in that election, and 14 seats in the following election in 1923. As the major opposition party in the 1923–7 Dáil (Cumann na nGaedheal held 63 seats and the abstentionist Sinn Fein 44), Labour tended to remain primarily a party of trade-union defence, largely ignoring the issues which divided the two major Treaty parties. In the election of June 1927, the last election preceding Fianna Fáil's entry into the Dáil, Labour scored its greatest success, winning 22 seats (i.e. 14 per cent) with almost 13 per cent of the popular vote. In general, the June 1927 election was to prove the high point of non-Treaty parties, that is for parties other than Cumann na nGaedheal, Fianna Fáil and Sinn Fein. The National League, a party formed in 1926 in an effort to build a coalition of former supporters of the Irish Parliamentary Party, and which was still opposed to Sinn Fein in all its versions, won eight seats (5 per cent); 11 seats (7 per cent) were won by the Farmers Party, a sectional agrarian grouping which had been represented in the Dáil since 1922. Non-party or independent candidates won 16 seats (10 per cent). Overall, the June 1927 election left the three Treaty parties with just 63 per cent of the seats (as against 70 per cent in 1923)—see Table 1.1 below.

By mid-1927, the Irish party system was experiencing what Schattschneider (1960) has referred to as a 'conflict of conflicts', in which the parties which mobilised around the Treaty question were confronted by a group of smaller parties and independents which sought to mobilise along alternate dimensions of conflict. Thus, while the contemporary Irish party system is now dominated by the heirs to Sinn Fein, it nevertheless did seem possible that an alternative alignment might have emerged. In June 1927, and arguably also in 1923, it appeared as if an alternative politics might gain ground, one in which farmers, trade-unionists and others unconcerned with the intra-nationalist conflict might establish a substantial foothold in the new party system.

In the event, the situation was to be changed utterly with the entry of Fianna Fáil into the Dáil, a move which accorded the Treaty opposition a sufficient degree of salience to more or less obliterate the alternative dimensions of conflict. In the election of September 1927, just one month after the legitimation of Fianna Fáil, the two Treaty parties won a combined total of 78 per cent of Dáil seats; Labour's share fell to just 9 per cent, with the Farmers Party winning just 4 per cent and the National League 1 per cent (see also below, pp. 47–51).

But to treat the renewed salience of the Treaty opposition simply as evidence of the recrudescence of strictly territorial or constitutional concerns is itself to exaggerate the situation in the 1920s, for it is important to recognise that the intra-nationalist conflict between Fianna Fáil and Cumann na nGaedheal was also complemented by a significant division on overall economic and social policy which acted to polarise the parties to an even greater degree. Fianna Fáil urged a radical programme of social and economic reform designed to appeal to the interests of small farmers and the working class. Pushing a strongly protectionist policy which gelled well with its radical nationalist politics, the party promised increased employment, lower taxes, improved state housing and a more equal distribution of national wealth. In June 1927, for instance, the Labour Party leader had claimed that 12 of Fianna Fáil's 15 manifesto pledges had been drawn from earlier Labour Programmes (Mitchell 1974, p. 224), while a recent commentator had described the Fianna Fáil approach to social welfare as 'more advanced than any proposed by a non-socialist party before the United States new deal' (O'Leary 1961, p. 22). Indeed, de Valera himself later admitted a concern that the party might be seen as *too* orientated towards working-class interests in these early years: 'In those days I believe we could be called Socialists, but not Communists', he recalled in a 1976 interview, adding that the decision to adopt the name Fianna Fáil was partly prompted by the need to stress a national appeal (McInery 1976). The first national organiser of the party was also to emphasise its radicalism: 'the backbone of Fianna Fáil was the dispossessed class', he recalled in an interview in 1976 (MacKenna 1976).

By contrast, the domestic policy of Cumann na nGaedheal was marked by an essential conservatism, stressing only a minimum of state intervention and pursuing a free trade policy based on the export of agricultural produce and the importation of manufactured goods. As Sinnott (1978, p. 41) has noted, support for the party 'derived as much from its conservative reaction to economic depression . . . as from its protreaty position' (see also Orridge 1983). The constituency of the party tended to reflect this conservative bias, as can be seen by its relative strength in areas dominated by large commercial farming interests, in sharp contrast to the support pattern for Fianna Fáil, which tended to dominate in those poorer and peripheral areas which were often characterised by subsistence farming (e.g. Garvin 1974, 1977a; Rumpf and Hepburn 1977).

The legitimation of Fianna Fáil in 1927 does not appear to have diminished the intensity of its opposition to Cumann na nGaedheal; indeed, by effecting a pragmatic recognition of the new state, and therefore by opening the possibility of a transfer of power, the legitimising strategy of Fianna Fáil served, if anything, to accentuate the relevance of its alternative programme. Following Sartori's (1976, pp. 131–45) terminology, Irish politics in the late 1920s bore many of the characteristics of polarised pluralism. Although the parties divided primarily along a nationalist as opposed to strictly left–right dimension, and although not characterised by the presence of 'bilateral opposi- tions' (see Sinnott 1984; and Mair 1979), Sartori's substantive criteria are clearly appropriate: the cleavage was deep, consensus was low, and the very legitimacy of the political system was itself in question (Sartori 1976, p. 135).

The degree of polarisation and the vulnerability of the political system can hardly be doubted. In August 1927 two parties confronted one another across a parliamentary debating chamber when just four years earlier they had opposed one another in a military struggle. And even allowing for the legitimising strategy of de Valera, it was evident, as one contemporary observer recalled, that 'the recognition by Fianna Fáil of the Government and Parliament of the Irish Free State was neither whole-hearted nor unequivocal' (O'Sullivan 1940, p. 224). In 1928 a senior figure in the party, Séan Lemass, addressed the Dáil in the following terms: 'Fianna Fáil is a slightly constitutional party. We are perhaps open to the definition of a constitutional party . . . Our object is to establish a Republican Government in Ireland. If this can be done by the present methods we have, we will be very pleased, but, if not, we would not confine ourselves to them' (Dáil Debates 22:1615– 1616, quoted by O'Sullivan 1940, p. 224). When the members of Fianna Fáil were later accused by a member of the government of having 'failed so far to make clear what is their attitude towards the authority of the Government in the Dáil', de Valera replied: 'I have on more than one occasion said exactly what our attitude was. I still hold that our right to be regarded as the legitimate government of this country is faulty, that this House itself is faulty. You have secured a *de facto* position . . . But as to whether you have come by that position legitimately or not, I say you have not come by that position legitim- ately. You brought off a *coup d'état* in the summer of 1922' (Dáil Debates, 28:460, quoted in full in Moynihan 1980, pp. 162–66).

In hindsight it is rather easy to underestimate the seriousness with which the Fianna Fáil challenge was viewed by the government, particularly given that Fianna Fáil was later to don the mantle of the 'natural governing party' in Ireland. Yet when the transfer of power did occur in 1932, less than a decade after the end of the civil war, it undoubtedly appeared as a momentous event. One commentator has even asserted that 'on the Fianna Fáil side, there were widespread rumours that elements in Cumann na nGaedheal would not allow them to take office. Accordingly, as the Fianna Fáil deputies filed into the government benches, almost every man of them carried a revolver in his pocket' (Coogan 1966, p. 70; the same assertion can be found in Williams 1967, p. 30). Certainly de Valera himself later expressed his trepidation as to what might have transpired: speaking to the Dáil on 15 March 1932 he commented favourably on the 'peaceful change of government', remarking that 'we heard of frightful things that would happen the moment that the Fianna Fáil government came into power' (quoted by Fanning 1983, p. 109).

Fianna Fáil first took office in 1932 as a minority government with Labour Party support. Following the snap election of 1933, the party won its first overall majority, and was to remain in office as either a majority or minority government until 1948. Fianna Fáil won power on the basis of a radical republican programme which aimed at severing the remaining constitutional and economic ties with the United Kingdom. In the long-term, the party was committed to the restoration of the Irish language and to the creation of an all-Ireland republic. In the shorter-term it intended to make the 26-county Irish Free State as independent as possible of British constitutional control. In power, the party abolished the oath of allegiance, substantially reduced in import-ance and later abolished the office of the Governor General—the representative of the British Crown in the Irish Free State, and, in 1937, won popular approval for a new Constitution which made the Irish Free State a republic in all but name. The 1937 Constitution, Bunreacht na hÉireann, which remains in force in a slightly amended form today, 'was almost literally de Valera's constitution' (Chubb 1982, p. 45), and claimed *de jure* jurisdiction over Northern Ireland while admitting that its *de facto* jurisdiction was valid only in the area of the Irish Free State (Arts 2 and 3). The actual declaration of a republic was not favoured in 1937 because of de Valera's belief that such a declara-tion would impede the prospect of eventual unification with Northern Ireland (Chubb 1982, pp 45–6), although such a declaration was eventually made in 1948 by the then incumbent coalition government of Fine Gael, Labour, and other minor parties.

Fianna Fáil in power also rapidly implemented its policy of economic protectionism. Wide-ranging tariffs were imposed on the import of manufactured goods, while incentives were offered to farmers to con-vert from the export-orientated cattle trade to the more domestically-orientated tillage farming. The land annuities, which were the monies

Table 1.1 Party share of electoral vote and number of Dáil seats, 1923–44

	1923		1927 June		1927 Sept		1932		1933		1937		1938		1943		1944	
	V*	S†	V	S	V	S	V	S	V	S	V	S	V	S	V	S	V	S
Sinn Fein	27.4	44	3.6	5	–	–	–	–	–	–	–	–	–	–	–	–	–	–
Fianna Fáil	–	–	26.1	44	35.2	57	44.5	72	49.7	77	45.2	69	51.9	77	41.9	67	48.9	76
Cumann na nGaedheal/ Fine Gael	39.0	63	27.5	47	38.7	62	35.3	57	30.5	48	34.8	48	33.3	45	23.1	32	20.5	30
Labour	10.9	14	12.6	22	9.1	13	7.7	7	5.7	8	10.3	13	10.0	9	15.7	17	8.8	8
National Labour	–	–	–	–	–	–	–	–	–	–	–	–	–	–	–	–	2.7	4
Centre Party	–	–	–	–	–	–	–	–	9.2	11	–	–	–	–	–	–	–	–
Farmers Party	12.1	15	8.9	11	6.4	6	3.1	4	–	–	–	–	–	–	–	–	–	–
National League	–	–	7.3	8	1.6	2	–	–	–	–	–	–	–	–	–	–	–	–
Clann na Talmhan	–	–	–	–	–	–	–	–	–	–	–	–	–	–	11.3	14	11.6	11
Others	10.6	17	14.1	16	9.1	13	9.4	13	5.0	9	9.7	8	4.7	7	8.0	8	7.6	9
Total	100.0	153	100.0	153	100.0	153	100.0	153	100.0	153	100.0	138	100.0	138	100.0	138	100.0	138

* V = percentage first-preference vote
† S = number of seats
Source: Mackie and Rose (1982).

collected by the Irish Government from those native landowners who had bought their farms on the basis of loans arranged through the tenant-purchase schemes of the pre-1921 Land Acts, were no longer paid to the United Kingdom government, but were now retained for use by the Irish exchequer. The United Kingdom government retaliated in kind, placing its own major tariffs on the import of Irish agricultural produce. The subsequent 'economic war' between the two countries persisted until 1938.

The new programme proved only partially successful. Industrial employment rose by almost 50 per cent between 1931 and 1938, and industrial output rose by some 40 per cent. On the other hand, the intended restructuring of Irish agriculture failed to materialise. Acreage under tillage increased by only some 10 per cent in this period, and there was an almost wholesale reconversion back to cattle at the end of the economic war. Moreover, per capita income also declined in this period, 2nd emigration had again begun to accelerate (e.g. Lyons 1973, pp. 610–24; Meenan 1967).

In political terms, the new government had managed to sever most of the remaining constitutional ties with the United Kingdom, but the solution to partition seemed as distant as ever. Moreover, as far as the more militant republicans of Sinn Fein and the IRA were concerned, de Valera in power proved as implacable an enemy as had the previous Cumann na nGaedheal administrations. De Valera was clearly in a difficult position *vis-à-vis* the IRA. The state which he was to head was that to which he had denied legitimacy less than a decade earlier, and which he and his supporters had challenged by force of arms during the 1922–3 civil war. Yet, although when assuming office he immediately ordered the release of those IRA members who had been imprisoned under the Cumann na nGaedheal government, de Valera made no move to disband the official state army or to replace it by his former comrades in arms. And as his grip on the institutions of government tightened, he himself initiated increasingly severe measures against the IRA. By mid-1935, more than 100 IRA members had been imprisoned, and the IRA paper, *An Poblacht* (literally The Republic), had been suppressed. In June 1936 the IRA was declared an illegal organisation (Bell 1979, pp. 99–141).

Yet if the Fianna Fáil record in office was to disillusion many of its more radical supporters, it was also to gain credibility among more moderate voters. The growth of industry and industrial employment also secured for the party a strengthened base among the growing urban middle class and working class, while its welfarist commitments further encouraged working-class support. As the party of government, it quickly allayed the fears of those who had viewed its advent to power as the harbinger of chaos, and its firm opposition to the semi-fascist Blueshirt movement, which had mobilised in opposition to Fianna Fáil and in defence of those interests threatened by the economic war (Manning 1970), and its increasing hostility to the IRA, reassured those who had felt that the regime itself was under threat. In short, Fianna Fáil in government proved itself to be both a stable and efficient administration, emphasising the symbolic rather than the violent side of militant republicanism, and pursuing an overall economic policy which managed to stave off the worst effects of international recession, even if it did not lead the anticipated growth in all sectors. While maintaining the populist 'small-man' rhetoric which initially swept it to power, Fianna Fáil when in office quickly took over from Cumann na nGaedheal the role of guarantor of governmental and regime stability: as Garvin (1977a, p. 179) puts it, the party conquered the 'ideological political centre' of Irish politics.

The increasing popularity of Fianna Fáil among moderate voters was accompanied by the electoral eclipse of Cumann na nGaedheal. In 1933, Cumann na nGaedheal and the Centre Party (the newly-formed successor to the Farmers Party) had together polled almost 40 per cent of the popular vote. Later that year the two parties merged, together with the Blueshirts, to form Fine Gael which, at its first electoral outing in 1937, polled only 35 per cent of the popular vote. The Fine Gael vote fell further in 1938, to 33 per cent, and continued to decline thereafter: to 23 per cent in 1943, to 21 per cent in 1944 and to just less than 20 per cent in 1948. Indeed, by the beginning of the post-war period the party seemed almost on the verge of extinction. In four of the five by-elections of 1945, for instance, it had been unable to find candidates who were willing to put themselves forward for election (Whyte 1980, pp. 112–13).

By the 1930s and 1940s, Fine Gael had lost its primary political *raison d'être*. The party had earlier enjoyed substantial electoral advantage as the party of government and as the guarantor of regime stability during a period in which the political system itself had seemed under threat (for a recent treatment, see Prager 1986). For a decade after the civil war, and in a period of severe crisis and limited but continued political violence, it had managed to establish an efficient administration and to consolidate the institutions of the new state. When Fianna Fáil then took over the reins of government in 1932, and when the threatened chaos failed to materialise, the earlier appeal of

Cumann na nGaedheal/Fine Gael lost much of its relevance, and the party was driven increasingly into a position of simple economic and social conservatism. In the 1930s and 1940s Fine Gael found itself reduced to voicing the criticisms of an essentially marginalised and right-wing constituency—the larger farmers and large commercial interests which had suffered during the economic war, the ex-Unionists who objected to the growing constitutional autonomy of the new state, and so on. It was a constituency which, by the end of the 1940s, constituted little more than a sizeable minority, and the party itself seemed to have little to offer in the way of a more widespread electoral appeal. By the end of the 1940s Fine Gael was a party 'firmly rooted in the past, lacklustre, moribund and, as far as policies were concerned, little more than a pale shadow of Fianna Fáil' (Gallagher 1976, p. 35).

By moving towards the centre of the political spectrum, Fianna Fáil had begun to marginalise Fine Gael as the representative minority right-wing opposition. At the same time, however, this centre-seeking strategy was to boost the declining fortunes of the small Labour Party, which now gained credibility among Fianna Fáil's more radical critics. Labour had initially provided the necessary support which allowed Fianna Fáil to form its first minority government in 1932, and even when Fianna Fáil went on to win an overall majority in 1933, Labour continued to offer it political support. The threat posed by the Blueshirts, together with a Fianna Fáil agreement to implement certain pledges from the Labour programme and to consult Labour on proposed legislation, was sufficient to bind the parties until the mid-1930s (Nevin 1967, pp. 62–3). Labour soon began to adopt a more critical stance, however, and a pronounced leftward shift in the new party constitution adopted in 1936 was reflected in a call for the establishment of a workers' republic. In the 1937 election, competing from a very critical position *vis-à-vis* Fianna Fáil, Labour's vote increased to more than 10 per cent, higher than at any election since June 1927. In 1938 its vote fell slightly, but in 1943 it increased to almost 16 per cent, and to more than 23 per cent in the province of Leinster where, among farm labourers, the party had maintained a reasonably strong basis of support throughout the 1920s and 1930s.

Hopes for further growth were quickly dashed in the wake of a major split in the party in 1944. Part personality conflict, part inter-union bickering, and part a conflict of left and right within the party, the result of the division was the secession of five Labour TDs who established a new party called National Labour. A general election called shortly after the split found the party in disarray, with Labour polling only 9 per cent and National Labour 3 per cent. The parties remained divided in 1948, together polling only 11 per cent, albeit enjoying an increase in their total number of seats from 12 (8.7 per cent) to 19 (12.9 per cent) in a newly-enlarged Dáil (the total number of seats was increased from 138 to 147). National Labour and Labour later merged in 1950 when both were partners in the then incumbent Fine Gael-led coalition government (on National Labour and the split see Lysaght 1970, pp. 158–63; Nevin 1969).

The election of 1943 also witnessed the emergence of Clann na Talmhan (literally 'Children of the Land') a new party which, like Labour, appealed to those disillusioned by the centre-seeking strategy of Fianna Fáil. But whereas Labour directed its appeal to the urban and rural proletariats, Clann na Talmhan focused almost exclusively on the small-farming constituencies of the West of Ireland. The new party was formed in 1938 in order to promote the interests of an agricultural sector which had suffered the 'terrible disillusionment of the past twenty years of native government under the political parties' (Clann na Talmhan 1944, p. 440). It later amalgamated with a similar group which had organised in the Eastern half of the country and which was called the National Agricultural Party. The first general election contested by Clann na Talmhan was that of 1943, when it won 11 per cent of the popular vote and 14 Dáil seats. Support for the party was concentrated in areas characterised by a dominance of poor or semi-subsistence farming, winning 18 per cent of the popular vote in Connaught-Ulster and 13 per cent in Munster, while it made no major electoral effort in the Dublin area or even in Leinster. With fewer candidates and a slightly increased vote, the party won 11 seats in the 1944 election, but thereafter declined to 6 per cent of the vote and seven seats in 1948, to 3 per cent of the vote and six seats in 1951, and to 3 per cent of the vote and just five seats in 1954. The party also contested the 1957 and 1961 general elections, winning 2.4 per cent and 1.5 per cent of the vote respectively, and three and then just two seats. During the lifetime of the 1961–5 Dáil one of these remaining Clann TDs died, and his son, who stood as a Fine Gael candidate, was successful in the ensuing by-election. The last remaining Clann TD retired in 1965.

Agrarian parties were no novelty in Irish politics (see Coakley 1983). Prior to the emergence of Clann na Talmhan, the Farmers Party and then the Centre Party had maintained a substantial Dáil presence between 1922 and 1933. What distinguished Clann na Talmhan, however, was its appeal to small farmers in particular, and its relative strength in Connaught-Ulster as against the more commercially-orientated farming areas of Leinster and parts of Munster (Garvin 1977a; Gallagher 1976). Moreover, while the earlier farmers' parties had competed primarily with Cumann na nGaedheal, Clann na Talmhan appears to have drawn votes from both Fine Gael and Fianna Fáil, and achieved its greatest electoral success in what had been the original western heartland of Fianna Fáil support. The electoral turnaround which gave Clann na Talmhan 18 per cent of the Connaught-Ulster vote in 1943, for example, was accompanied by a decline in the Fine Gael vote in the same area from 33 per cent to 23 per cent, and by a decline in the Fianna Fáil vote from 52 per cent to 42 per cent.

In a sense, the short-lived success of Clann na Talmhan was as much a symptom of the disillusion with the new Fianna Fáil administration as was the contemporary success of Labour. The 'small-man' rhetoric of Fianna Fáil had generated substantial expectations among both the working class and small farmers who had felt themselves neglected by the policies pursued by Cumann na nGaedheal, and despite the continued support which Fianna Fáil enjoyed from both groups throughout the 1930s, there emerged a sufficient level of dissatisfaction to boost the fortunes of both Labour and Clann na Talmhan. But while Labour couched its protest in relatively radical ideological terms, Clann na Talmhan saw itself as little more than the political expression of a marginalised vocational interest. For Clann na Talmhan, the national interest and the farmers' interest were as one, and the key to national prosperity lay in the prosperity of the agricultural sector which, the party believed, was being neglected by Fianna Fáil. Its policies included little beyond this, save for an unequivocal opposition to excessive state interference in the economy and a standard commitment in favour of Irish unity. According to the party's own figures, the agricultural sector accounted for only 36 per cent of the national income, while employing some 65 per cent of the working population. The party's programme also urged the establishment of a 'Christian and National Social Order based on a minimum economic income for all citizens', and called for a reduction in the salaries and/or benefits paid to members of the government (Clann na Talmhan 1944, pp. 37–43).

Were it not for its participation in the Fine Gael-led coalition governments of 1948–51 and 1954–7, Clann na Talmhan might in hindsight appear as simply an ephemeral protest party which emerged from the disillusioned politics of the small farmers. Yet it can also be argued that this minor party offered a clear example of an ideological current which has permeated much of the political life of post-independence Ireland, a current which is redolent of the anti-party, corporatist imagery not often associated with the politics of twentieth-century Europe (see, for example, Malloy 1974; see also Chapter 4 below). Clann na Talmhan was always eager to dissociate itself from the politics of party and to deny a partisan purpose. The terms used by its deputy leader in his first speech to the Dáil offers an appropriate instance: 'as a new party, coming into this House without any feelings of hatred, spite, malice or bitterness, we appeal to the older Deputies to forget these feelings. We appeal to each and every Deputy to do his part in contributing to the solution of the economic problems which confront us' (quoted in Clann na Talmhan 1944, p. 36). The same emphasis is evident in the party's statement that it was 'fully determined to remain independent of all parties and to vote for or against a motion according as to whether it is for the betterment of the country or not' (ibid., p. 37). A more graphic instance is quoted by Garvin (1977a, p. 181), when he refers to a speech by the party leader in Galway in which he claimed to represent people who were 'determined to drive from power the politicians'.

The most interesting aspect of this rhetoric is the echo which it finds in both Fianna Fáil and Fine Gael. For, despite 'the central place of party in Irish politics' (Garvin 1981a, pp. 179–85), the Irish political leadership has always seemed curiously keen to dissociate itself from the notion of party. In the Fianna Fáil case, de Valera and other party leaders continually stressed that they represented a national movement rather than a political party. In the Fine Gael case, the leadership has always been keen to emphasise that its goal was neither party political nor partisan of any kind, but represented some 'higher' and more generalisable collective good. This aversion to parties is part of an older tradition once familiar in Europe (e.g. Daalder 1983, pp. 3–5), in which the party 'as part' was seen as inimical to the interests of the nation or the people 'as whole'. In the Irish case, however, this aversion to party was to prove at once more pervasive and more persistent through time.

The second new party which was to emerge from the shadow of disillusion was Clann na Poblachta (literally 'Children of the Repub-lic'), which won 13 per cent of the popular vote and ten Dáil seats at its first electoral outing in 1948. Despite achieving a higher national profile in Irish politics than did Clann na Talmhan, its success proved no less transient. In 1951 its vote fell to just 4 per cent and it won two seats. Thereafter it contested the 1954, 1957 and 1961 elections, winning just 4 per cent, 2 per cent and 1 per cent of the popular vote, and three, two and then just one Dáil seat.

Clann na Poblachta was formed in Dublin in 1946 by a group of former republican activists, many of whom had been interned by the Fianna Fáil government during World War II. The party was led by Séan MacBride, a former Chief of Staff of the IRA. The party also enjoyed the support of a number of prominent social reformers who favoured a greater expansion of the welfare state and a more vigorous drive against unemployment and emigration. For a time the party seemed set to inherit the role adopted by Fianna Fáil when the latter posed a major challenge to Cumann na nGaedheal in the 1920s and early 1930s. Socially radical and unequivocally republican, it seemed set to build an alliance of the various strands of leftist opposition to Fianna Fáil which were then dissipated among the divided Labour parties and Clann na Talmhan, as well as those who had remained in the more radical wing of Fianna Fáil itself. In the event, the election of 1948 proved too precipitate to allow the party to build the necessary organisational momentum (Manning 1972, p. 103), although with 13 per cent of the poll it exceeded the combined total of Labour and National Labour, and far exceeded that of Clann na Talmhan. In the Dublin area Clann na Poblachta polled more than 19 per cent, while the vote of Fianna Fáil fell by 13 per cent, and that of the two Labour parties by almost 3 per cent. Clann na Poblachta also polled well in Connaught-Ulster, polling 14 per cent as against a loss of almost 7 per cent by Clann na Talmhan and a loss of just over 7 per cent by Fianna Fáil.

The leadership of MacBride, and the strong republican voice in the party—the provisional executive of which 'sounded like a roll-call of the 1930s IRA' (Farrell 1983, p. 26)—have always left the impression of Clann na Poblachta as an essentially radical nationalist opposition to Fianna Fáil. Manning (1972, p. 102), for example, identifies republicanism as the party's 'dominant characteristic', while in his excellent study of minor parties in Ireland, Coakley (1983) treats Clann na Poblachta as first and foremost a republican party. Yet, to judge by its election literature, the explicitly nationalistic component of the appeal received relatively little emphasis. Of the seven policy statements in its 1948 manifesto, the national problem—headed 'Partition'—was accorded last place and included only two statements. The first, its phrasing reminiscent of the statement by Clann na Talmhan in the 1944 election, emphasised the need for economic progress as a key to the eventual unification of North and South: 'until we set up social services and an economic system that are at least as good as those offered to the people of the Six Counties by the British Labour Government, no serious advance can be made towards the ending of Partition' (Clann na Poblachta 1948). The second statement was more vigorous, urging that the Dáil should be open to the participation of elected representatives from Northern Ireland.

In general, however, the tenor of the party programme was welfarist rather than republican, calling for full employment, a basic minimum wage, comprehensive social insurance, free education, and the raising of the minimum school leaving age to 16 years (ibid.). Thus, although the stimulus to form the party undoubtedly derived in part from republican disillusion with the failure of Fianna Fáil to effect the unification of North and South, it was also in part due to developments in the United Kingdom, where the Beveridge report of 1942, and the election of a Labour government in 1945, had offered Irish radical politics a guide for the future development of public policy. Yet despite this relative radicalism, the authors of the 1948 election programme were also at pains to demonstrate their adherence to prevailing Catholic teaching. Thus the preamble to the programme began by stating that 'the structure of the Christian State is based on the family. Sociologically and morally the family life is essential to the Nation' (ibid.).

It was this curious ambivalence between social radicalism on the one hand and obeisance to Catholic teaching on the other which eventually was to destroy the party. In 1951 the Clann Minister for Health, Noel Browne, came into direct conflict with the Catholic hierarchy which opposed his plans to introduce free health care for mothers and children (Whyte 1980, pp. 196–238; Farrell 1983, pp. 33–6). Mac-Bride eventually demanded Browne's resignation, a move which divided the party and prompted the resignation of two additional Clann na Poblachta TDs. An election was called quickly after the incident in which Clann na Poblachta managed to win only two seats while three dissidents—including Browne—were elected as Independent TDs.

Had the party remained loyal to Browne in 1951 and ignored the hierarchy's opposition to what was the first major step towards a national health service along British lines, it might well have established an enduring presence in Irish politics. Its record in government had been otherwise quite impressive (e.g. Farrell 1983), and it seemed as if there then existed a potential constituency for reformist opposition to Fianna Fáil. Of course, this was not to be. While a modified version of the coalition again took office in 1954, this time with the external support rather than full involvement of a much-reduced Clann na Poblachta, the party system was already well on the way towards a long-term consolidation of the traditional alternatives. In the wake of the 1954–7 coalition government, Fine Gael and the now reunited Labour Party determined to pursue independent and party specific strategies, while the two Clann parties gradually faded to oblivion.

An Overview of Post-war Trends

The renewed dominance of the 'traditional' party system is clearly evident from the data in Table 1.2, which reports the various parties' shares of the vote at each general election between 1948 and 1987, and which emphasises the marginalisation of the minor parties. Clann na Poblachta declined from 13 per cent to just 4 per cent between 1948 and 1951, and thereafter continued to decline until its eventual disappearance in 1969. Clann na Talmhan also declined steadily until its disappearance in 1965. National Labour merged back into the Labour Party in 1950, since when a united Labour Party has persisted—with varying degrees of electoral success—through to the present. And while Sinn Fein—sporadically—and the Workers Party—more consistently—have emerged to challenge the three traditional parties, as has the new Progressive Democratic Party in 1987, one of the most striking features of post-war electoral development remains the long-term monopoly of Fianna Fáil, Fine Gael and Labour. Having won just 73 per cent of the vote (this figure includes the National Labour vote) in 1948, the three main parties together polled 97 per cent in 1965, and averaged almost 94 per cent over the two elections of 1982, before then falling back to just 78 per cent in 1987, the lowest combined total since 1948. This trend is also reflected in the changing levels of the Rae (1971) fractionalisation index, which falls from 0.730 in 1948 to 0.631 in November 1982—although note also the low score in 1954—and then rises to 0.710 in 1987.

Fine Gael virtually doubled its vote between 1948 and 1982, increasing from just less than 20 per cent in 1948 to just over 39 per cent in November 1982, and then falling back to 27 per cent in 1987, its lowest national vote since 1957. Labour support has also proved quite volatile, rising from just over 12 per cent in 1948 (the figure includes National Labour) to 17 per cent in 1969, when it also won 28 per cent in Dublin, before falling back to just over 9 per cent in 1982 and to less than 7 per cent in 1987, its lowest poll since 1933. The Fianna Fáil vote has also fluctuated, ranging erratically between 42 per cent (in 1948) and 51 per cent (in 1977). In general, and again in contrast to the trend in Western Europe (cf. Pedersen 1979; 1983), average volatility peaks

Table 1.2 Party share of electoral vote (per cent), index of electoral fractionalisation, and index of volatility, 1948–87

Elections	1948	1951	1954	1957	1961	1965	1969	1973	1977	1981	1982 Feb	1982 Nov	1987
Fianna Fáil	41.9	46.3	43.4	48.3	43.8	47.7	45.7	46.2	50.6	45.3	47.2	45.2	44.1
Fine Gael	19.8	25.8	32.0	26.6	32.0	34.1	34.1	35.1	30.5	36.5	37.3	39.2	27.1
Labour	8.7	11.4	12.1	9.1	12.0	15.4	17.0	13.7	11.6	9.9	9.1	9.4	6.4
National Labour	2.6	–	–	–	–	–	–	–	–	–	–	–	–
Progressive Democrats	–	–	–	–	–	–	–	–	–	–	–	–	11.8
Clann na Poblachta	13.2	4.1	3.8	1.7	1.1	0.8	–	–	–	–	–	–	–
Clann na Talmhan	5.6	2.9	3.1	2.4	1.5	–	–	–	–	–	–	–	–
National Progressive Democrats	–	–	–	–	1.0	–	–	–	–	–	–	–	–
Sinn Féin*	–	–	–	5.3	3.1	–	–	–	–	2.6	1.0	–	1.9
Workers Party†	–	–	–	–	–	–	–	1.1	1.7	1.7	2.2	3.3	3.8
Others	8.2	9.5	5.6	6.6	5.5	2.0	3.2	3.9	5.6	4.0	3.2	2.9	4.8
Total	100.0	100.0	100.0	100.0	100.0	100.0	100.0	100.0	100.0	100.0	100.0	100.0	100.0
Turnout (%)	74.2	75.3	75.7	70.6	69.9	74.5	76.9	76.6	76.3	76.2	73.8	72.8	73.3
Electorate (thousands)	1,800	1,785	1,763	1,738	1,671	1,683	1,735	1,784	2,119	2,275	2,275	2,336	2,446
Index of fractionalisation‡	0.750	0.695	0.589	0.680	0.687	0.632	0.645	0.643	0.634	0.649	0.628	0.631	0.710
Index of volatility§	13.9	14.4	7.1	11.3	9.3	9.4	2.8	3.3	6.7	8.6	3.2	3.3	16.1

* Anti-H-Block Committee in 1981
† 1973, Official Sinn Fein
‡ As defined by Rea (1971)
§ As defined by Pedersen (1979)
Sources: Mackie and Rose (1982); Gallagher (1985); official figures published by the Stationery Office; *Irish Times*, 20 February 1987.

in the early post-war years, then declines, before suddenly rising to a post-war high in 1987.

Finally, it is also necessary to underline that the relative consolidation of the traditional party and the decline in average volatility through to 1982 was accompanied by a substantial increase in the size of the electorate and thus by a large increase in the number of new voters. Having fluctuated around 1.7 million in the period 1948 to 1973, the electorate in 1977 increased to over 2.1 million (this was the first election to incorporate the newly-enfranchised 18–20 year olds), and to over 2.2 million by 1982. By 1987, the electorate had increased to almost 2.5 million. Turnout has remained reasonably stable throughout the post-war period, recording its lowest levels in 1957 and 1961.

A similar pattern of consolidation is observable at the legislative level from the data in Table 1.3, which reports the distribution of Dáil seats between 1948 and 1987. Since the demise of Clann na Talmhan and Clann na Poblachta, only four other parties have managed to win a plurality of Dáil seats following an election: the National Progressive Democrats, which Gallagher (1985, p. 114) describes as little more than a collective label for two ex-Clann na Poblachta TDs who later joined the Labour Party in 1961; Sinn Fein, which pursued an abstentionist policy, in 1957 and 1981 (on the latter occasion under the label of the 'Anti-H-Block Committee'); the Workers Party, formerly Official Sinn Fein and later Sinn Fein—the Workers Party, in the 1980s, and the new Progressive Democratic party in 1987.

The latter two parties represent perhaps the most serious and sustained challenge to the traditional party system since the disappearance of the two Clann parties. The Workers Party derives from the majority wing following a split in Sinn Fein in 1969 and, having since abandoned much of the old Sinn Fein nationalist rhetoric, has moved towards what might be considered a Eurocommunist position. The bulk of its support is to be found in Dublin working-class constituencies, where its radical policies and active grass-roots campaigns have won it a quite significant following among former Labour Party supporters who have become disenchanted with Labour's commitment to coalition (see below). In the local elections in 1985, and in the general election of 1987, the Worker's Party narrowly outpolled Labour in the borough of Dublin and may yet displace the latter as the leading left party in the city (on the Workers Party see Rooney 1984; Gallagher 1985, pp. 114–18).

More recently, in early 1986 two dissident Fianna Fáil TDs launched a new party, the Progressive Democrats. By early summer 1986 the

Table 1.3 Distribution of Dáil seats, index of legislative fractionalisation, and turnover of seats, 1948–87

Elections	1948 N	1948 %	1951 N	1951 %	1954 N	1954 %	1957 N	1957 %	1961 N	1961 %	1965 N	1965 %	1969 N	1969 %
Parties														
Fianna Fáil	68	46.3	69	46.9	65	44.2	78	53.1	70	48.6	72	50.0	75	52.1
Fine Gael	31	21.1	40	27.2	50	34.0	40	27.2	47	32.6	47	32.6	50	34.7
Labour	14	9.5	16	10.9	19	12.9	12	8.2	16	11.1	22	15.3	18	12.5
National Labour	5	3.4	–	–	–	–	–	–	–	–	–	–	–	–
Progressive Democrats	–	–	–	–	–	–	–	–	–	–	–	–	–	–
Clann na Poblachta	10	6.8	2	1.4	3	2.0	1	0.7	1	0.7	1	0.7	–	–
Clann na Talmhan	7	4.8	6	4.1	5	3.4	3	2.0	2	1.4	–	–	–	–
National Progressive Democrats	–	–	–	–	–	–	–	–	2	1.4	–	–	–	–
Sinn Féin*	–	–	–	–	–	–	4	2.7	0	0	–	–	–	–
Workers' Party†	–	–	–	–	–	–	–	–	–	–	–	–	–	–
Others	12	8.2	14	9.5	5	3.4	9	6.1	6	4.2	2	1.4	1	0.7
Total	147	100	147	100	147	100	147	100	144	100	144	100	144	100
Index of fractionalisation‡	0.717		0.683		0.670		0.632		0.643		0.620		0.592	
Turnover of seats§ (%)	27.9		21.1		19.7		22.4		25.2		22.4		30.6	

Elections	1973		1977		1981		1982 Feb		1982 Nov		1987	
	N	%	N	%	N	%	N	%	N	%	N	%
Parties												
Fianna Fáil	69	47.9	84	56.8	75	45.2	81	48.8	75	45.2	81	48.8
Fine Gael	54	37.5	43	29.1	65	39.2	63	38.0	70	42.2	51	30.7
Labour	19	13.2	17	11.5	15	9.0	15	9.0	16	9.6	12	7.2
National Labour	–	–	–	–	–	–	–	–	–	–	–	–
Progressive Democrats	–	–	–	–	–	–	–	–	–	–	14	8.4
Clann na Poblachta	–	–	–	–	–	–	–	–	–	–	–	–
Clann na Talmhan	–	–	–	–	–	–	–	–	–	–	–	–
National Progressive Democrats	–	–	–	–	–	–	–	–	–	–	–	–
Sinn Fein*	–	–	–	–	2	1.2	0	0	–	–	0	0
Workers' Party†	0	0	0	0	1	0.6	3	1.8	2	1.2	4	2.4
Others	2	1.4	4	2.7	5	3.0	4	2.4	3	1.8	4	2.4
Total	144	100	148	100	166	100	166	100	166	100	166	100
Index of fractionalisation‡	0.614		0.578		0.633		0.608		0.608		0.654	
Turnover of seats§ (%)	19.4		31.8		33.7		17.5		15.7		25.3	

* Refers to anti H-Block Committee candidates in 1981
† In 1973, Official Sinn Fein
‡ Based on the formula in Rae (1971)
§ Percentage of TDs who were not members of the outgoing Dáil
Sources: Mackie and Rose (1982); Nealon and Brennan (1981); Browne (1981; 1982); Trench (1983); official figures published by Stationery Office; *Irish Times*, 20 February 1987.

Dáil strength of this new party had increased to five, with the addition of two other dissident Fianna Fáil TDs and one dissident Fine Gael TD. At its first electoral outing in 1987 the party polled almost 12 per cent of the vote and won 14 seats, making it the third largest party in the Dáil. Despite its largely Fianna Fáil origins, the new party proved a greater threat to Fine Gael (see Chapter 5 below), mobilising a distinctly middle-class appeal based on calls for fiscal austerity, tax cuts, and reductions in government spending. As yet, its capacity to provide an enduring alternative remains uncertain.

In three other cases individual independent TDs have adopted party labels in the Dáil. Neil Blaney, expelled from Fianna Fáil in 1970, sits as a self-styled representative of Independent Fianna Fáil. Noel Browne, who on different occasions has represented Clann na Poblachta, Fianna Fáil, the National Progressive Democrats and the Labour Party, has also represented the small and short-lived Socialist Labour Party. More recently an independent left Limerick TD, Jim Kemmy, formed a new party called the Democratic Socialist Party, and was elected under this label in 1987.

The Dáil strength of the three traditional parties is slightly greater than that at aggregate electoral level. In 1948, for example, the three parties (including National Labour) won 80 per cent of Dáil seats with just 73 per cent of the popular vote. Since then their combined Dáil strength has averaged over 90 per cent, with a high of 99 per cent in 1969 and a low of 87 per cent in 1987. These figures also reveal a slight bias towards the larger parties in the translation of votes into seats. Fianna Fáil has enjoyed a clear advantage in this regard, winning a disproportionately high share of Dáil seats following each post-war election, and winning an overall majority of seats without a corresponding electoral majority in 1957 and in 1969. Fine Gael has also enjoyed an advantage in the translation of votes into seats, being overrepresented at Dáil level following all but two elections—those of 1965 and 1977. Labour, on the other hand, has been generally disadvantaged, winning a disproportionately high share of seats only in 1948, 1954, November 1982, and 1987. Figures on the proportionality of electoral outcomes with reference to the three parties are shown in Table 1.4.

More importantly, however, the balance of Dáil strength throughout the post-war period has maintained Fianna Fáil in a position where it is the only party which can credibly claim a capacity to govern on its own. Fine Gael, despite its post-war growth, remained obliged to pursue an alliance strategy in order to win office, either by forming a coalition with or by gaining support from another Dáil party. Between 1957 and

Table 1.4 Irish elections 1948–87: indices of proportionality for the three main parties*

Year	Mean vote 1948–87 (%)	1948	1951	1954	1957	1961	1965	1969	1973	1977	1981	1982 Feb	1982 Nov	1987‡	Mean
Party															
Fianna Fáil	45.8	110	101	103	111	112	105	113	103	113	103	103	101	111	107
Fine Gael	31.5	107	107	107	103	103	96	103	108	96	108	102	108	113	105
Labour†	11.4	115	96	102	82	91	95	74	97	94	92	99	102	113	96

* The index of proportionality was devised by Cornelius O'Leary, and is calculated on a base of 100 by dividing the percentage of seats by the percentage of votes. Full proportionality is therefore 100, while 100+ signifies disproportionately high representation and 100– disproportionately low representation (O'Leary, 1979, Chapter 9)

† Includes National Labour in 1948

‡ The relevant figure for the Progressive Democrats is 71

Source: O'Leary (1979); official figures published by the Stationery Office, Dublin; *Irish Times*.

1969, however, both Fine Gael and Labour pursued go-it-alone strategies and eschewed the possibility of coalition and, as noted above, this period also witnessed major electoral successes for both parties. Yet despite their growing support, neither party amassed sufficient support to pose a single-party alternative to Fianna Fáil government, and in 1973 they reverted to a coalition strategy. Since then, Labour has experienced a secular decline in its overall electoral support, while Fine Gael grew erratically through to 1982, before falling back in face of the PD challenge in 1987 (cf. Table 1.2). Labour eventually rejected the coalition strategy, and its withdrawal from government on 20 January 1987 precipitated the election in February of that year.

In this crucial sense, although the period from 1948 to 1982 witnessed the consolidation of the traditional party system and the waning of alternative political forces, nevertheless the *logic of governance* persisted: the alternatives have been either *monocolore* Fianna Fáil administrations or Fine Gael-led coalition administrations. The only change has been in the composition of the latter. Initially, non-Fianna Fáil administrations involved a broad, multi-party alliance of Fine Gael, Labour, National Labour, Clann na Talmhan, Clann na Poblachta and Independent TDs, while in the 1970s and early 1980s the alternative to Fianna Fáil has involved just Fine Gael and Labour.

It is also necessary to underline that this represents a significant shift from the pattern in the late 1920s and 1930s. In the earlier period, party competition revolved primarily around the opposition of Fianna Fáil and Cumann na nGaedheal/Fine Gael, with other parties struggling for a foothold. In the post-war period, by contrast, party competition has revolved around the opposition of Fianna Fáil and more or less *all* the other parties, with the opposition to Fianna Fáil initially being spread around a heterogeneous and rather motley range of minor parties in the late 1940s and 1950s, and later concentrated on the more cohesive alliance of Fine Gael and Labour. Thus, as far as the governing alternatives are concerned, the degree of change since 1948 has been perhaps of *less* significance than is the contrast between the post-war period *as a whole* on the one hand, and the period of the late 1920s and 1930s on the other (Mair 1979). Despite the Progressive Democrats' appeal to voters to 'trust us with the balance of power', there is little sign that the emergence of this new party will fundamentally alter the Fianna Fáil versus the Rest pattern of opposition.

Between 1948 and March 1987, as can be seen from Table 1.5, Fianna Fáil formed eight of the 14 administrations, holding office from 1951 to 1954, from 1957 to 1973, from 1977 to 1981, and from

Table 1.5 Patterns of government formation, 1948–87

Period	Type of government	Percentage of Dáil seats*	Parties involved in government	Duration in months
1948–51	Minority coalition	46.3	Fine Gael, Labour, National Labour, Clann na Talmhan, Clann na Poblachta one Independent	40
1951–4	Minority single party	46.9	Fianna Fáil	36
1954–7	Majority coalition	50.3	Fine Gael, Labour, Clann na Talmhan, (with pledge of support from Clann na Poblachta)	34
1957–61	Majority single party	53.1	Fianna Fáil	55
1961–5	Minority single party	48.6	Fianna Fáil	42
1965–9	Majority single party	50.0	Fianna Fáil	51
1969–73	Majority single party	52.1	Fianna Fáil	44
1973–7	Majority coalition	50.7	Fine Gael, Labour	51
1977–81	Majority single party	56.8	Fianna Fáil	48
1981–2	Minority coalition	48.2	Fine Gael, Labour	8
1982 (Mar)–1982 (Dec)	Minority single party	48.8	Fianna Fáil	9
1982–7	Majority coalition	51.8	Fine Gael, Labour	49
1987 (Jan)–1987–(Mar)	Minority single party	41.8†	Fine Gael	2
1987	Minority single party	48.8	Fianna Fáil	na

* At time of taking office ·
† Calculated on a base of 165, since one of the seats in the 166-seat Dáil was vacant pending a by-election

March to December 1982, and with an average term of office of 41 months. Coalition administrations have governed in the interim (excluding the single-party Fine Gael caretaker administration of January–March 1987), with an average term of office of 36 months. Thus not only has Fianna Fáil governed more often, its governments have also proved more durable, thus underlining its claim to be the 'natural party of government' (Mair 1979; see also Chapter 4 below). However, the regular alternation in office has done much to undermine this. More recently between 1948 and 1973, for example, Fianna Fáil governed for 20 out of 26 years. Between 1973 and 1987, on the other hand, it was in government for only five out of 14 years. The credibility of the non-Fianna Fáil alternative in this period has also been increased by the sheer simplification of the coalition option—from being a relatively uneasy multi-party alliance in the late 1940s and 1950s, it became a simple and quite cohesive two-party coalition in which, in 1973 and 1977, the two parties even campaigned on a joint manifesto.

It is also worth noting that executive durability in post-war Ireland seems largely a function of the initial level of Dáil support enjoyed by the different governments. Seven out of the 14 administrations have enjoyed an overall majority (this includes the 1965 Fianna Fáil government which held exactly 50 per cent of the seats), and these have persisted for an average of 48 months. The five minority administrations formed before 1987 have persisted for an average of only 23 months, although this figure increases to 39 months if the two exceptionally short-lived administrations of 1981 and 1982 are excluded. Nevertheless, commanding only a minority of Dáil seats does not necessarily imply a vulnerability to parliamentary defeat, since Independent deputies can normally be relied upon to support the incumbent government rather than to precipitate an early election. On only two occasions since 1948 have governments felt obliged to resign following a Dáil defeat: in February 1982 the minority coalition government resigned when its budget was rejected by the Dáil, and in November 1982 the minority Fianna Fáil administration resigned following its defeat in a vote of confidence. In both cases, independent socialist TDs voted against the incumbent government, reflecting a more critical and policy-orientated approach than was normally the case with Independent TDs in the past, many of whom had been almost wholly orientated towards local constituency politics (Farrell 1985). Following each of these defeats an election was called prior to any attempt to form a new government. On two other occasions in the post-war period, in 1951 and 1957, both involving coalitions, incumbent governments resigned in anticipation of parliamentary defeat or because of dissension within the coalition ranks (Chubb 1974, p. 56), while in 1987 the withdrawal of Labour from the coalition government left Fine Gael in an unsustainable position.

The final topic which needs to be treated in this rather cursory overview of party-system development concerns the contemporary sociology of party support. For Whyte (1974), the contemporary Irish party system is one characterised by 'politics without social bases'. Notwithstanding the initial radical-conservative opposition which reinforced that of territorial nationalism, post-war politics appears to have been dominated by catch-all parties which seem to eschew the establishment and maintenance of enduring links with specific social sectors. To be sure, there are evident biases. Fine Gael for long retained a distinct middle-class appeal which was complemented by its relative electoral weight among larger farmers, while Labour has enjoyed a distinct advantage—or suffered less of a disadvantage—among working-class voters. Such a pattern emerged clearly in 1969 in the first major opinion survey to be carried out in the Irish Republic (see Table 1.6) and at the time of Labour's greatest post-war electoral success. The social profile of each party's support shown by this poll has since informed much of the literature on Irish electoral behaviour, including the seminal study by Whyte (1974) cited above.

Table 1.6 Social class and party support, 1969 (per cent)

	Fianna Fáil	Fine Gael	Labour	Others/ don't know
CLASS				
Upper/middle (AB)	37	37	10	17
Lower-middle (C1)	48	26	15	11
Middle (ABC1)	*45*	*28*	*14*	*13*
Skilled manual (C2)	40	21	27	12
Unskilled manual (DE)	43	14	28	15
Working (C2DE)	*42*	*16*	*28*	*14*
Farmers (30+ acres) (F1)	38	46	2	14
Farmers (30− acres) (F2)	53	26	5	16
Farmers (F)	*42*	*40*	*3*	*15*
All classes	*43*	*25*	*18*	*14*

Source: Gallup opinion poll, 1969.

As can be seen from the data in Table 1.6, Fianna Fáil in 1969 enjoyed virtually identical levels of support among the three main social categories—the middle class (ABC1), where the party recorded 45 per cent support, the working class (C2DE), where it recorded 42 per cent, and the farmers (F) where it recorded 43 per cent. Fine Gael, on the other hand, found its greatest support among farmers, followed by the middle class, and recorded relatively little support among the working class. Finally, it was among working-class voters that Labour found its greatest support, followed by the middle class, with the party barely registering any support among farmers.

Taking all three parties together, therefore, political preferences seem remarkably unstructured by social class. In comparative terms, Rose (1974, p. 17) employed the data from this survey to show that Ireland ranked at the bottom of a list of 15 Western democracies in terms of the capacity of social structure to account for inter-party variations in electoral support. Social structure variables explained just 3.1 per cent of the variance in the Irish case, as against an average of 39.8 per cent in the other 14 democracies. Yet as is also evident from the data in Table 1.6, the poor explanatory value of social structures derives largely from the cross-sectional appeal of Fianna Fáil. Opposing this party to Fine Gael and Labour is to create two broad coalitions of diverse social groups, two large catch-all electorates which are more or less indistinguishable from one another in terms of class, region, or whatever. Removing Fianna Fáil from the equation, on the other hand, reveals a not insubstantial class effect in terms of the competition of Labour versus Fine Gael, with the former evincing a strong bias towards the working class and the latter an equally strong bias towards the middle class and the farmers. Applying the same method as that used by Rose and Whyte to this 'subset' of the party system reveals that as much as 3.19 per cent of variance is explained by social structure, ranking Ireland quite highly in the range of 15 Western democracies (see Mair 1979, pp. 457–9).

Of course this is a wholly artificial exercise: Fianna Fáil cannot simply be abstracted from the system, while in terms of party competition Fine Gael and Labour were allies, participants in a joint coalition which, in the combination of their support patterns, proved as socially heterogeneous as the constituency of Fianna Fáil. Moreover, as will become clear, the class bias of Labour versus Fine Gael was to be quickly eroded as the latter recorded substantial gains among working-class voters in the late 1970s and early 1980s.

Table 1.7 reports data from surveys carried out on the eve of

Table 1.7 Social class and party support, 1977–87 (per cent)

Class	Fianna Fáil				Fine Gael				Labour				Others/don't know			
	1977	1981	Nov 1982	1987	1977	1981	Nov 1982	1987	1977	1981	Nov 1982	1987	1977	1981	Nov 1982	1987*
Middle (ABC1)	46	40	32	30	30	37	38	19	7	8	7	3	16	15	23	48
Working (C2DE)	50	46	38	39	21	26	28	15	14	13	10	5	15	15	24	43
Large farmers (>50 acres)	48	40	35	34	42	43	51	35	1	2	4	2	8	15	10	29
Small farmers (<50 acres)	48	56	43	44	38	31	36	24	5	4	5	3	8	9	15	30
All farmers	48	49	38	39	40	36	44	29	3	3	4	2	8	12	14	29
All classes	*49*	*44*	*36*	*36*	*28*	*31*	*35*	*19*	*9*	*10*	*8*	*4*	*14*	*15*	*21*	*42*
% Vote at election	*51*	*45*	*45*	*44*	*31*	*37*	*39*	*27*	*12*	*10*	*9*	*6*	*6†*	*8†*	*7†*	*22†*

* Includes Progressive Democrats (ABC1 = 16; C2DE = 7; LF = 8; SF = 5; AllF = 6; AllC = 10

† Percentage vote received by candidates/parties other than FF, FG or Lab

Sources: 1977: amalgamation of three NOP election polls, May–June 1977 (adapted from Sinnott 1978, p. 53), *N* = 1,788; 1981: amalgamation of three IMS election polls, May–June 1981, *N* = 3,147; 1982: amalgamation of three MRBI election polls, October–November 1982, *N* = 3,026; 1987: amalgamation of two IMS election polls, 2 & 14 February 1987, *N* = 2,097.

the elections of 1977, 1981, November 1982 and 1987, where the trends in overall party support are immediately evident. First, the general level of stated Fianna Fáil support has declined from 49 per cent in 1977 to just 36 per cent in 1987. Second, the decline of Fianna Fáil is matched by a steady increase in Fine Gael support through to 1982, a rise commensurate with the aggregate electoral fortunes of that party. Finally, Labour remains reasonably steady in the 1977–82 period, though with an average support far below that recorded in 1969 (Table 1.6), and barely registers in 1987. A closer comparison of the data in Table 1.7 with those in Table 1.6 reveals much of the source of these general changes. Fianna Fáil has experienced a loss of support across all social categories, and especially among middle-class voters (ABC1) where it has fallen from 45 per cent in 1969 to just 30 per cent in 1987, most of this loss initially appearing to benefit Fine Gael which rose from 28 per cent middle-class support in 1969 to 38 per cent in 1982, and which then fell to just 19 per cent in 1987. Labour's steady losses among working-class voters—from 28 per cent in 1969 to just 5 per cent in 1982—also initially appeared to act to the advantage of Fine Gael, which recorded an increase in support among this group from 16 per cent in 1969 to 28 per cent in 1982. Again, there was a falling back in 1987. Working-class support for others—the Workers Party and Sinn Fein in particular—has increased, as has the proportion of working-class respondents refusing to state a preference.

Working-class support for Fianna Fáil has proved quite volatile, rising from 42 per cent in 1969 to 50 per cent in 1977, and then falling back to 38 per cent in 1982 and 39 per cent in 1987. Despite this erratic pattern, however, Fianna Fáil in 1987 remains—as it had been in 1969—the most popular single party among working-class voters. Support for Fianna Fáil among farmers has also proved somewhat volatile, increasing in 1977 and 1981, but evincing a sharp decline in 1982 and 1987. Among large farmers there is evidence of a steady decline, while the party support among small farmers—the traditional Fianna Fáil heartland—is more erratic.

It is also necessary to underline the increased proportion of respondents registering support for 'others' or for no candidate or party. This is particularly important in 1982 and 1987 and among both middle- and working-class respondents, with the latter drifting towards the Workers Party and to a lesser extent Sinn Fein, and with the former turning eventually towards the PDs. In part also, this appears to reflect the general decline in the intensity of partisan identification in Ireland in recent years, which can be expected to have been more pronounced in urban areas (see Chapter 2 below).

In general terms these data suggest that the Irish party system is characterised by a politics which is now even more free of social bases than was the case in 1969. This shift to a more classless pattern of voting is also evident in the changing values of the Alford (1963) index of class voting when applied to all three parties, and which is reported in Table 1.8. In the Labour case, where one would expect it to record its highest levels, the index has fallen from just 14 in 1969 to as little as 2 in 1987. In the case of Fine Gael, the (negative) values of the index have fallen from −12 in 1969 to −4 in 1987. Only in the case of Fianna Fáil does the index register an increase—from −3 in 1969 to 9 in 1987, reversing the relative Fianna Fáil–Labour class positions of 1969—but here the change is less a consequence of increased working-class support than of decreased middle-class support. Relatively speaking, the PDs evince quite a pronounced class profile in 1987, registering the lowest value of any of the four parties, and a new class bias may emerge if this trend should continue.

Table 1.8 Index of class voting, 1969–87*

Party	1969	1977	1981	1982	1987
Fianna Fáil	−3	4	6	6	9
Fine Gael	−12	−9	−11	−10	−4
Labour	14	7	5	3	2
Progressive Democrats	na	na	na	na	−9

* The figures refer to the index of working-class voting devised by Alford (1963), and record the percentage of working-class respondents favouring a certain party *less* the percentage of middle-class voters supporting that party. In the case of Labour in 1969, for instance, the value of 14 is calculated by subtracting 14 (the proportion in the ABC1 category supporting Labour) from 28 (the proportion in the C2DE category supporting Labour).

The Freezing of Alternatives?

Notwithstanding the fluctuations in the fortunes of the parties in the past 60 or so years, and despite the recent emergence of the Progressive Democrats, the most striking impression which remains from this overview is the sheer similarity between the configuration of the party system in the latter post-war years and that which prevailed more than half-a-century before. Fianna Fáil remains the largest party in the system, even though its claim to be the natural party of government has been severely undermined in recent years. Following a period of decline, Fine Gael was gradually restored to a major role in the party system, while Labour, despite short-term periods of growth, still remains on the margins of mainstream politics. But to admit the similarity is one thing; to identify the actual processes which may explain it is quite another. Is the contemporary configuration of the party system simply the result of historical inertia? Why was the Irish party system in the later post-war years yet again characterised by this Fianna Fáil–Fine Gael 'duopoly', and why has Labour remained in such a marginal position?

Rather like a latter-day Freud, the student of modern party systems will often search for an understanding of contemporary political align-ments in the early and formative phases of mass political mobilisation. Party alternatives persist through decades and even through genera-tions, and the language of contemporary political debate often seems to differ only marginally from that which stabilised some 60 or 70 years before. Having reviewed the origins of the Irish party system, and having presented a cursory overview of post-war developments, I will now therefore attempt to assess the extent to which Ireland is characterised by just such a historical inertia. In particular, the relative strength of Fianna Fáil and Fine Gael, and the relative weak-ness of Labour, will be assessed both in the context of the original mobi-lisation of post-independence politics and in the light of subsequent developments, in an effort to offer a clearer understanding of the basis of the contemporary configuration.

In 1967, in a most cogent and persuasive presentation, Lipset and Rokkan (1967, p. 50) argued that the party systems of Western Europe reflected, 'with few but significant exceptions, the cleavage structures of the 1920s'. Cleavage structures, and the party systems which embodied these cleavages had more or less 'frozen' in the 1920s in the wake of the final extension of the franchise to the working class and the property-less. Europe was then characterised by fully mobilised electorates expressing a set of political terms of reference which were to remain intact and relatively unchallenged through subsequent decades. With the final incorporation of the last block of the citizenry the political debate was more or less stabilised, and subsequent conflict and divisions revolved around variations on already stated themes. Thus, surveying the party landscape in the late 1960s, Lipset and Rokkan (1967, p. 5) found that 'the party alternatives, and in remarkably many cases the party organisations, are older than the majorities of the national electorates'. Alignments had frozen into place.

Although a wave of electoral volatility in the 1970s was seen to challenge the validity of this conclusion (e.g. Pedersen 1979; 1983; Maguire 1983), nevertheless the Irish case appeared to offer one of the clearest examples of such party-system maintenance, exemplified most clearly in the almost identical electoral outcomes of 1932 and 1982. Indeed, the level of volatility between the 1932 election, on the one hand, and the two elections of 1982, on the other, is perhaps less than that experienced by many Western European countries over consecutive elections in the 1970s! Going back even further, the particular strength of Fianna Fáil and Fine Gael has been traced to the virtual electoral monopoly enjoyed by Sinn Fein in the 1918 Westminster election (Farrell 1970; 1971), while the current weakness of the Labour Party is also seen to derive from this crucial contest, in that Labour's contemporary failure can be partially explained by its decision not to nominate any candidates in 1918, but rather 'to allow a demonstration of unity on the issue of self-determination' (Farrell 1971, p. 42).

But why do party systems persist? A crucial explanatory variable in the persistence theory advanced by Lipset and Rokkan concerns the timing of the extension of the franchise and of the introduction of universal male suffrage. It was the particular balance of political forces prevailing at that time which was to be frozen into place through its mobilisation into mass politics by the newly participant unpropertied and working-class voters. In these terms, the 1918 election in Ireland appears at just such a critical juncture. The extension of the franchise to the unpropertied and to women over the age of 30 had the effect of almost tripling the electorate—from some 700,000 voters at the previous election in 1910 to some 2 million in 1918 (Farrell 1971, p. 46).

The 1918 contest therefore had the potential to be a mobilising election *par excellence*, and the politics which it mobilised were nationalist politics. The only parties which competed in 1918 were those whose primary concern focused on the issue of self-determination. Sinn Fein sought immediate and total independence. The Irish Parliamentary Party sought Home Rule. The Unionists, whose major successes were achieved in what is now Northern Ireland, sought to prevent the secession of Ireland from the United Kingdom. Labour, as has been seen, withdrew. In addition, the election itself provided a massive victory for Sinn Fein. In Ireland as a whole, the movement won 73 of the

105 seats, with 26 for the Unionists and six for the IPP. In the 26-county area which was to become the Irish Free State, the Sinn Fein victory was even more convincing, winning 71 of the 76 seats, with three going to the Unionists and two to the IPP. Nationalist politics was clearly paramount in 1918, and given that this contest involved the mobilisation of an almost wholly new electorate, it seems that it is here that we must seek the key to understanding the subsequent dominance of Sinn Fein's successors—Fianna Fáil and Fine Gael.

Yet to treat 1918 as *the* mobilising election and as *the* source of a subsequent freezing of alternatives is, to say the least of it, problematic. There are four main difficulties involved in such an interpretation. First, the actual extent of popular mobilisation in 1918 was relatively low. Approximately one in three of the Sinn Fein victories were in uncontested seats, which in itself implies that some one in every three voters had no opportunity to register an electoral preference. Moreover, even in the contested constituencies turnout was not exceptionally high. Indeed, of those registered to vote in 1918, only some 47 per cent actually did vote, with some 53 per cent absenting themselves from the polls due to being unable or unwilling to register a preference (Mackie and Rose 1982, p. 192).

Second, even if we accept that nationalist politics had been frozen into place in 1918, we are then faced with the problem of accounting for the relatively high level of *non*-nationalist voting in June 1927, when the various strands of nationalist opinion—Fianna Fáil, Cumann na nGaedheal and the rump of Sinn Fein—together polled just 57 per cent of the popular vote which, given the low turnout, accounted for just 38 per cent of the registered electorate.

Third, even if June 1927 is read as a temporary aberration, there remains the problem of accounting for the outcome of the 1948 election, when the combined vote of Fianna Fáil and Fine Gael came to just 62 per cent, and in which the latter seemed almost on the verge of extinction. Finally, even if these points can be explained away, there is still the problem of explaining the relative decline of Labour after 1969 and, to a lesser extent, the relative growth of Fine Gael. Since 1969, the Labour vote has fallen by two-thirds, and while it now commands a similar level of support to that which it won in the early 1930s, its most recent debility can hardly be explained away by reference to events half-a-century before. In short, while an emphasis on the 1918 election is necessary for an understanding of the contemporary party system, by no means does it offer a sufficient explanation of the alignment. Too much has happened between then and now.

To be sure, all of these variations could be exaggerated. The support for Clann na Poblachta in the 1948 election, for instance, could be read simply as a variation on the 'frozen' nationalist theme given that in many ways the new party replicated the original appeal of Fianna Fáil. In a similar sense, the emergence of the PDs in 1987 can be read as simply a variant on traditional Fine Gaelism. But this in turn begs another question, which was already raised in the Introduction (p. 4): what exactly is meant by the freezing of party systems? Is it the politics and the cleavage structure which is frozen, or is it simply the party organisations themselves? If the former is the case, then one can envisage a situation of essential continuity which none the less is *also* character- ised by immense organisational fluctuation and electoral volatility. If the latter is the case, then even the most stable party configuration may conceal a wholesale transformation.

For the moment, however, I have chosen to concentrate on the persistence of the party organisations themselves for, as the historical overview makes clear, even the electoral dynamics of these organisa- tions clearly belies the notion that the contemporary political alignment is simply the product of historical inertia and of the freezing of an alignment initially mobilised in the first years of independence. Indeed, as will be argued throughout this study, the post-war consolidation of the traditional party system owed at least as much to the actual strategies of these parties as to any inherited legacy of the past. Three episodes stand out in particular in this regard: the crucial period following the legitimation of Fianna Fáil in 1927; the challenge of the new parties in the 1940s; and the decision of Labour and Fine Gael to coalesce in 1973.

Party Competition, 1927–33: The Failure of the Non-Nationalist Challenge

Let us begin with a truism: the relative success of non-nationalist parties and candidates in June 1927 was a reflection of the low degree of salience accorded to the intra-nationalist conflict of Fianna Fáil and Cumann na nGaedheal, while the subsequent decline of the non-nationalist alternative in the elections of September 1927, 1932 and 1933 was a symptom of the renewed salience of the intra-nationalist conflict after June 1927. The crucial watershed was the entry of Fianna Fáil into the Dáil in August 1927. As long as the major anti-Treaty opposition had persisted with an abstentionist strategy and had remained in the extra-parliamentary wilderness, the alternative non- nationalist opposition mounted by Labour, the Farmers Party and the

National League had achieved a particularly heightened profile. While never absent from the politics of the new state, the divisions over the Treaty had been at least at one remove from the day-to-day political agenda prior to August 1927. The resultant vacuum was rapidly filled by the demands of those concerned with the more immediate problems generated by social and economic policy.

Nor was this simply a case of a potential Sinn Fein/Fianna Fáil body of voters who were unwilling to waste their votes on an abstentionist party. Had that been the case, the entry of Fianna Fáil into the Dáil in August 1927 would have seen a surge in its vote while leaving that of Cumann na nGaedheal more or less unchanged. In fact, the legitimising strategy of Fianna Fáil led to a surge of votes for *both* of the Treaty parties, with Cumann na nGaedheal increasing from 28 per cent of the popular vote in June 1927 to 39 per cent in September 1927, while support for Fianna Fáil grew from 26 per cent to 35 per cent. In other words, the new strategy of Fianna Fáil increased the salience of the nationalist *cleavage* itself, a change which was to lead to a major increase in votes for both parties organising along that cleavage, and to a concomitant erosion of support for those parties mobilising along alternate dimensions of conflict. In June 1927 non-nationalist parties and Independents had won 43 per cent of the total vote; in September 1927, one month after the entry of Fianna Fáil into the Dáil, they won just 26 per cent. The legitimation of the anti-Treaty opposition not only served to emphasise the polarisation of nationalist politics, but also accorded that polarisation a degree of salience which was sufficient to defuse the potential for any alternative mobilisation. Moreover, as can be seen from Table 1.9, it began a trend which was to continue over the subsequent two elections and which was to underline the marginalisation of non-Treaty politics in the new state.

The second point to note here is that the growth of the Treaty parties coincided with the final stage of political mobilisation. Turnout increased marginally from 68 per cent to 69 per cent between June and September 1927, and then jumped to 77 per cent in 1932 and to 81 per cent in 1933, a level of participation which was to remain unsurpassed in the subsequent history of the state. The effect of this was to take Fianna Fáil and Cumann na nGaedheal from a position in which they commanded the support of 54 per cent of voters and 36 per cent of the electorate in June 1927 to one in which they won more than 80 per cent of the voters and 64 per cent of the electorate in 1933. Moreover, if we add to this latter figure the support of the Centre Party, which was to merge with Cumann na nGaedheal to form Fine Gael later in 1933, the

Table 1.9 Voting percentages, 1927–33

	June 1927	Sept. 1927	1932	1933
Sinn Fein	3.6	–	–	–
Fianna Fáil	26.1	35.2	44.5	49.7
Cumann na nGaedheal	27.5	38.7	35.3	30.5
Labour	12.6	9.1	7.7	5.7
National League	7.3	1.6	–	–
Farmers' Party	8.9	6.4	3.1	–
Centre Party	–	–	–	9.2
Others	14.1	9.1	9.4	5.0
Index of volatility*	na	20.3	9.6	14.4
Index of fractionalisation†	0.806	0.705	0.662	0.646
% valid votes	66.3	67.7	75.3	80.4

* The index of volatility is based on the formula in Pedersen (1983)
† The fractionalisation index is based on the formula in Rae (1971)
Source: Mackie and Rose (1982).

Table 1.10 Electoral mobilisation: party shares of electorate, 1927–33

	June 1927	Sept 1927	1932	1933	
Sinn Fein	2.4	–	–	–	
Fianna Fáil	17.3	23.8	33.5	40.0 }	31.9†
Cumann na nGaedheal	18.2	26.2	26.6	24.5 }	
Centre Party	–	–	–	7.4	
Labour	8.3	6.1	5.8	4.6	
Others*	20.0	11.6	9.4	4.0	
Non-voters/Invalid votes	33.7	32.3	24.7	19.6	
Total electorate	100.0	100.0	100.0	100.0	

* Includes National League, Farmers' Party and Independents
‡ In 1933, after the election, Cumann na nGaedheal and the Centre Party merged to form Fine Gael
Source: Mackie and Rose (1982).

results are even more striking, amounting to 89 per cent of the vote and 72 per cent of the electorate (see Table 1.10). By 1933, therefore, the predecessors of the two parties which currently dominate the party system had achieved an extraordinarily high level of electoral penetration—*double* that achieved in June 1927 and significantly greater than that achieved by Sinn Fein in 1918.

Do the elections of 1927–33 therefore constitute a new critical juncture which, together with that of 1918, was to freeze the political alternatives into place? As Sinnott (1978, p. 37) rightly points out, there are three central aspects involved in the Lipset–Rokkan thesis. First, there is the actual timing of the introduction of universal adult male *suffrage* which, in the Irish case, immediately preceded the 1918 election, when 75 per cent of the adult population was enfranchised; the remaining 25 per cent, including women aged between 21 and 30, were enfranchised in 1923. The second aspect concerns the timing of full electoral *mobilisation*. In the Irish case, there were really three waves of mobilisation: the first occurred in 1918, and involved the participation of just less than half the enfranchised electorate; the second came between 1923 and 1927, when approximately two-thirds of the electorate participated; and the third occurred in 1932–3, when participation reached its effective maximum of 80 per cent. The final aspect concerns the particular *cleavage* or cleavages which formed the basis of that mobilisation. In the first phase, the nationalist cleavage was clearly the only relevant one, in that non-nationalist parties did not even offer any candidates for election. The second wave, however, was characterised by a significant concern for non-nationalist issues, and occurred at a time when it seemed that the non-nationalist opposition might actually force a substantial realignment. The final phase of mobilisation was again dominated by the nationalist cleavage, in the form of a polarised conflict between those supporting and those opposing the Treaty settlement.

But it is also important to recognise that the division in this final phase of mobilisation was not *wholly* nationalist, at least in the sense that it involved more than simply territorial or constitutional issues. The Fianna Fáil–Cumann na nGaedheal opposition also revolved around the crucial conflict of free trade versus economic autarchy, with a general but nevertheless substantial radical-conservative overlay. Moreover, particularly in so far as it began to find expression in the violent confrontations between the pro-Fianna Fáil IRA and the pro-Cumann na nGaedheal Blueshirts, it was also a conflict which involved the legitimacy and the authority of the regime itself. A division marked by such intensity and pervasiveness would inevitably impact on future generations.

To treat the period from 1927 to 1933 as an extended period of alignment is also inadequate, however, since the party system proved as unstable after this period as it had before. In other words, there is still a considerable degree of unexplained variation. As has been noted, Fine Gael entered a period of steady decline after 1933, its vote finally falling below 20 per cent in 1948. Labour, adopting a more independent position in the late 1930s, seemed set to challenge for a new major role in the party system, while the 1940s also witnessed the emergence of the two new Clann parties. In short, while Fianna Fáil was to maintain the dominant position which it first gained in the early 1930s, the other parties seemed as much in flux *after* the 'aligning period' as before. Far from being wholly frozen by 1933, the party alternatives remained unsettled.

Party Competition in the 1940s

The essence of the original division within Sinn Fein was undoubtedly nationalist. Fianna Fáil sought full independence from the United Kingdom, while Cumann na nGaedheal/Fine Gael proved content to work within the confines of dominion status—at least in the short term. That said, I have also emphasised the importance of the social and economic components of the division, and the sense in which it was also characterised by a significant radical-conservative overlay. Fianna Fáil not only mobilised more militant republican feeling, but it also voiced a radical opposition to the status quo which allowed it to harness the dissatisfaction of the more deprived and disadvantaged sectors in the new state. Fianna Fáil was not simply a nationalist party; it was also the party of the 'have-nots', winning the support of the small farmers and the nascent urban working class. 'Although we stand for all sections of the people', remarked de Valera in 1951 (*Irish Press*, 30 May), 'nevertheless the sections for which we have a special regard . . . are the small farmers on the one hand, and the workers on the other'. In this sense the original conflict went beyond mere territorial and constitutional questions to approximate, in a very loose fashion, a left–right opposition.

However, Fianna Fáil's advent to office in 1932, supported—appropriately—by the Labour Party, was soon followed by an extension of its appeal into the former heartland of Cumann na nGaedheal. As noted earlier, Fianna Fáil's first decade of government was characterised by a centre-seeking strategy which won it new respect among those who had originally viewed it as a harbinger of chaos. Garvin (1981a, pp. 166–7) offers a brief but incisive account of the change, documenting the shift from the politics of protest in the early 1930s to a position in the 1940s where it had moved into 'a central position in Irish society' and had established 'an extraordinary electoral empire ... [which] defied class distinctions'. The most evident consequence of this change was the gradual erosion of Fine Gael support. More importantly, however, this centre-seeking strategy was to have an additional impact elsewhere in the party system, as other parties emerged in a major attempt to succeed in the leadership of Ireland's disadvantaged constituency. For, as Fianna Fáil became increasingly incorporated as the party of government and as the party of the status quo, a space began to open on its left which seemed to allow for a new radical mobilisation. This new mobilisation occurred in the 1940s, in what was almost a mirror-image of the earlier mobilisation which had carried Fianna Fáil to victory in 1932 and 1933. But whereas Fianna Fáil had managed to aggregate the differing strands of protest under one broad political programme, the new mobilisation was dispersed across three parties. Labour, Clann na Talmhan and Clann na Poblachta, with the latter appearing to offer the most potent possibility of realignment.

Consider the situation. Fianna Fáil had shifted towards the centre, if not towards the centre-right of the political spectrum, and was threatening the very existence of Fine Gael. In so doing, it had opened up a space for a new radical politics on its left, making available once more elements of the 'have-not' constituency which it had initially mobilised in the 1920s and early 1930s. Three parties, two new and one old, then began an attempt to win over that constituency, or at least its component parts. Clann na Talmhan attempted to harness the grievances of the disillusioned small farmers. Labour sought to consolidate its own appeal among the rural proletariat and attempted to woo the urban working class, an attempt which was severely curtailed by the 1944 split within the party. Finally, Clann na Poblachta sought to marry republican discontent and a strong commitment to social justice in a replication in miniature of the earlier Fianna Fáil appeal.

To be sure, this tripartite assault on Fianna Fáil's now neglected constituency was neither ideologically cohesive nor unambiguous. Clann na Talmhan may have reflected the genuine grievances of marginalised small farmers, for example, but in no other sense could it be described as a very radical party. Moreover, the three components vied with one another almost to the same extent as they vied with Fianna Fáil, and it is likely that a number of voters viewed them simply as part of an alternative to Fianna Fáil rather than as the expression of a new radical opposition. In this sense, the parties were often grouped with the more conservative and ever-declining Fine Gael, and certainly Clann na Talmhan won voters from that party. Nevertheless, for a large segment of voters, whether small farmers, farm labourers, trade-unionists or republicans, the new parties must inevitably have been seen as a vehicle for the implementation of reform and as articulators of the needs of those who felt themselves neglected by both Fine Gael and Fianna Fáil.

The dynamic which created Clann na Talmhan and boosted the fortunes of Labour, and which later was to provide the impetus for Clann na Poblachta, eventually waned away. Had it continued, the map of contemporary Irish politics might well have looked remarkably different. For this to have occurred, however, two related trends evident in the 1940s would have had to continue: first, Fine Gael would have had to continue to decline; and second, as a consequence, Fianna Fáil would have had to continue to drift to the right as it steadily absorbed Fine Gael's more conservative constituency. Had this occurred, there would have remained some scope for a new radical opposition. In such circumstances, it is not impossible to conceive of a new alignment in which a centre-right Fianna Fáil would have been confronted by a centre-left coalition or amalgam of Labour and Clann na Poblachta (and possibly even Clann na Talmhan, although this is more arguable), a coalition which might not only have been sustained over time, but which also might have induced an alternative language of politics.

This is all mere speculation of course, and the reality proved quite different. Fine Gael recovered, Fianna Fáil drifted back towards the centre or centre-left, and the challenge of the new opposition came to nothing. I would argue, however, that the processes which led to this restoration of 'normality' owe less to historical inertia, and rather more to the actual alliance strategy adopted by the smaller parties.

In the 1948 election Fianna Fáil had won just 42 per cent of the popular vote and 46 per cent of the Dáil seats. Although remaining the largest party, it was thus possible for an alternative government to emerge. Fine Gael had won just less than 20 per cent of the popular vote and 21 per cent of the seats. Labour and National Labour had won 11 per cent of the vote and 13 per cent of the seats. Clann na Poblachta had won 13 per cent of the vote and 7 per cent of the seats, and Clann na Talmhan had won 6 per cent of the vote and 5 per cent of the seats. Independent candidates had won 8 per cent of the votes and also 8 per cent of the seats. The question of government formation was therefore completely open. Fianna Fáil could govern on its own as a minority administration, with support from either the Independents or one of the other parties. Alternatively, it could attempt to form a coalition, but to do so would be to undermine its own emphasis on single-party government as an essential prerequisite of stability. As against this, the other parties could attempt to form their own coalition, involving the participation or support of the Independent TDs.

Labour and the other new parties faced a crucial choice. They could either allow Fianna Fáil to remain in office as a minority administration, and thus allow themselves more time in which to mobilise an alternative politics; or they could subordinate their differences in the interests of forming a broad anti-Fianna Fáil alliance which, inevitably, would involve and also be dominated by Fine Gael as the largest of the potential allies.

In the event, the smaller parties opted for the latter alternative and, with the support of the Independents, they created a minority coalition government under the Fine Gael leadership which commanded 46.3 per cent of the Dáil seats (cf. Table 1.5). The rest, as they say, is history. The coalition eventually resigned; the combined vote of the two Clann parties fell to just 7 per cent in the next election; Labour—now reunited—retained its vote, and Fine Gael was set back on the road to electoral recovery, gaining some 6 per cent of the votes with respect to 1948. Thereafter the trend continued, with a second faltering coalition holding office between 1954 and 1957, and with Fine Gael and Labour steadily growing until they more or less enjoyed a virtual monopoly of the opposition to Fianna Fáil. By 1969, Fine Gael and Labour together accounted for 94 per cent of the non-Fianna Fáil vote.

In terms of the crude left–right or radical–conservative continuum, the logic was even more evident. The experience of coalition had restored Fine Gael to relative electoral health, and reinstated the party as the favoured exponent of centre-right opinion. This, in turn, discouraged Fianna Fáil from encroaching further on the right. At the same time, the experience of coalition was also sufficient to discredit and almost destroy Clann na Poblachta, and thus opened up some space to the left of Fianna Fáil which encouraged the latter to compete once more for its old radical constituency. In short, competition to the right no longer seemed rewarding for Fianna Fáil, whereas competition to the left seemed immediately more attractive. The Fianna Fáil choice was clear and, as Bew and Patterson (1982) ably document, the party's response was unequivocal: despite opposition from more conservative elements in the party, the Fianna Fáil deputy leader, Séan Lemass, launched a drive towards social and economic reform which, *inter alia*, was to cement its alliance with the working class and the trade unions.

In effect, the alliance strategy of the smaller parties had had three major consequences. First, by choosing to ally with the conservative Fine Gael, the radical elements in the coalition had effectively denied their earlier emphasis on reformist politics and thereby weakened their own opportunity for future reformist mobilisation. Second, their alliance with Fine Gael had allowed the latter a necessary lease of life which, in turn, halted the rightward drift of Fianna Fáil and so curtailed the space for a new radical mobilisation. Third, by aligning themselves into a broad anti-Fianna Fáil alliance, they had encouraged a view of politics as organising around simply two camps—those who supported Fianna Fáil and those who did not. Within such a simple bipolar opposition, there seemed little or no room for any new or distinct appeal.

Finally, as Labour was to rediscover after 1969, the legacy of the anti-Fianna Fáil alliance meant that it now proved increasingly difficult for a minor party to appeal for votes if the only strategic option for that party lay in joining a Fine Gael-dominated coalition. Strategically constrained by the need to form a governing alternative in a context where one of the major parties, Fianna Fáil, eschewed coalition, it seemed as if there could be little opportunity for minor party growth.

Labour after 1969

Between 1957 and 1973 the Labour Party had pursued an independent strategy which was accompanied by an increasingly radicalised electoral appeal. In a sense, the party adopted a style similar to that which had characterised its growing alienation from Fianna Fáil in the 1930s. During the 1960s the party found itself blanketed in a new and quite unprecedented wave of optimism. 'The Seventies Will be Socialist' was a frequent catchcry and, rhetorically at any rate, the party experienced a significant turn to the left. By the late 1960s it had begun to speak of 'a new Republic', and had begun to see itself as the primary voice for socialist policies and working-class demands. Party membership rapidly increased, it began to attract a new generation of intellectuals and radicals, and enjoyed a substantial electoral growth, particularly in Dublin. The national Labour vote increased from 9 per cent in 1957 to 17 per cent in 1969, and in Dublin it increased from 8 per cent to 28 per cent, making it the second largest party in the city. Once again, Labour seemed on the threshold of majority-party status.

Yet what appears as a relative success in hindsight was viewed by the party itself as a relative failure. Despite the increased vote in 1969, Labour found itself no closer to what some of its more optimistic ideologues had hoped would be a single-party Labour government. Indeed, in 1969, despite a large increase in the number of Labour seats in Dublin, the overall Dáil representation of the party actually declined from 22 to 18, as rural TDs were defeated in what they believed to be a conservative reaction to the new socialist rhetoric. Faced with this outcome, and despairing of every achieving majority status, Labour reverted to a coalition strategy in 1973 when, despite a decline in its overall vote, the party did gain one extra seat. This, together with Fine Gael gains, was sufficient to put the coalition in office and to displace Fianna Fáil for the first time in 16 years. The coalition alliance persisted through to January 1987, and the two parties were returned to office in 1981 and again in November 1982.

Labour's reversion to a coalition strategy was certainly under-standable. To the extent that a minority party with governing ambitions believes it impossible to achieve majority status, it will be obliged to forge alliances with other minority parties. Labour had seen its electoral support grow in the 1960s, but found itself unable to translate this growth into Dáil seats. The result was the continuance of Fianna Fáil in office while both Labour and Fine Gael grew increasingly frustrated with the persistent politics of opposition. If Labour was intent on having its policies adopted at governmental level, and if it could not hope to form a government on its own, then the next best option was coalition. And since Fianna Fáil completely eschewed any possibility of coalition, Labour was then obliged to revert to an alliance with Fine Gael. Hence the decision in 1973 and its reaffirmation in later years.

The problem with such a strategy, however, has been that it has weakened Labour's independent appeal. There is an evident logic here. As long as Labour remained committed to its alliance with Fine Gael, a vote for Labour became a vote for coalition. Moreover, and barring any electoral earthquake, a vote for coalition was also a vote for a Fine Gael-dominated coalition. Thus Labour not only appealed for votes on its own behalf, but also on behalf of an alliance of which it was a minority partner. In such circumstances, the logic of voting for Labour *rather than voting for Fine Gael* proved difficult to sustain; since a vote for Labour was a vote for a Fine Gael-dominated coalition, then in many ways it may make more sense simply to vote for Fine Gael *per se*.

Of course, this logic might not hold true if Labour were seen to have a discernible and independent impact on the policies of the coalition. Thus, while a vote for Labour would still be a vote for a Fine Gael-dominated coalition, it would at least make sense as a means of increasing Labour's voice within that coalition. In practice, however, for much of the coalition period Labour did not appear to make its voice heard—this was to change somewhat during the 1982–7 government which collapsed when Labour withdrew from coalition—and allowed itself to be subsumed within the alliance to the extent that in 1973 and 1977 both parties campaigned on a joint manifesto. And while Labour could and eventually did threaten Fine Gael with withdrawal from coalition, the party has not been in a position to threaten an *alternative* alliance, since Fianna Fáil had eschewed coalition. In this sense, it is in a very different position from some other Western European minor parties which find themselves as junior partners in coalition, for, unlike the German FDP, for example, Labour is not a *pivotal* party—at least as far as coalition-making is concerned (offering external support for alternative minority governments is another matter altogether). Lacking an independent role, Labour thus finds there is little to emphasise in favour of its own case. It also finds itself with few strategic options: either it faces a loss of power by returning to opposition, or it faces a loss of identity by subsuming itself within coalition. In short, Labour finds itself strategically constrained by the logistics of party competition.

Labour's unfortunate position has been reflected in a steady electoral decline since 1973. In national terms, Labour's vote has fallen from 17 per cent in 1969 to 14 per cent in 1973, to 12 per cent in 1981, to 9 per cent in each of the elections of 1982, and to just over 6 per cent in 1987. But even these are not the most telling figures.

Viewed as part of the coalition alliance, Labour has experienced an even more severe decline. In 1969 Labour won 30 per cent of the combined Fine Gael–Labour vote. In 1973 and 1977 this fell to 28 per cent, and to just 21 per cent in 1981. In the two elections of 1982 it fell to below 20 per cent, and finally fell to just 19 per cent in 1987. The persistence of coalition in this period acted to reinforce the bipolar pattern of Irish politics. In so doing it has encouraged a drift from Labour to Fine Gael as the increasingly dominant partner of the non-Fianna Fáil side of the divide. Tangentially, it is also worth recording that in October 1982 the then leader of the Labour Party not only resigned his leadership, but also resigned from the party itself, and one week later joined the ranks of Fine Gael (Gallagher 1985, p. 82).

Nor is the failure to compete with Fine Gael the only source of Labour decline. Viewed as part of the left, Labour's debility is even more evident. In 1969, as effectively the only party on the left, Labour won virtually 100 per cent of the left vote. Since then, its monopoly has been challenged by independent socialist candidates, by minor left parties such as the Socialist Labour Party which split from Labour over the coalition question, and by the Workers Party, which outpolled Labour in Dublin in the 1987 election. In 1973 Labour won 92 per cent of the left vote. This fell to 81 per cent in 1977, to 79 per cent in 1981, to 73 per cent in February 1982, to 69 per cent in November 1982, and to just 58 per cent in 1987.

Labour's position is hardly enviable. The evidence suggests that it has suffered an erosion of its pro-coalition support, which drifted towards Fine Gael, and an erosion of its anti-coalition support, which drifted towards the Workers party and other independent socialist candidates. Within such a context, the question for Labour becomes not one of future growth but rather of sheer survival. Moreover, if this analysis is accepted, then it can be suggested that this current debility derived in large part from its commitment to coalition. Had Labour proved less impatient—a similar impatience had arguably curtailed the growth of Clann na Poblachta in the 1940s—and had it maintained its independent strategy after 1969 in an effort to build on the electoral gains of the 1960s, it is not inconceivable that it might have supplanted Fine Gael as the second party in the system. Such a diagnosis is also shared by the party's recent commission on electoral strategy (Labour Party 1986), which argued that Labour growth necessitates a rejection of future coalition options.

Whether Labour would have broken through to major party status had it rejected the coalition option in 1973 is, again, mere speculation. What is undeniable, however, is that Labour's marginal role in the Irish party system cannot simply be explained by historical inertia and by reference to the legacy of 1918, of the late 1920s, or even of the 1940s. Rather, it is in large part due to the logic of party strategy, and to the choices and decisions of the Labour leadership as well as to the choices and decisions of the leaderships of its competitors. The dynamics of party competition, together with the inevitable pressures of an office-seeking strategy, have left Labour with little discernible voice in contemporary Irish politics. To suggest that this is the fault of those Labour leaders who stood aside for Sinn Fein in 1918, or even of those leaders who opted for coalition with Fine Gael and the other minor parties in the 1940s, is to ignore the importance of contemporary political realities. The strategy adopted by the present Labour leadership, as well as that of the leadership of Fianna Fáil and Fine Gael, is at least as relevant as the decisions made by their respective predecessors.

Persistence, Change and the Relevance of Party Competition

These arguments are not intended to challenge the general theory of Lipset and Rokkan (1967). On the contrary, cleavages do persist and the parties which organize along these cleavages maintain a hold and a momentum which stretches far beyond the point at which they initially mobilised. But while parties and party systems persist, it is also necessary to emphasise that they do not persist *per se*, but persist under certain conditions and within certain circumstances. These conditions and circumstances may be environmental—that is, they may relate to the social structure, the prevailing value system, the institutional context, and so on—but they may also belong in the party arena itself, and have much to do with the strategy of the parties, their ideological appeals and the manner in which they compete.

In other words, the capacity of parties to persist is not predetermined, and the rules of the political game are not necessarily set irrevocably from the beginning of mass politics. Parties do not survive simply because of the circumstances which surround their take-off, while other parties do not fail simply because they got off to a bad start. Rather, parties *also* persist because of their own independent and continuing capacity to structure mass electoral attitudes and behaviour.

This emphasis on the independent impact of the parties and the party systems owes much to the innovative argument of Sartori (1969: 1976). Addressing the analysis of Lipset and Rokkan and the question of the freezing of party systems, Sartori essentially turns the problem on its head, arguing that the freezing of a system is only intriguing if one persists in viewing parties as dependent variables; it is not intriguing, however, if it is accepted that a frozen party system is simply 'a party system that intervenes in the political process as an independent *system of channelment*, propelled and maintained by its own laws of inertia' (Sartori 1969, p. 90). As should be evident from the discussion of the shifting dynamics of party competition in the late 1920s and early 1930s, in the 1940s, as well as more recently in the post-1969 phase, the Irish case offers what is virtually a text-book example of such

independent channelment. In all three cases it can be argued that the
potential for major change was frustrated by the strategic decisions of
the parties themselves, and as a consequence of the logistics of government formation.

In short, there is nothing inevitable about the persistent dominance
of Fianna Fáil in contemporary Irish politics. Nor is it inevitable that
Fine Gael remained the main challenger to Fianna Fáil, nor that Labour
remains on the margins. While the fact that Sinn Fein won a landslide in
1918 and that Labour failed to involve itself in that crucial contest may
be of immense importance, it seems hardly a sufficient explanation for
the continued success of Sinn Fein's offspring and the continued
weakness of Labour through to the 1980s. In the mid- to late 1920s it
appeared that an alternative politics might emerge, but this was
frustrated by the legitimising strategy of Fianna Fáil. In the 1940s, a
major realignment of the party system also seemed possible, but was
arguably frustrated by the alliance strategy of the smaller and more
radical parties and particularly by Clann na Poblachta's loss of nerve
over the Mother and Child scheme. Again in the late 1960s it seemed
possible for Labour to emerge as a major political force, but its decision
to opt for a coalition strategy appears to have frustrated its potential
growth. In other words, what the parties themselves have done, and the
manner in which they compete, must also be included as central
components in any equation which attempts to explain the persistence
and freezing of alignments. This is not simply to indulge in a series of
'what if' speculations. Rather, the point is to emphasise that the
persistence and consolidation of the traditional parties is more contingent than much of the existing literature would have us believe. In short,
party strategy matters.

If this overview of the Irish party system says anything, therefore, it is
that a full understanding of the contemporary political alignment
requires less emphasis on the inertia of tradition and on the sheer force
of history, and correspondingly more emphasis on the parties as well as
on the party system itself. The partisan balance is not a given; rather,
individual parties may also win or lose support as a result of their
respective electoral strategies, organisational capacities, and their
ideological appeals. Competition is crucial, and an analysis of the
patterns of competition in the Irish party system will be the task of the
following chapters.

2
DO IRISH PARTIES COMPETE?

The suggestion that parties compete involves two major assumptions: first, it assumes that *parties* are actually relevant to voting behaviour; and second, it assumes that voters actually *choose* between parties. Such assumptions may appear quite straightforward, and indeed they are accepted by almost the entire literature on party competition. In the Irish case, however, there are two quite compelling reasons to challenge these basic assumptions.

The first and most evident difficulty is the ambiguity created by the Irish electoral system, in that voters indicate preferences for individual candidates rather than for parties as such. Since independence, voting in Ireland has been carried out by means of the Single Transferable Vote (STV) in multi-member constituencies. Voters are presented with ballot papers listing the names of the individual candidates in alphabetical order and voters then rank these candidates on a 1, 2, 3, etc. basis in order of preference. The ballot papers are then collated and grouped according to the first-preference votes shown thereon. Any candidate who receives a quota (see below) of votes on the basis of these first preferences is declared elected. If he/she wins more first preferences than is required for a quota, the resultant *surplus* is then distributed to the remaining candidates in proportion to the distribution of second preferences across the total number of ballot papers of the successful candidate. If no candidate receives sufficient first preferences to reach the quota, then the candidate with the lowest number of first preferences is eliminated and his/her votes allocated to the remaining candidates according to the distribution of second preferences on his/her ballot papers. The count continues in this way until all the seats are filled, gradually electing candidates who reach or surpass the quota and distributing their surpluses, and/or eliminating candidates and redistributing all of their votes. Where a candidate is eliminated or has a surplus, and where no subsequent preference is indicated on the ballot paper, that ballot is deemed non-transferable. To the extent that votes do become non-transferable, and so diminish the pool of votes available for distribution, it becomes possible for one or more candidates to be elected without actually reaching the quota. Where one seat remains to be filled, for instance, and where there are only two candidates remaining in the running, the candidate with a plurality of votes is deemed elected regardless of whether he/she has reached the quota (for an example of a constituency count, see Table 2.3 below).

The quota itself is calculated by dividing the total number of valid votes by one more than the number of seats, and then by adding one to the resulting figure. For example, in a four-seat constituency with a total valid poll of 40,000, the quota is $[40,000/(4 + 1)] + 1 = 8,001$. The quota is therefore the smallest number of votes which at the same time will ensure that only the requisite number of seats is filled. In the above example, 8,001 is the smallest figure which will allow only four seats to be filled, in that the next number below this—8,000—could allow for the election of five candidates. All constituencies in Ireland are multi-member constituencies. During the inter-war period, some of these constituencies were particularly large, involving seven, eight, and in one case even nine seats. Over the post-war period, however, no constituency has been allocated more than five seats or less than three seats. Tangentially, it can be noted that as the number of seats in a constituency increases, there is a corresponding decrease in the quota as a percentage of the total valid poll. In a three-seat constituency, for example, the quota is obtained by dividing the total valid poll by four, and then adding 1 to the result, thus making the quota some 25 per cent of the valid poll. Conversely, in a nine-seat constituency the divisor is ten, and so the quota is only 10 per cent of the valid poll. The larger the number of seats in a given constituency, therefore, the lower is the effective threshold of representation.

The ambiguities presented by such an electoral system in any discussion of the *parties* competing for votes is obvious, for it is perfectly conceivable that voters may orientate only to individual *candidates*. Certainly the relatively enormous body of literature on the incidence of clientelism and brokerage in Irish politics (from Chubb 1963 to Komito 1984) would seem to indicate the importance of personalistic rather than partisan links between voters and politicians. To be sure there is a presence of party in so far as both Fianna Fáil and Fine Gael almost always nominate more than one candidate in each constituency and voters can link these candidates through the medium of their common party label[1] ranking, say, candidate A of Fianna Fáil in first position, candidate B in second, candidate C in third, and so on. But voters are under no obligation to rank in terms of party, and they may choose instead to rank by gender, locality, or whatever, ordering the different candidates regardless of their party affiliation.

In addition to the candidate versus party problem, however, there is a second difficulty which seems to militate against any easy application of notions of party competition to the Irish case, and this is the problem of electoral *choice*. For even if it can be shown that a substantial number of voters do orientate primarily to parties rather than to candidates, it does not necessarily follow that they *choose* between parties on election day. To the extent that those voters who orientate to party are *also* strong party loyalists, for example, then their presence does not of itself indicate the existence of competition within a electoral market. For such an electoral market to exist, it is necessary that at least some of those voters who are orientated to party also choose between the competing parties at elections, rather than simply expressing a long-standing affective attachment.

As far as the Irish case is concerned the essential problem here is the interplay of personalistic politics on the one hand and party orientations on the other.[2] Both elements have been widely discussed in the literature on Irish politics, and most recently have enjoyed an extensive analysis by Carty (1981). For Carty, however, as in other analyses of Irish voting, the party *orientation* component is almost entirely reducible to a notion of party *loyalty*. In other words, those voters who orientate primarily to parties are *also* party loyalists with enduring affective ties to a particular party, and are therefore not part of an electoral market as such. Carty thus presents two distinct models of Irish voting behaviour: 'the first, emphasising the parochial and particularistic character of electoral competition, argues that voters are mobilised by the personalised appeals of local notables . . . The second . . . contends that the electorate has a highly developed set of partisan allegiances, so that individual voting reflects a voter's party identification' (Carty 1981, p. 62). Both interpretations are plausible. The problem, however, is that by emphasising candidate and non-party voting, on the one hand, and partisan loyalty, on the other, they effectively combine to prevent the applicability to the Irish case of any real notion of party competition *per se*. To the extent that a voter is orientated to candidates rather than to parties, then the party as such can do little to win that voter's support. Conversely, to the extent that a voter has a highly developed sense of partisan loyalty, there seems little point in an alternative party seeking to win over that voter. To adopt these interpretations is therefore to rule out the existence of an electoral market, and to deny the possibility that voters may also be *in competition* between the parties.

In a seminal discussion of patterns of polarisation and fragmentation in Western European party systems, Giacomo Sani and Giovanni

Sartori (1983, pp. 329–35) identify a crucial distinction between that which is in competition and that which is not. Their concern is primarily with issues and ideologies, that is with the substantive content of party competition (for which see Chapter 4 below), but the distinction may also be usefully applied to voters themselves. Thus, sections of the electorate may be seen as winnable by the parties through competition, and as such may be considered to be in competition. Different sections of the electorate, on the other hand, may be considered as more or less unwavering in terms of their pre-existing commitments or political loyalties, and as such considered to be out of competition. Different sections again may not be orientated to party at all, but rather to candidates, personalities or whatever, and these also may be considered to be out of competition as far as the *parties* are concerned. This latter category seems particularly appropriate to the Irish case where, given the electoral system and given that parties often nominate more than one candidate in a constituency, candidates choice may not be the same as party choice.

Following this distinction, therefore, the general thrust of this chapter is to argue that there is indeed a substantial and growing body of voters in competition between the parties. In other words, this chapter argues that there is not only a pervasive orientation to party in the Irish electorate, but also that a substantial proportion of party voters actually choose which party to support as opposed to simply expressing long-standing affective loyalties. Finally, I will argue that the parties themselves are becoming increasingly aware of the importance of these voters in competition and are modifying their electoral strategies accordingly, as well as their general organisational styles (see Chapter 3 below).

Of course if the parties are to find the competition for votes worthwhile, then it is necessary to show that they are likely to be rewarded in terms of seats as well as votes: if the parties are to compete, they must have something to gain. In this sense, while the presence of voters in competition may be a necessary condition for the adoption of competitive electoral strategies by the parties, it is hardly sufficient, since the winning of additional party voters must also lead to winning additional seats and, perhaps, to winning government office itself. The basic problem here is that, for a number of reasons, Irish elections have often been seen to be non-competitive—at least in terms of party. First, over the entire post-war period, alternation in government has depended on the capacity of the non-Fianna Fáil parties to form a coalition, an option rejected by these parties in the period from 1957 to 1973. Thus even if

Fianna Fáil suffered substantial electoral losses, which it sometimes did, and even if these resulted in a loss of seats to other parties, the party was still more or less guaranteed a return to office as the only party in a position to form a government. Second, as a result of both the peculiarities of the STV electoral system and the nomination strategies of the parties, many constituencies have been seen as essentially non-competitive between parties, in that the struggle for the final seat in many multi-member constituencies has been fought out between competing candidates from the same party. In a related vein, a substantial amount of the turnover of seats at elections has resulted from *intra*-party competition, in which an incumbent candidate from a given party has been displaced by a running-mate from the same party. Between 1951 and 1977, for instance, some 30 per cent of competitive seat changes were accounted for in this fashion (Carty 1981, p. 114).

However, there is evidence to suggest that this view of Irish elections as non-competitive between the parties cannot be wholly justified. Since the formation of the Fine Gael–Labour coalition of 1973, for example, there has been a practical governing alternative to Fianna Fáil and there has been a regular alternation in office. Fianna Fáil victory is no longer so assured as was once the case: between 1932 and 1973, for instance, Fianna Fáil had been in office for all but six years; since 1973, on the other hand, it has actually been in office for only some five years. Over the past decade or so, the gain or loss of simply a handful of seats has determined the composition of the incoming government, and thus the parties now have a lot at stake.

Second, despite high levels of intra-party competition, an average of more than two-thirds of constituencies since 1961 have in fact been subject to *inter*-party competition for the final seat. In other words, the winner of the last seat in contention in these constituencies has been subject to challenge from a candidate competing from an alternative platform. The relevant figures are shown in Table 2.1, which shows the proportion of constituencies where the runner(s)-up was *not* from the same party as the candidate who won the final seat. The proportion varies from a low of 52 per cent of constituencies in 1973 to a high of 76 per cent in 1961, averaging 68 per cent over the 1961–87 period as a whole. Nor is the gap between the winner of the last seat and the runner(s)-up insubstantial: in more than half of all constituencies and in three in every four of the inter-party competitive constituencies the number of votes separating the final victor from the opposing party's runner(s)-up was less than 30 per cent of the quota, thus often involving substantially fewer than 2,500 votes.

Table 2.1 Inter-party competitiveness of Irish constituencies, 1961–87

Year	Constituencies with inter-party competition for final seat* %	Marginal constituencies as a percentage of those with inter-party competition for final seat† %	Marginal constituencies as a percentage of all constituencies %	N
1987	70.7	69.0	48.8	(41)
1982 (ii)	73.2	66.6	48.8	(41)
1982 (i)	70.7	79.2	56.1	(41)
1981	75.6	74.2	56.1	(41)
1977	64.3	92.5	59.5	(42)
1973	52.4	68.2	35.7	(42)
1969	69.0	72.3	50.0	(42)
1965	63.2	75.0	47.4	(38)
1961	76.3	75.8	57.9	(38)
Mean	68.4	74.8	51.1	

* Defined as such where the runner(s)-up competes from a different platform than the candidate who wins the final seat.

† Marginal constituencies are here defined to be those where the margin of votes separating the last candidate to be elected and then runner-up is less than 30 per cent of the quota.

Putting both these points together, it can be suggested that the competing parties do indeed have much to gain from an improvement in their electoral performance: party seats can be won or lost and the resultant shifts *can* make the difference between government and opposition. Thus, it is in the parties' interests to compete for and to win over those voters in competition. Who these voters might be, and how the parties hope to attract them, will be the subject of the remainder of this chapter.

Voters in Competition

There are two levels of competition in Irish elections. On the one hand, parties compete with one another to accumulate the greatest possible amounts of first-preference votes and to ensure that their voters rank all of the party's candidates in the highest possible positions. On the other hand, there is a significant degree of intra-party competition in which the individual candidates of a given party in a given constituency compete with one another to see who occupies any seats won by that party. Obviously these considerations apply only when the parties nominate slates of candidates; where a party nominates only one candidate, there will be no intra-party competition and the voter will be unable to separate candidate preference from party preference: to choose the party is to choose the candidate and vice versa. In practice, of the three parties considered in this study, only Labour has frequently tended to nominate single candidates in the individual constituencies, while both Fianna Fáil and Fine Gael normally nominate a plurality of candidates. Where there is a plurality of party candidates, then the voter not only must choose which party to support, if any, but also which candidate within the party to rank in the highest position. Hence, for a party voter, party preference is only the first step; thereafter a ranking of the candidates within that party's list must be determined.

Parties versus Candidates

The first problem to confront is therefore the extent of party voting as opposed to non-party voting, with party voting being defined here as the ranking of all the candidates from a given party in the highest possible positions. On the face of it, there are a number of reasons why one might anticipate a high level of party voting. First, the sheer importance of party to the politics of Ireland since independence, as well as evidence of a consolidation of the party system in the post-war period, suggest a pervasive concern for party rather than simply for individual candidates (Chapter 1). Second, voting behaviour of TDs in the Dáil itself is remarkable for the extent to which it follows party lines, and, with the exception of church–state and moral issues (see, e.g., Cooney 1986 for a recent review), there are very few instances of backbenchers defying their party position on legislative divisions or of governments suffering defeats at the hands of dissenting TDs (Chubb 1982, Chapter 10). Finally, and most crucially, a survey of the relatively poor electoral results of candidates who leave established parties and attempt to win seats as independents suggest that there is not much life outside party, and that the prior success of these individuals derived mainly from their original party affiliation (cf. Table 2.2). Of the 17 candidates who left one of the three main parties between 1948 and 1982 and stood at the subsequent election on an independent ticket or with only a nominal party label, only four managed to increase their personal first-preference total vote. The total first-preference vote won by these 17 candidates fell by more than one-third, while their average share of the total valid poll—a more meaningful measure which takes account of changes in voter turnout—fell from 13.3 per cent to just 8.8 per cent. Tangentially, it can also be noted that eight of these candidates were Fianna Fáil defectors, and of these only one managed to increase his personal vote.

Table 2.2 Electoral record of party dissidents, 1948–87*

Number of dissidents	Former party	First pref. vote at last election as party candidate		First pref. vote at consecutive election as Independent	
		Total	Mean percentage of TVP	Total	Mean percentage of TVP
8	FF	43,172	17.5	27,256	11.1
6	FG	22,945	9.2	13,538	5.8
3	Lab	12,286	10.6	11,371	8.6
17	Total	79,003	13.3	52,165	8.8

* This excludes the dissidents who competed on the Progressive Democrat ticket in 1987, since they did so with the backing of a fully-established, well-financed political party. However, the three Fianna Fáil dissidents who competed under this Aontacht Éireann label in 1973 are included, since this was effectively only a nominal label. Excluding them from the table would change the Fianna Fáil figures to: 5 28,053 17.3 21,274 14.0.

Yet despite the seeming importance of party, the literature on Irish politics is overwhelming in its emphasis on the importance to both voters and politicians of what are essentially non-partisan clientelistic, localistic and personalistic orientations (see, e.g., Chubb 1963; Bax 1976; Sacks 1976; Higgins 1982; Komito 1984). Survey evidence also suggests the importance of such concerns to the voter, in that respondents frequently indicate that their preferred action when seeking to remedy a particular grievance is to contact their local TD or councillor rather than bureaucratic or other institutionalised agencies. In addition, TDs tend to have a very localistic orientation: most not only reside in the constituencies which they represent, but were also born there. Many combine their Dáil membership with membership of a local authority, and devote much of their activity to simple constituency service rather than to the more generalised role of a legislator (e.g. Chubb 1963; Higgins 1982). Many also attribute their continued electoral success to such constituency service rather than to a more partisan appeal, which suggests that their political affiliation is at most a secondary feature in the mobilisation of popular support.

This emphasis has been further reinforced by a number of in-depth studies of individual constituency voting patterns. Thus Parker's (1982) study of the Galway West constituency revealed a clear localistic bias in the distribution of first-preference votes among the individual candidates, in that the farther one got from the home area of a particular candidate, the fewer first preferences that candidate obtained. Sacks's (1976) exhaustive study of politics in Donegal recorded a similar phenomenon, in that candidates from within the same party divided the constituency into bailiwicks, each bailiwick being based around the candidate's home area. The actual results of this strategy were that, within the same party, one candidate received the vast majority of the party's first preferences within his own bailiwick, while the other candidate received the vast majority of party's first preferences within the other bailiwick.

The localistic bias of Irish electoral behaviour is also recognised in the nomination strategies of the parties as they strive to effect a geographical balance in their constituency slates. When nominating candidates in constituencies which cross county boundaries, such as Carlow-Kilkenny or Sligo-Leitrim, both Fianna Fáil and Fine Gael will ensure that at least one candidate comes from each county area. Beyond this, they will also try to ensure that each of the major towns or distinct areas in a constituency is represented by at least one candidate in their constituency lists. The four-seat constituency of Sligo-Leitrim in the election of February 1982 (the count for which is reported in Table 2.3) affords a useful example of this process. One-third of the population lives in Leitrim, with two-thirds in Sligo, and with a majority of the latter in Sligo town and its immediate environs, the remainder being in the southern end of the county. There are thus three distinct areas, a fact which is reflected in lists of candidates nominated by both Fianna Fáil and Fine Gael in February 1982. Each party nominated one candidate from the Leitrim area (Ellis for Fianna Fáil and McCartin for Fine Gael—jointly accumulating 13,915 first preference votes); one each from Sligo town (McSharry and Nealon—jointly accumulating 18,296 first preferences), and one each from southern County Sligo (Brennan and Cawley—with 9,283 first preferences). Of the other minority party or Independent candidates, Bree and Kennelly were based in Sligo town, and McGirl in Leitrim. The logic of the Fianna Fáil and Fine Gael nominating strategies seemed to stem from the recognition that localistic considerations were of such importance that if, say, Fianna Fáil did not nominate a Leitrim candidate while Fine Gael did, then the latter would enjoy a major electoral advantage. If no Leitrim candidate were nominated by any party, of course, or if there were no independent Leitrim candidate, then no party would enjoy an undue advantage. But neither party can afford to take such a risk and so, for safety's sake, they try to balance their tickets from the outset.

What is more interesting in this regard, however, is first, that the attempted balance also included the southern part of County Sligo, containing considerably fewer votes than either Leitrim or Sligo town, which suggests that a party will be willing to represent a specific locality on its ticket even if there are insufficient votes in that locality to guarantee the election of that candidate, and even if that candidate is likely to be eliminated at an early stage in the counting process (as was Cawley in the example in Table 2.3), a decision which is presumably based on the assumption that these votes will transfer to other candidates from the same party. This is a crucial point which indicates a great deal of the parties' understanding of voter behaviour, and it is something to which we shall return below. For now, suffice it to note that in order to achieve a geographic balance, a party seems to be willing to nominate a candidate who is very likely to be unsuccessful. In some cases, this strategy is carried to such an extreme that, as with Fianna Fáil in the Louth constituency in 1981, a party will actually nominate more candidates than there are *total* seats available (in that election, there were three seats in competition in the Louth constituency, yet Fianna Fáil nominated four candidates—one was elected).

Such a concern with balancing local interests suggests a belief by the parties that many voters orient to candidate, locality or whatever, rather than to party as such. The problem, however, and the essential paradox is that when it comes to transferring lower-preference votes, voters appear to rank the various candidates by party rather than by some other criterion. Over all the general elections between 1948 and February 1982, for example, an average of some 82 per cent of Fianna Fáil lower-preference votes in all constituencies were transferred to other Fianna Fáil candidates when these were still in the running and available to receive transfers, while the corresponding figures in Fine

Table 2.3 Constituency count in Sligo-Leitrim, February 1982

Valid poll 45,700
Number of seats 4
Quota 9,141

Candidates	First count Votes	Second count Transfer of Bree's and Kennelly's votes	Second count Result	Third count Transfer of Cawley's votes	Third count Result	Fourth count Transfer of McGirl's votes	Fourth count Result	Fifth count Transfer of Nealon's surplus	Fifth count Result
Bree, Declan (Ind.)	1,035	−1,035	–	–	–	–	–	–	–
Brennan, Matty (F.F.)	7,500	+216	7,716	+415	8,131	+458	8,589	+45	8,634*
Cawley, Patrick Joseph (F.G.)	1,783	+127	1,910	−1,910	–	–	–	–	–
Ellis, John (F.F.)	7,654	+91	7,745	+62	7,807	+1,070	8,877	+16	8,893*
Kennelly, Seamus (Lab.)	339	−399	–	–	–	–	–	–	–
McCartin, John Joseph (F.G.)	6,261	+132	6,393	+1,228	7,621	+669	8,290	+233	8,523
McGirl, John Joe (S.F.)	2,772	+320	3,092	+85	3,177	−3,177	–	–	–
MacSharry, Ray (F.F.)	9,214	–	9,214	–	9,214	–	9,214	–	9,214*
Nealon, Ted (F.G.)	9,082	+422	9,504	–	9,504	–	9,504	−363	9,141*
Non-transferable	–	+126	126	+120	246	+980	1,226	+69	1,295
Total	45,700	–	45,700	–	45,700	–	45,700	–	45,700

* Elected candidates. Note that both Brennan and Ellis were elected without reaching the quota of 9,414, since both had a plurality over the last remaining candidate, McCartin. Note also that when a candidate reaches the quota, as did MacSharry on the first count and Nealon on the second count, they are no longer considered eligible for receipt of the lower-preference votes of eliminated candidates.
Source: Official results, published by the Stationery Office.

Gael and Labour were 75 per cent and 64 per cent respectively (Gallagher 1978; Browne 1982, p. 11). Indeed, party voting even extends into coalition voting, in that voters indicating Fine Gael or Labour first-preferences in the period since these parties entered coalition in 1973 have tended to give their lower-preferences to candidates from the other coalition party once they have already ranked the candidates from their own favoured party. Between 1973 and February 1982, for example, an average of 75 per cent of Fine Gael lower-preferences have transferred to Labour when no Fine Gael candidate has remained in contention, while the comparable figure for Labour lower-preferences is 62 per cent (Browne 1982, p. 11).

Furthermore, the partyness of lower-preference voting is such that when looking at the transferred votes of specific candidates, and when one can control for the competing appeals of party versus locality, party tends to prove the dominant force. In the example in Table 2.3, for instance, the elimination of Cawley occurred when a candidate from the locality but not from the party was still in the running (i.e. Brennan), and when another candidate from the party but not from the locality was still in the running (i.e. McCartin). In the event, 64 per cent of Cawley's votes transferred within the party rather than within the locality, while only 22 per cent transferred within the locality rather than within the party. In the same vein, a study of transfer patterns in the 1977 general election which controlled for both locality and party concluded that the former was at best a secondary consideration for voters (Marsh 1981, p. 285).

This, then, is the essence of the problem: studies of the distribution of first preferences suggest the primacy of locality over party, an emphasis apparently shared by party strategists who attempt to effect geographically balanced tickets; studies of the transfer patterns of lower preferences, on the other hand, are unanimous in demonstrating the primacy of party over locality. In addition, and what is even more important, the logic of a localist nomination strategy is pursued to the extent that parties will seek to include candidates from given localities even if those candidates have little or no chance of being elected. And the only rationale which appears to explain this strategy is that the parties expect to retain the transferred lower-preferences which follow from the elimination of unsuccessful candidates, an expectation which appears to run counter to the original emphasis on balancing localities. For, to the extent that locality is indeed that important, then the votes of such a candidate when eliminated should be expected to stay within the locality and therefore to transfer to a competing party. If, on the other hand, the votes transfer within the party and are expected to transfer within the party, then this suggests that party is more important than locality, and so belies the necessity to effect a geographic balance of candidates in the first place!

More specifically, and staying with the above example, the justification for Cawley's nomination by Fine Gael would have been that, if there were no local Fine Gael candidate, many voters from South Sligo would have voted for a local Fianna Fáil candidate such as Brennan. But if these voters were so concerned with locality, then even if they did give their first-preferences to Cawley rather than to Brennan, surely Fine Gael would also have anticipated that they would then give their second-preferences to Brennan rather than to a second, and necessarily non-local, Fine Gael nominee. Thus their votes would not benefit Fine Gael in the last analysis. On the other hand, to the extent that they would give their second-preferences to another Fine Gael candidate, albeit one from a different locality, then they could be regarded as primarily Fine Gael voters rather than South Sligo voters. And in so far as they were Fine Gael voters rather than South Sligo voters, why would it then be necessary to nominate a local Fine Gael candidate for their benefit?

All of this may seem quite complicated and not a little arcane, but it actually does relate to a very central point: do voters accord primacy to the candidate, the locality or whatever, or do they accord primacy to the party? While the parties' nomination strategies reflect an emphasis on locality, their willingness to spread their vote by including candidates who are very unlikely to be successful suggests that they also expect to retain the transfers of eliminated candidates, which in turn suggests an expectation that votes will transfer by party. Thus the localistic bias in the distribution of first preferences, as well as the parties' efforts to achieve a geographically balanced slate of candidates, suggest a primacy of candidate or locality. Transfer patterns, on the other hand, suggest a primacy of party. How can we resolve this apparent contradiction?

The solution is to postulate the existence of a group of voters who are party voters, but whose commitment to party is mediated by candidate or localistic considerations. Such voters are partisans in the sense defined above, in that they rank all of a particular party's candidates in the highest possible position, but they are essentially *clientelistic partisans*. In other words, they will vote as partisans *only* if the party nominates a particular candidate or type of candidate. They like party X and will vote for party X, but only because it is the party of candidate

A. And if candidate A is not nominated, but a similar candidate—B—is nominated by the alternative party Y, then these voters will give their first-preferences to candidate B of party Y and go on to give their lower-preference votes to the running-mates of B on the list of party Y. To postulate the existence of this type of voter is the only way in which one can account for *both* the localistic bias in first-preference voting *and* the partyness of lower-preference transfers. More importantly, perhaps, it seems that party strategists implicitly believe in the existence of such clientelistic partisans, in that it is the only way in which one can make sense of a nomination strategy which, within reason, seeks to incorporate representatives from as many areas as possible, even in the knowledge that not all those nominated can expect to win election.

It can be suggested, therefore, that there exists a body of voters in the electorate who, though orientated primarily to candidate rather than to party, nevertheless are in competition between the parties. That is, they can be won by the *party*, and transfer within the party, through the nomination of particular candidates. The next step is then to see if there are also other voters, who are not necessarily primarily orientated to candidate, but who may also be considered to be in competition between the parties.

The National Competition for Votes: Affective versus Instrumental Partisanship

As a first step in this enquiry it is necessary to distinguish between those 'party voters' who are party loyalists and those party voters who are not party loyalists. Convinced party loyalists may be considered to be effectively out of competition and as not part of the electoral market. While an alternative party might seek to win their support, opportunity costs and the inevitable scarcity of campaign resources suggest that no party would really consider such a strategy to be worth the effort. To the extent that those orientated to party are *not* loyalists, on the other hand, then they can be seen to *choose* between the alternatives according to the competing programmes, records, appeals and strategies. As such, they may be considered to be in competition, and a strategy to win their support would then be worthwhile for the parties. The key problem then becomes that of determining the extent to which party voters do indeed choose between the competing alternatives, and thus the extent to which these party voters are in competition. Unfortunately, given the lack of really adequate survey evidence, it is impossible to solve this problem in a precise way, and the presence of party voters in competition can only be imputed indirectly. That said, this indirect supportive evidence is compelling.

To begin with, and on a priori grounds alone, one would anticipate that there are voters who do actually choose parties on the basis of past performance or future promises, particularly given that, in recent years, there has been a regular alternation in government. Since the early 1970s, a choice of government has been a real possibility, and one can therefore assume that voters weigh up the merits of the competing alternatives before deciding how to vote. In other words, one can assume the development of a certain degree of pragmatic or instrumental voting.

Second, the relevance of government activity is now such that one can also assume that many voters have an immediate and very practical interest in the policies which are on offer from the competing parties. Given that so many citizens now depend on the state for either welfare benefits or for their employment, it is likely that a very instrumental attitude towards partisan choice will have been engendered. In short, and as elsewhere in Western Europe, government activity is becoming ever more relevant to the lives of ordinary citizens. Between 1950 and 1980, for instance, total public expenditure grew from 30 per cent of Gross Domestic Product to 55 per cent, while social expenditure alone grew from 15 per cent to 29 per cent (Maguire 1985, pp. 295–7). One recent estimate suggests that recipients of social security and their dependents now amount to almost one-third of the population, while the number of public employees in the health and education sectors alone constitute approximately one-seventh of the total labour force (Coughlan 1984, pp. 41–2). Indeed, aggregate public employment has increased substantially over the past decades. Between 1971 and 1981, for instance, aggregate public employment increased from 21.7 per cent of total persons at work to 27.7 per cent (Census of Population 1981, Vol. 4, Table 7; Ross 1986, p. 305). What government does, how much it spends, and the various policies which it proposes, are all therefore of crucial importance to an immensely large proportion of the electorate. Within such a context, one could easily anticipate that a certain proportion of voters will look at the record in government and the campaign promises, will carefully weigh up the competing alternatives, and will vote accordingly.

Third, while survey evidence consistently emphasises the importance of local candidate appeal in determining voter choice, it also indicates a substantial concern with such national issues as the choice of Taoiseach, of Cabinet ministers and of policies. Some 47 per cent of respondents in a NOP–*Irish Times* survey in 1977, for instance, indicated that the choice between the different party leaders or between the competing policies would be the most important factors in determining their vote, as did 59 per cent of respondents in an IMS survey in 1981.[3]

Fourth, and as I have noted elsewhere (Mair 1987a), the imputed concern with policies and performance appears to be sustained by patterns in aggregate electoral data, and in the reasonably strong relationship between the electoral record of incumbent parties and the general level of economic well-being. This in turn suggests that voters express rational choices as to which party to support. If things are going well, the governing parties tend to gain more votes—or at least they tend to lose fewer votes—whereas if things are going badly, they tend to suffer a major erosion of their electoral support. To illustrate this trend, Figure 2.1 plots the changes in the vote of governing parties (excluding the short-lived governments of 1981 and 1982) against changes in the levels of real per capita disposable income, a useful summary measure of economic well-being.[4] On only two occasions in the post-war period have incumbent governments actually increased their electoral support, in 1965 and in 1973, and on both occasions there had been a substantial growth in the level of per capita personal disposable income. On other occasions, they have tended to lose less when personal disposable income has increased, and to lose more when personal disposable income has decreased. In general, the correlation between the two variables is .31, which suggests that some 10 per cent of the variance in the electoral record of incumbent governments can be explained by changes in the level of personal disposable income.

Finally, and most crucially, the scope for pragmatic or instrumental voting can be imputed from evidence which shows that Ireland is not characterised by unusually high levels of partisan loyalty. Quite the reverse: a survey reported by Inglehart and Klingemann (1976) indicated that Ireland recorded the lowest level of partisan identification of nine European Community countries, while a more recent comparison of levels of attachment to party in the European Community showed Ireland to have a lower level of partisan identification than all countries other than Belgium or France (Mair 1984), countries where the fissiparous nature of party organisation (France) or the recent history of party splits and divisions (Belgium) would lead one to expect a weak sense of party allegiance.

All of these factors suggest the presence of an available party electorate which is likely to be motivated in voting choice by the

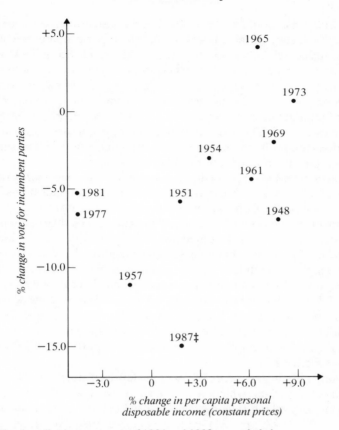

* The short-lived governments of 1981 and 1982 are excluded.

† PDI = total personal expenditure on consumer goods and services and personal savings, calculated at constant prices on a per capita basis. The level of change is that between the year of the election or, if in the first six months of the year, the year before the election, less the previous year.

‡ Estimate of PDI; loss of vote refers to Fine Gael and Labour.

Figure 2.1. The relationship between economic well-being and the electoral performance of incumbent parties, 1948–87* (r = .31)

competing policy appeals, performance records, and propaganda of the alternative governments. In other words, they suggest the importance of instrumental rather than simply affective partisanship. What is even more significant, however, is that the evidence also suggests that this available electorate is *increasing* as a proportion of the total voting public. The evidence here is sparse, but again it is consistent.

The first indication that the available electorate is increasing can be seen in the decline of the already low levels of partisan identification. This point has recently been disputed by Marsh (1985, p. 194) who, given the general lack of appropriate survey data in Ireland and the necessarily sparse evidence concerning party identification, simply reports responses to the question 'do you usually think of yourself as Fianna Fáil, Fine Gael, Labour or whatever?', and records an upward trend in these data. The problem with this simple question, however, is that it does not probe the *intensity* of identification, and while a similar or even greater proportion of the electorate may now think of themselves in terms of a particular party, this does not necessarily imply that they feel as close to that party as they once did. For data at this level one must turn to the Eurobarometer surveys which, between 1978 and 1985, included a more or less identical question about degrees of party attachment in each of its bi-annual polls. Here the evidence of a decline in the level of party attachment is striking, albeit over a relatively short period. Applying an index of party identification to these data[5] shows that the level of party identification has declined reasonably steadily from 38.2 in October 1978 to just 26.1 in 1984, in a range where 0 indicates no sense of attachment to party while 100 indicates that all respondents feel a 'very close' sense of attachment to party. The unmistakable trend in this index of intensity of party identification is shown in Figure 2.2.

Second, one can get a sense of declining levels of attachment to party through survey data which probe past as well as present voting intentions, and which thus measure *consistency* of voting behaviour. Here Marsh's (1985, p. 181) evidence is quite unequivocal: in 1969, some 90 per cent of voters indicated a preference for the same party as in the previous election; in 1973, this had fallen to 78 per cent, and in 1981 to just 75 per cent. And while the trend was reversed in the February 1982 election, when the figure rose to 84 per cent, this could have been expected given that the two elections involved were separated by just eight months.

More generally, however, the shifting ecology of Irish politics suggests an increasingly available electorate, as demographic changes accord a greater electoral weight to the more urban areas, particularly in the eastern half of the country. Between 1961 and 1971, for example, the proportion of the population living in urban areas increased from 42 per cent to 52 per cent, rising to almost 56 per cent by 1981, while between 1971 and 1981 the greater Dublin area alone increased by 18 per cent and included almost one-third of the total population (Census

Source: Eurobarometer Surveys

Figure 2.2. Index of intensity of party identification, 1978–85

of Population 1981, Vol. 1, Table 8). As a consequence of these shifts, the proportion of Dáil seats elected from the Dublin area increased from 20 per cent to 29 per cent between 1961 and 1987, while the proportion elected from Connaught-Ulster fell from 25 per cent to 19 per cent in the same period. In and of themselves, these demographic changes might appear to have little bearing on political attitudes. In practice, however, they are likely to create the conditions for a decline in the sense of party attachment in that, as Borre and Katz (1973) have argued, affective orientations to parties tend to thrive in more rural communities, which are often characterised by lower educational levels and a generally poorer standard of living. A more instrumental attitude, on the other hand, can be associated with urban environments, and with higher levels of education and a more developed sense of civic competence (e.g. Barnes 1984).

Certainly, in the Irish case, parties do seem to have a greater 'hold' in the more rural and peripheral areas (where they also have a greater organisational presence—see Chapter 3 below). The evidence here is also sparse, but again it is consistent. For example, the comprehensive 1976 survey quoted earlier, which included questions on party identification, reveals that the sense of party attachment is greater, albeit only slightly so, in more rural and peripheral areas. In Connaught–Ulster some 52 per cent of respondents stated that they felt 'very' or 'fairly' strongly attached to a party, as against less than 45 per cent in the Dublin region. In urban–rural terms, the imbalance was almost identical, with 53 per cent of rural respondents indicating that they were very or fairly strongly attached to a party as against 45 per cent in urban areas. To be sure, this slight imbalance may be simply a reflection of the imbalance in Fianna Fáil support, given that Fianna Fáil tends to record a higher proportion of the vote in rural and peripheral areas, and given also that a higher proportion of Fianna Fáil voters identify with their chosen party than is the case among Fine Gael voters (see p. 87). But while this may explain the imbalance, it does not detract from its implications, and from the general sense that the rural and peripheral electorate has a greater sense of party attachment than the more urban and 'central' electorate. This point is further sustained by a comparison of levels of aggregate electoral volatility across the regions, shown in Table 2.4. While volatility in general is higher both in the earlier post-war period at the time of the rise and fall of such parties as Clann na Talmhan and Clann na Poblachta as well as in 1987 with the emergence of the Progressive Democrats (cf. Chapter 1 above), it also tends to be higher in the almost wholly urbanised Dublin region, declining as one moves west towards the predominantly rural region of Connaught–Ulster. The average value of the volatility index in Dublin is 11.9, almost half as much again as the figure of 8.3 in Connaught–Ulster, with the bias being particularly evident between 1969 and 1982.

In conclusion, and if it is accepted that a more volatile and less 'party-attached' electorate tends to emerge in urban and eastern areas, the growing demographic bias in favour of these areas seems to imply a potential increase in the available electorate as a proportion of the total voting public (for an early assessment, see Mair 1981). And if this is so, then one should expect an awareness of this change to be reflected by the parties expending a greater effort in election campaigning. While this will be dealt with primarily in Chapter 3, nevertheless one particular element which does deserve attention at this point is the new emphasis on manifesto politics.

The emergence of a manifesto politics in the 1970s offers a very real indication of a more nationally competitive politics, particularly in the

Table 2.4 Aggregate volatility by region, 1948–87*

Year	Region			
	Dublin	Rest of Leinster	Munster	Connaught/ Ulster
1948	19.5	13.7	13.7	15.5
1951	16.3	15.6	18.4	10.5
1954	11.8	11.1	5.2	8.2
1957	14.3	11.7	12.4	9.3
1961	7.4	11.4	10.5	10.5
1965	13.8	6.3	5.2	17.7
1969	11.1	3.5	2.7	4.3
1973	7.9	3.2	3.0	4.3
1977	11.1	8.5	7.7	2.8
1981	10.7	10.8	9.5	4.1
1982 (i)	4.9	3.6	3.3	3.5
1982 (ii)	5.3	4.3	1.8	3.5
1987	20.9	14.3	17.4	13.1
Mean	11.9	9.1	8.5	8.3

* The index of volatility is that defined by Pedersen (1979; 1983)

Source: Calculated from election figures in Gallagher (1985, pp. 156–60), and in *Irish Times*, 20 February 1987.

case of Fianna Fáil. Fianna Fáil for long had been the least competitive of the three parties, not least because for many years it could take its victory for granted (see below). The party vote consistently remained above 40 per cent in the post-war period, and for much of this period its opposition remained divided and unwilling to coalesce into a potential alternative government. The emergence and subsequent success of the coalition in 1973 was thus to lead to a major strategic rethink, among the most crucial components of which proved to be the formation of the new policy committee and eventually the publication of a full election manifesto in 1977. Fianna Fáil had traditionally relied on party leaders' speeches, newspaper advertising and radio broadcasts as a means of publicising its election policies (see Chapter 4), and had deliberately eschewed manifesto politics. Indeed, explaining the absence of a formal manifesto in 1969, the party's national director of elections had suggested that 'manifestos have a marxist ring about them' (Gallagher 1982, p. 91). The 1977 election was to change this. Almost as soon as the election was announced, the party issued a glossy, 47-page reflationary programme which promised, *inter alia*, the abolition of domestic rates, the abolition of car tax, and the introduction of a £1,000 grant to first-time buyers of new houses. The logic behind the strategy was as direct as the promises themselves: Fianna Fáil felt the need actually to win new votes rather than simply rely on the mobilisation of its core supporters, and one of the key methods in this process was the formulation of an attractive package of policies. In other words, the party needed to compete and could no longer take its support for granted.

Fine Gael and Labour, which from a traditional position of opposition had always been more competitive than Fianna Fáil, had regularly published election programmes, although, as will be seen in the case of the *Just Society* (see, p. 121), they did not necessarily make a great effort to publicise them. In 1977, however, and perhaps ironically, the two parties did not enter the campaign in a very competitive mood (Farrell and Manning 1978, pp. 137–8). The constituency redistricting (see, pp. 90–1) had perhaps made them somewhat complacent. Although they did produce a manifesto, it was not published until after that of Fianna Fáil and, as one journalist remarked at the time, was presented 'as if victory were certain and the issues didn't matter ... (and) with a suave and smiling confidence which was staggering' (quoted in ibid., p. 138). Their unexpected defeat was of course to shatter this complacency as effectively as the complacency of Fianna Fáil had been shattered following its defeat in 1973, and the 1981 election was to witness the publication of manifestos by all three parties with, in the Fine Gael case, an exceptionally well publicised and carefully costed national programme (which included the promise of a weekly allowance for housewives) as well as a separate manifesto directed explicitly at voters in greater Dublin.

A more nationally competitive stance is also evident in the increased role of the parties' head offices in the organisation and publicity of recent election campaigns. As part of its preparations for the 1981 election, for example, Fianna Fáil had established an organisation committee which met regularly for the two years prior to the election and which was intended to facilitate the party's adaptation to the new constituency boundaries devised by the independent commission. In the two months before the election this became an election committee proper, which decided on the number of candidates to be nominated in each constituency and eventually added a total of some ten candidates to the locally selected lists. Party head office arranged for the printing of some 25,000 'Notes for Speakers', a brief guide to Fianna Fáil election policies, which were distributed throughout the country. Each constituency was given 500 national party posters, and some 2.75 million local leaflets were prepared. Overall, the party employed some 40 people on a full-time basis in its head office, and ended up with an election budget almost twice as large as that in 1977, and which was estimated by the national director of elections at some I£600,000 (interview with the author, 10 June 1981). According to an estimate in the *Irish Times* (11 June 1981), the party spent some I£400,000 on newspaper advertising alone. In February 1982, when again campaigning from opposition, the General Secretary claimed that the party employed some 75 full-time workers, and over and above the local leaflets, produced some 500,000 party posters and 1.5 million national leaflets (interview with the author, 19 February 1982), while in 1987 the party campaign budget was loosely estimated at around I£2 million (O'Reilly 1987, which also reviews the 'high-tech' and extraordinarily costly campaign preparations of Fine Gael and the PDs).

The campaigning zeal of Fine Gael proved no different. In preparation for the 1981 election, Fine Gael had also begun its groundwork at least two years prior to the election itself. Three committees have been established, for strategy, communications and finance respectively, each of which included the new General Secretary. In 1980 a special director of elections for the Dublin area was appointed, who enjoyed a considerable degree of autonomy, and part of whose brief was to prepare a special manifesto for Dublin voters. Some 30 full-time workers were employed by head office for the duration of the campaign and again, as in the case of Fianna Fáil, much effort was expended in the production of publicity material. Some 200,000 posters were published, as well as some 750,000 copies of a special election issue of the internal party newspaper, the *National Democrat*. In general, party workers estimated that the head office election budget totalled some I£600,000 as opposed to just I£350,000 in 1977 (interviews with the author, 8 June 1981), while the *Irish Times* (11 June 1981) estimated that the budget for national newspaper advertising alone amounted to I£300,000. In February 1982 an assistant organiser reported that head office employed more than 40 full-time workers, published some 150,000 posters and issued three national leaflets, one for each week of the campaign, and with an average circulation of 1 million (interview with the author, 17 February 1982. For a more general account of the marketing of Fine Gael, see Farrell 1986; and O'Byrnes 1986. O'Reilly 1987 estimates the 1987 national campaign budget at I£750,000).

Labour's efforts paled by comparison. In 1981, the national director of elections was appointed less than three months before the election was called, and during the campaign itself the party employed only nine full-time workers. Head office published some 45,000 national posters, as well as some 300,000 local posters, the costs of which were met by the local parties. The party at national level did fund advertising, but even then financial restrictions forced an emphasis on the provincial rather than the national press. Head office was also responsible for the production of some 25,000 national leaflets designed to attract the youth vote (Labour laid substantial emphasis on this in 1981), as well as for some 200,000 give-away party newspapers (national director of elections, interview with the author, 10 June 1981). In February 1982 the position was even weaker. Nine full-time workers were employed by head office, and only some 100,000 posters were produced, although this allowed for a recycling of the 1981 posters, since according to the national director of elections, not all of these had been used at the time (interview with the author, 15 February 1982). Finally, according to an estimate in the *Irish Times* (6 November 1982), Labour's head office budget during this election amounted to only I£150,000, which, according to the Assistant General Secretary (interview with the author, 29 January 1987), was the same figure budgeted in 1987, when party head office employed some 14 full-time workers. One interesting curiosity from the 1987 election was that, according to Advertising Statistics of Ireland Ltd, the proportion of moneys spent by all the political parties on newspaper and outdoor advertising was 49 per cent for Fianna Fáil, 27 per cent for Fine Gael, 19 per cent for the Progressive Democrats and 5 per cent for the Labour Party (O'Reilly 1987) which, in the event, quite closely reflected their respective shares of the national vote!

The result of this increasingly competitive approach was a national-isation of electoral campaigning. As Carty (1981, p. 125) has pointed out, 'the national dimension of the campaign has come to dominate much of the parties' electoral activity. It has now become about as important as the local campaign in influencing voter response'. Elections are increasingly fought out by the national leaderships of the parties and by their head offices: not only do these now exert a greater and greater control over local strategy (see Chapter 3), but they are also responsible for those competing policies, proposals and issues which are of increasing concern to an ever-growing proportion of the electorate. As elections have become more competitive, so too has competition become more nationalised.

In conclusion, and returning to the central theme of voters in competition, the combination of all these factors—low and arguably decreasing levels of party identification; survey evidence which indicates quite a substantial concern with national political leadership and the competing policies; the increasing relevance of government policy to the lives of ordinary citizens, and the reasonably strong relationship between the aggregate electoral record of incumbent parties and the level of personal economic well-being—suggests that there is indeed a category of voter who is orientated to party but who is *not* a party loyalist. In short, we can postulate the existence of a second group of voters, who may be termed *partisan pragmatists*, who are also in competition between the parties, albeit this time at national level.

Types of Irish Voter

Building on these arguments, we can now begin to elaborate a typology of voters. There are two dimensions involved here. First, there is the distinction between voters who are orientated to *candidates* as against those who are orientated to *parties*. Second, there is the distinction between those who are *in competition* and those who are *out of competition*. Combining these two dimensions yields the fourfold typology shown in Figure 2.3, which distinguishes: I Clientelistic Non-Partisans, who are orientated *only* to the candidate and who are thus *out of party competition*; II Clientelistic Partisans, who are orientated to the candidate but who will then transfer their lower-preferences to that candidate's running-mates rather than cross party lines, and who are therefore *in party competition*; III Partisan Loyalists, who are

		Voters are	
		Not In Competition	*In Competition*
Voters orientate primarily to	*Candidates*	I Clientelistic Non-Partisans	II Clientelistic Partisans
	Parties	III Partisan Loyalists	IV Partisan Pragmatists

Figure 2.3. Typology of Irish voters

orientated to party but whose sense of identification is such that they would not consider voting for an alternative party, that is they do not choose between parties and are therefore *out of party competition*; and IV Partisan Pragmatists, who are also orientated to party but who do not have a highly developed sense of party allegiance, and who therefore choose between parties and as such are *in party competition*.

It must be emphasised that this typology does not imply that types III and IV in Figure 2.3, who are primarily orientated to party, are wholly free from particularistic concerns. Rather, the point is that, while they may be concerned to express personalistic or localistic preferences, these are *secondary* to their party preferences. They vote the party first, and thereafter choose which candidate within that party to rank highest within the list, and this latter choice may indeed be determined by particularistic motives. In this sense they differ from those voters who may be categorised as types I or II, since these choose the candidate first and only then, if at all, switch to party voting. Moreover, the typology is not intended to categorise voters for once and for all, in that individuals may shift between the categories over time. Rather, the point is that at any one election, voters may be divided into these four categories, and that party campaigning efforts will be directed towards types II and IV, as those voters who are in competition, while I am also suggesting that these voters are increasing as a proportion of the total electorate, and that, as the system becomes more competitive, they are becoming increasingly important to the parties.

Towards a More Competitive System?

Although the clearest example of the emergence of a more competitive orientation to Irish electoral politics can be seen in the case of Fine Gael, the most significant change is perhaps that registered by Fianna Fáil. Fianna Fáil has traditionally been the least competitive of the main parties, appearing to take its vote for granted for much of the post-war period, and eschewing attempts to win new recruits in favour of a primary reliance on the mobilisation of its core support. This approach derived in part from its much-flaunted position as 'the natural party of government', and in part from a general conviction that with a core vote of some 40 per cent, and with a divided opposition, it was more or less guaranteed a return to office.

In addition, however, party confidence also derived from a realisation that it enjoyed quite a strong sense of loyalty within its constituency. Quite simply, more Fianna Fáil voters were more commited to their party than was the case with Fine Gael or Labour. Why should this have been the case? To some extent, the more intense sense of loyalty derived from the party's nationalist appeal. As Richard Sinnott (1978, p. 39) has argued, the initial alignment in the formative years of the party system saw Cumann na nGaedheal moderating rather than abandoning the original nationalist politics of Sinn Fein, a development which

> enabled the antitreaty party (i.e. Fianna Fáil) to inherit the platform, the symbols, and the mystique of the earlier phases of the independence movement. By contrast, the protreatyites, in spite of the fact that they held power and in spite of their considerable practical achievements, were forced into an ambivalent, reactive, and even negative position on the national issue . . . It was in this sense that the political conflict was asymmetrical and uneven. Deep-seated loyalties are formed around clearcut, positive symbols rather than around the qualified aspirations and successes of the compromiser.

Yet it was not simply the monopoly of the symbols of nationalism which created a larger and more committed constituency for Fianna Fáil as opposed to Fine Gael (although this was to prove of crucial importance—see Chapter 4). Rather, the party also benefited from those crucial predictors of political loyalty—time and stability (Converse 1969; 1976). In brief, Fianna Fáil supporters tended to turn to the party earlier in the life cycle and tended to stay with it thereafter, and, in the process, developed a deeper sense of partisan attachment than many of those who turned to Fine Gael. In part this also relates to Sinnott's emphasis on the importance of symbols: as Mishler *et al.* (1974, p. 423) have noted,

> the earlier a party identification develops the more likely it is to be motivated by a non-rational, affective attachment to a symbol rather than by any rational calculus . . . The more emotional and affective the motivation for a party identification, the more persistent and immutable the identification is likely to be. Relatedly, party loyalties developing later in the life-cycle, which presumably are products of a more rational calculus, are more likely to be discarded.

Even such a cursory review of development of the party system as that provided earlier (Chapter 1) points to the likelihood that a higher proportion of Fine Gael supporters than Fianna Fáil supporters will have developed any sense of loyalty later in the life cycle. Quite simply, the Fine Gael vote has proved remarkably less stable than that of Fianna Fáil and has tended to fluctuate according to the ebbs and flows of minor parties and independents. In the first place, a significant proportion of those voting for Fine Gael in its early years would have previously voted for such parties as the National League, the Farmers Party and the Centre Party. Later, as the party climbed out of its electoral trough in the earlier post-war years, it tended to absorb many of the votes previously cast for Clann na Talmhan and Clann na Poblachta. Between 1948 and 1951, for instance, Clann na Poblachta's vote dropped by some 7 per cent, while Fianna Fáil remained stable and Fine Gael increased by 8 per cent. If, as Rumpf and Hepburn (1977, pp. 145–7) suggest, the situation developed whereby 'a vote for Clann na Poblachta was seen to be no more in practice than a vote for an anti-Fianna Fáil coalition', then it would have made perfect sense for Clann voters to transfer their allegiance to the most powerful component of that coalition, Fine Gael. In 1965, with the final departure of Clann na Talmhan and a sharp decline in the support for Independent candidates, Fine Gael also made noted advances in the western periphery, with the loss of 18 per cent by the Clann and the Independents being accompanied by an increased Fine Gael vote of 10 per cent and by a growth in Fianna Fáil and Labour of just 5 per cent and 3 per cent respectively. And while one must be cautious in making individual-level inferences from such aggregate data, it should also be noted that a number of individual Clann na Talmhan candidates later stood for election under the Fine Gael label (Gallagher 1976, pp. 39–40).

The general picture is of a volatile Fine Gael vote, periodically rising and falling according to the fluctuations in the support for minor parties and independents, and, more recently, rising also as the fortunes of Labour declined and then falling in the face of the electoral mobilisation of the Progressive Democrats (see Chapter 1). By contrast, the Fianna Fáil vote remains reasonably stable throughout its history (between 1932 and 1977, for example, the standard deviation of the national Fianna Fáil vote is just 3.1, as against 5.1 for that of Fine Gael), a stability which is quite congruent with the party's relatively pronounced degree of organisational penetration and presence (see Chapter 3). Without wishing to push it too far, it was as if there existed a Fianna Fáil electorate for which Fianna Fáil alone 'competed' (although occasionally it experiences a minor challenge from Sinn Fein), and a non-Fianna Fáil electorate for which Fine Gael, Labour, the Progressive Democrats and a host of minor parties competed.

Given this circumstance, it is not, then, surprising to find that Fine Gael identifiers tend to be fewer in number and to have developed their party loyalty later in the life cycle. Thus a survey of party activists in Dublin noted that some 65 per cent of Fine Gael respondents had fathers with the same party preference, as against 73 per cent in Fianna Fáil; 36 per cent were 'self-recruited' as against 30 per cent in Fianna Fáil; 35 per cent mentioned the family as a source of political involvement, as against 63 per cent in Fianna Fáil, while 20 per cent first joined the party when more than 30 years of age, as against just 6 per cent in the case of Fianna Fáil (Garvin 1977b). The differences may be small in some cases, but they do all point in the same direction. More significantly, Marsh's (1985, pp. 181, 194) evidence shows that an average of 78 per cent of Fianna Fáil voters between 1969 and 1982 had voted for the party in the previous election, whereas the comparable figure in Fine Gael was only some 64 per cent, and that an average of 40 per cent of respondents in three surveys in 1976, 1981 and 1982, 'usually thought of themselves' as Fianna Fáil, as against just 26 per cent usually thinking of themselves as Fine Gael.

The general conclusion to be drawn from these disparate data is that the traditional and in many ways only *potential* Fine Gael constituency contains a higher proportion of what we have termed 'voters in competition', whereas Fianna Fáil has enjoyed a greater proportion of loyalists, who are out of competition. The result was that while Fine Gael was obliged to woo voters *de novo* at each election, and often was obliged to woo simply those voters who might otherwise have voted for Labour or the other minor parties or independents, Fianna Fáil could rest content with simply mobilising its core support.

All this was to change in the 1970s, however, as the coalition alternative emerged with some electoral force, and as affective loyalties declined and the core Fianna Fáil vote proved inadequate to ensure victory. From that point onwards Fianna Fáil felt obliged to compete. As Jack Lynch later remarked somewhat wistfully (in an interview with the author, 19 November 1980), the party could no longer afford to rest on its laurels: 'in the old days, one was either pro-de Valera or anti-de Valera, or pro-Lemass or anti-Lemass, or neither, and then one supported Labour'. By the mid- to late 1970s, those days had passed.

But while a competitive orientation to electoral politics has become significantly *more* intense over the past decade or so, this should not be taken to suggest that competition is itself a wholly *new* phenomenon. On the contrary, the parties, and more particularly the governments, have long attempted to create conditions favouring their return to office. For example, fine-tuning the economy as a means of generating a more favourable view of government policy is a time-honoured technique of governments the world over and, as can be seen from the pattern in Figure 2.1, the Irish case seems no exception to such a rationale.

Electoral engineering is also a familiar technique for ensuring a return to office, and there is sufficient evidence of gerrymandering to show that here too the Irish case is no exception. In Ireland, however, the most effective form of gerrymandering is also perhaps the least blatant, in that it does not involve the transfer of certain pockets of voters from one constituency to another, but rather involves the adoption of, say, three-seat rather than four-seat constituencies, or four-seat rather than five-seat constituencies, in order to gain the maximum value from one's vote. As noted earlier, the effective threshold of representation declines as the number of seats in a constituency increases: in a three-seat constituency, the quota is approximately 25 per cent of the valid vote, in a four-seat constituency it is 20 per cent, and in a five-seat constituency 17 per cent. If a party is reasonably sure of getting slightly more than 50 per cent of the vote, therefore, it will gain its most favourable result in a three-seat constituency, winning two of the three seats in contention. In a four-seat constituency, on the other hand, it will also win only two seats, while in a five-seat constituency it will win three of the five seats in contention. Thus with 51 per cent of the vote, it will win either 67 per cent, 50 per cent or 60 per cent of the seats, according to whether there are three, four, or five seats in contention. Any governing party which is reasonably assured of winning a majority of votes in a given area will therefore tend to favour the adoption of three-seat constituencies as a means of maximising its return in that area; if, on the other hand, it expects to win less than 50 per cent of votes it will tend to favour four-seat constituencies as a means of minimising the return of its opponents; and, if it is unsure, it will tend to favour five-seat constituencies. Perhaps the most obvious example of this electoral engineering was the constituency map drawn up by the outgoing coalition government in 1977, and which was characterised by a heavy reliance on three-seat constituencies in the greater Dublin area where the coalition parties anticipated winning an overall electoral majority. In the event, the plan misfired, and the swing to Fianna Fáil in Dublin allowed that party to enjoy the advantage which the coalition parties had intended for themselves, and partially contributed to its record

Dáil majority of 20 seats. Partly as a result of this backfiring gerry-mander, decisions on redistricting have since been taken out of the hands of the government of the day and are now the prerogative of an independent, non-partisan boundary commission (Mair 1986b).

Finally, over and above the intensely competitive stance with which Labour approached the 1969 election (Gallagher 1982, Chapter 5), the decision of Labour and Fine Gael to form a pre-election coalition pact in 1973 can also be seen as a reasonably early symptom of the increased competitiveness of Irish elections. Each of the parties urged their supporters to transfer low-preferences to their coalition ally with the intention of maximising the value of their combined vote. The strategy proved to be successful. Whereas in 1969 only 33 per cent of the Fine Gael lower-preferences passed to Labour, and only 35 per cent of Labour lower-preferences passed to Fine Gael, the equivalent figures in 1973 were 71 per cent and 72 per cent respectively. The result was a far more effective vote and a greater return in terms of seats for the two parties: whereas each Fine Gael–Labour seat had cost an average of 9,915 first-preference votes in 1969, the equivalent figure in 1973 was only 9,026. The contrast in Fianna Fáil fortunes was even more striking, with each of its 1969 seats costing 8,138 first-preference votes, as against each costing 9,184 votes in 1973. With a combined vote of just over 51 per cent in 1969 the two coalition parties had won a total of 68 seats; in 1973, with a combined vote of just under 49 per cent they won a total of 73 seats.

Yet it is really only since 1973 that the parties appear to have developed a genuinely competitive edge and have begun to develop more sophisticated techniques for the mobilisation of electoral support. It is also in this period that they have begun to have something to compete for—a Fianna Fáil victory is no longer assured, affective loyalties have declined, and there is now an increasingly available electorate. And in so far as this available electorate—the voters in competition—falls into two broad categories, clientelistic partisans and partisan pragmatists, the parties have developed a two-pronged strategy, asserting national control over local strategy, on the one hand (see Chapter 3), and developing nationally appealing policy packages, on the other.

In both cases, therefore, the move towards a more competitive politics has placed the onus of election campaigning ever more firmly on the shoulders of the party head offices, and has been accompanied by the increased nationalisation of electoral politics. In contemporary election campaigns, as Chubb (1982, p. 79) has argued in the case of political information in general, local variation has declined and 'there are [now] no great differences in the picture with which people are presented whatever they read, see, or hear'. The organisational developments which reflect this more competitive orientation will be reviewed in the next chapter.

Notes

1. Party labels were first permitted on ballot papers following the Electoral Amendment Act 1963.
2. The following arguments incorporate and build on notions originally developed in the wake of the November 1982 election, written up in 1983, and which may yet be published in 1987 (see Mair 1987a).
3. Responses to survey questions probing motivations for voting choice should be treated with caution. In 1987, for example, Michael Laver and Richard Sinnott (in the *Irish Times*, 9 February 1987), concluded that voters were looking for 'good candidates' rather than policies or governments when deciding how to vote. However, the evidence for this conclusion rested solely on the 75 per cent of voters who had indicated in a recent poll that 'choosing a TD who will look after the local needs of the constituency' would 'influence them a lot' in deciding how to cast their *first-preference* vote. (Policies were mentioned by only 45 per cent of respondents and choosing a Taoiseach by only 27 per cent). It goes without saying, however, that this high proportion will also include those voters who had already decided a party preference—on the basis of policy, leadership or whatever—and who would then have to choose to which candidate within the party they would allocate their first preference. It is not at all difficult to conceive of a voter who will choose party on the basis of policy, and then prefer a particular candidate within the party on the basis of local constituency needs. The problem is that this crucial distinction is clouded by asking respondents only about their *first*-preference voting intentions. A prior question which asked the respondent to accord primacy to party or candidate would have proved more revealing.
4. The measure for personal disposable income is calculated by summing overall expenditure on consumer goods and services and overall personal savings, and then calculating this on a per capita basis. It is a very crude measure, made even more so by the absence of reliable quarterly data, which means that only a very generalised annual index can be derived. None the less, despite its crudity, it is positively associated with changes in the vote of incumbent parties, and thus does (albeit cautiously) sustain the overall argument.
5. The index of intensity of party identification is calculated by multiplying the percentage of those claiming to be 'very close' to a party by 3, those 'fairly

close' by 2, those 'merely sympathising' by 1, and those reporting 'no ties' to any party by 0, and then dividing the sum by 3. The range is thus from 0—all respondents claim 'no ties', to 100—all respondents claim to be 'very close' to a party. See Mair (1984, p. 179).

3

HOW THE PARTIES ORGANISE

One of the key assumptions underlying this study is that the parties matter. Politics cannot be reduced to a wholly dependent outcome of autonomous social forces, and the configuration of the contemporary party system cannot be viewed simply as the inevitable product of historical inertia. The parties are cause as well as consequence: what they say and do is of significant account.

If parties matter, then how they organise also matters, and it is also reasonable to suggest that an appreciation of their respective organisational structures, strengths and styles may facilitate an understanding of their relative performance. To what extent, for example, may the long-term dominance of Fianna Fáil be attributed to its organisational strength and skills? To what extent may the post-war growth of Fine Gael, and particularly its electoral advance in the late 1970s and early 1980s, be attributed to organisational revitalisation? Is the persistent weakness of Labour to some extent a consequence of organisational incapacity?

This chapter will attempt to offer answers to these questions and will also assess organisational responses to the increasingly competitive environment in which the parties find themselves. But since the organisational dimension is among the most neglected areas of party research in Ireland—three brief articles by Murphy (1967; 1968a; 1968b) and a short assessment by Gallagher (1985, pp. 121–31) constitute virtually the entire corpus of available literature—it is also necessary to offer an account of the party structures in and of themselves. As such, I will deal first with organisational structure and party finance, and then go on to assess organisational style and adaptation. The data which are included have been supplied by the parties' head offices or obtained from party documents or through interviews with senior party officials. Unless otherwise stated, therefore, the relevant source is the respective party head office.

Party Structures in General

The basic organisational unit of all three parties is the *branch* which, except in particular circumstances, is organised on a strictly territorial basis. Fine Gael on occasion has permitted the organisation of branches along functional lines. In the 1950s and 1960s, for instance, an influential group in the party was organised as the 'central branch', which had no territorial remit as such and which acted as a semi-intellectual think-tank for the party. Fine Gael in the 1950s also permitted the formation of separate women's branches, particularly in the West of Ireland, although this practice has now been discontinued.

The second major organisational unit in the parties is the *constituency council* (constituency executive in Fine Gael and cómhairle Dáilcheanntair in Fianna Fáil), composed of delegates from the individual branches, which represents the party at the level of the Dáil constituency. In the case of both Fianna Fáil and Fine Gael there is also an intermediary organisational unit (cómhairle cheanntair and district executive respectively) between the branch and the constituency council, which represents the party at the county electoral area, that is at the level of the local government constituency, and which is composed of delegates from the local branches. At both county electoral and constituency level, the role of these units is primarily to organise elections and to ensure the nomination and selection of candidates at the appropriate level.

The next stage in the organisational structure is the *national conference* or árd fheis which again is a delegate body and which, in theory at any rate, is the supreme policy-making body. Each party normally holds a national conference annually, although additional special meetings may also be called. Each party also maintains a *national executive* which is responsible for managing the party, and for devising policy and strategy in the period between national conferences. It is within these party executives that the real locus of power lies. In part elected by the national conference and the constituencies, in part by the Oireachtas (i.e. parliamentary) party, and in part also composed of representatives of relevant ancillary organisations (e.g. the youth section), the size, power and relative autonomy of the national executive varies from one party to another. The Fianna Fáil executive, which is arguably the most popularly constituted of the three, is also the largest, currently having 86 members. The Labour executive has a membership of 36, and that of Fine Gael 44 although, in the case of Fine Gael since 1970, executive functions have been divided between the executive proper and a National Council which is largely composed of constituency delegates.

Fianna Fáil

Each Fianna Fáil branch—or cumann (the plural is cumainn)—should have a minimum of ten members but, since the members are registered at a local level rather than with head office, it is impossible to ascertain the extent to which this rule is maintained. The secretary and two (formerly one) delegates from each cumann, together with delegates from the youth organisation (see below) form the cómhairle cheanntair, which is responsible for party organisation at the local electoral level. The chairman, secretary and three (formerly two) delegates from each cómhairle cheanntair then combine at the Dáil constituency level as the cómhairle Dáilcheanntair, which also includes the local TDs, delegates from the youth organisation and the constituency delegates to the national executive. All three local units send delegates to the party's árd fheis, which also includes the elected members of the Oireachtas party, Fianna Fáil members of the European Parliament, delegates from the youth organisation, all local councillors (since the 1970s), and the members of the national executive.

The national executive itself is in part composed of the ten party officers elected by the árd fheis and fifteen other delegates elected by the árd fheis. These latter represent the old 'committee of fifteen', a body originally developed during the early years of the party as an efficient but representative organisation which, given that transport was often difficult, was composed by people who could meet regularly and at reasonably short notice. While the original logistic intention behind the formation of the committee of fifteen is no longer relevant, membership remains a highly treasured honour with the party. The remainder of the national executive is composed of three members of the party's front bench who are nominated to the Executive by the party leader; five backbenchers elected by the Oireachtas party; three non-Oireachtas party members who are co-opted by the executive; four (formerly two) delegates of the National Youth Conference, and one delegate from each constituency (or administrative county where a constituency incorporates more than one county), elected directly by the cumainn in a postal ballot in which each cumann has one vote (since the number of constituencies varies from time to time, the total number of members on the executive also varies). Those elected in this fashion must be resident in their constituencies. The executive normally meets once a month, and members must attend 60 per cent of meetings to be eligible for re-election.

Given that effective power within Fianna Fáil rests with the executive, it is necessary to underline the extent to which it is open to popular election. Of the 86 members currently on the executive, only 11 (13 per cent) owe their membership to elite nomination or election—the three front-benchers, the five backbenchers and the three co-opted members. Fianna Fáil is also the only one of the three parties to facilitate—through a postal ballot—the direct participation of its members in the election of the party executive.

Fine Gael

Since 1970, all individual members of Fine Gael must be registered with head office and, following a 1982 reform, each branch must have a minimum of nine paid-up members. The branches themselves are represented on both the district and the constituency executive, as are local councillors and local members of the Oireachtas. There is no formal link between the district and constituency executives, although Fine Gael does place a lot of emphasis on the constituency officer board, which is similar to the national executive in miniature, and which is composed of the officers of the constituency executive, local public representatives and representatives of either the district executive or the branches.

The branches play a direct role in the National Council, a body unique to Fine Gael, the stated purpose of which is 'to review the working of the organisation of the Party'. Although the National Council is in part composed by certain officers of the party and members of the front bench, only the two (non-Oireachtas) representatives from each constituency have voting rights. In this sense the Fine Gael system can be seen to be as open to popular control as that of Fianna Fáil, in that ordinary members through their constituency organisation carry at least equivalent weight in the National Council as do the cumainn in the Fianna Fáil executive. Against this, however, while real power in Fianna Fáil rests with the executive, the National Council appears to play a relatively insignificant role in the day-to-day management of Fine Gael.

According to the constitution of Fine Gael, the árd fheis is the 'governing body' of the party. It is currently composed of the members of the national executive, the National Council, the Oireachtas party and local councillors, the officers of the constituency and district executives, and four delegates from each branch. The árd fheis then elects seven of the eleven officers of the party (the remaining four are appointed to the party leader) who, together with twelve other árd fheis delegates, form part of the national executive. Ten other members of the executive are elected by the various ancillary organisations, two by the National Council, and nine by the Oireachtas party. Of the 44 members, therefore, 23 (52 per cent) are selected by elite groups within the party—the leadership, the Oireachtas party, the National Council and the ancillary organisations (excluding the youth organisation)—a much higher proportion than in the Fianna Fáil case.

Nevertheless, Fine Gael has become more open over time. Prior to 1978, for instance, the árd fheis had no direct role in the selection of the executive beyond that of electing the party officers. The executive was then composed of the officers, twelve delegates from the National Council, eight delegates of the Oireachtas party, and three co-opted members. Moreover, prior to 1970 each constituency executive was entitled to just one delegate on the National Council, while the party leader nominated ten members. Finally, prior to 1978, each branch was entitled to send only two delegates to the árd fheis, while even at the constituency executive level branches could fail to win representation at the expense of the district executives.

Labour

Since 1979, Labour branches are expected to have a minimum of five members in rural areas and ten members in urban areas, and since 1971 the party head office has maintained a central register of members. The constituency council (there is rarely an intermediary organisation at local electoral level) is almost entirely composed of branch delegates, although corporate members may also be repre- sented and the youth organisation of the party may send four delegates to the constituency council. Labour also maintains a loose system of regional councils composed of delegates from the constituency council. These bodies have little effective power, however, and have been described by one General Secretary of the party as being 'more a debating society than a source of organisational input' (interview with the author, 3 November 1978).

The National Conference of the party is the supreme policy-making body and is generally reckoned to be a more effective forum than the equivalent in the other two parties. Delegates to the Conference are drawn mainly from the branches and the corporate membership. Each branch is entitled to send a minimum of two delegates, the actual number varying according to the number of registered members.

Corporate members, in this case affiliated trade unions, are repre-sented according to the numbers of members whom they have affiliated but, unlike the corporate members of the British Labour Party, these delegates do not enjoy a block vote. Rather, each union delegate, who must also be an individual member of the party, is entitled to only one vote. Each affiliated union may send at least two delegates to the Con-ference, with one additional delegate for every 500 and later 1,000 affiliated members. In 1969, for example, 95 (11 per cent) of the 850 delegates represented affiliated trade unions. Other delegates to the Conference include one representative from each of the constituency and regional councils and—without voting rights—the members of the Administrative Council (i.e. the party executive) and a representative of Labour's National Women's Council.

Despite the relative importance of the National Conference, the key forum in the Labour Party—as in Fianna Fáil and Fine Gael—is the national executive or Administrative Council. The Council is com-posed of 36 members, 20 of whom (including the three national officers) are elected by the Conference. The remaining members are the two leaders of the party (elected by the Oireachtas party), six members of the Oireachtas party (who are also elected by the Oireachtas party), two delegates elected by the National Youth Confer-ence, two appointed by the affiliated unions, two appointed by the National Women's Council, and two other co-opted members. Exclud-ing the Youth Conference delegates, this means that 14 (36 per cent) of the 36 members are subject to elite selection. Moreover, this propo-rtion has increased over time. The Oireachtas party delegation was increased from two to six in 1960 in an effort to improve liaison between the two bodies, while the co-options from the National Women's Council and the affiliated unions date from 1980 and 1978 respectively.

Ancillary and Affiliate Organisations

Fianna Fáil lays the least emphasis of all the parties on the mobilisation of support through ancillary organisations. Certainly the party has long had informal links with sections of industry, both through its fund-raising network as well as earlier links with such organisations as the National Agricultural and Industrial Development Association in the 1930s (Bew and Patterson 1982, p. 44). In addition, it was the only one of the three parties to have a 'tied' national daily newspaper, the *Irish Press*, which was established under the control of the de Valera family in 1931. Although it remains in the effective control of the de Valera family today, and although in the last analysis it can be relied upon to urge support for Fianna Fáil, the *Press* is now largely autonomous of the party.

Formally speaking, the only ancillary organisation attached to Fianna Fáil is Ógra Fianna Fáil, the youth section of the party which held its first conference in 1975 and which was formally established in 1978. Ógra Fianna Fáil is open to members of the party who are under 25 years of age and in this sense is a parallel rather than independent organisation. By the end of 1978, reported membership was some 5,600 and youth committees had been established in each county and constituency electoral area. Each constituency youth organisation (coiste ógra) sends 12 delegates to an annual national conference, and the conference in turn elects four delegates to the party executive. The party also appointed a full-time youth officer in 1981. Since 1984 Fianna Fáil has also begun to organise a National Women's Conference.

Fine Gael, by contrast, relies heavily on ancillary organisations, and by the early 1980s there were five such groups. The first and most important of these is Young Fine Gael, the youth section of the party, which was established in 1977. As is the case with the Fianna Fáil equivalent, Young Fine Gael is a parallel organisation to the main party, although youth members need not be members of an ordinary branch. Branches of Young Fine Gael need to have a minimum of eight members, and send delegates to both the district and constituency executives. Where possible, autonomous constituency youth executives are also established and, again as in the case of Fianna Fáil, there is a national youth conference, which elects delegates to a national youth executive as well as to the executive of the party proper. Fine Gael also appointed a full-time youth officer in 1978. Membership of Young Fine Gael in 1980 was reported to be 2,847, and some 6,000 in 1985.

The second ancillary organisation is the Trade Union Group, which was initiated in 1978. Initially organised by constituency, it is increasingly and inevitably restricted to the larger urban areas, and has the right to elect two delegates to the executive of the party. In a similar vein, the third ancillary organisation is the Agricultural Advisory Council, which was established in 1979 and which is organised by constituency. By 1986, branches of the Council had been established in all rural constituencies. The Council organises its own National Delegate Conference and, since 1984, has had the right to elect two delegates to the party executive.

The fourth group is the Council of Local Representatives, an organisation esablished in 1978 in order to facilitate and coordinate the activities of some 500 local Fine Gael councillors. The councillors meet by area and each area elects a delegate to the CLR itself which, in turn, elects four delegates to the party executive. Finally, though less formally, the party maintains a Women's Group with its own National Council which was established in 1979 to act as a consultative body liaising with the party's women TDs and ministers. The Women's Group is organised by constituency and, by 1984, had been established in a total of 17 constituencies.

Labour also places relative weight on the development of ancillary or affiliate organisations. The most important link is that with the trade-union movement. Seventeen unions are currently attached to the Labour Party, together affiliating some 175,000 members or 34 per cent of the unionised labour force. This figure is even more significant given that, with the exception of the Post Office Workers Union, public service unions (representing some 36 per cent of the unionised labour force) are prohibited from affiliating to political parties. Union affiliation to the Labour Party has increased substantially over the past two decades. Although 12 unions were affiliated in 1961, these did not include the three largest unions, the Workers Union, the Transport and General Workers Union, and the Amalgamated Transport and General Workers Union, which affiliated in 1965, 1968 and 1969 respectively. Despite this increased affiliation, however, Labour is probably more autonomous of the trade-union movement than was the case in the early post-war years. During the 1950s and early 1960s the party had few non-union members and acted as little more than the fairly tame political wing of the trade-union movement. As late as 1963, for instance, many of the party branches were simply branches of trade unions and non-union members were treated with immense suspicion (Gallagher 1982, p. 52).

Nowadays the unions carry little weight within the party. They play no formal role in the selection of candidates for public office, and do not enjoy block voting rights at the national conference. They elect— since 1978—only two members of the Administrative Council. But although union conferences frequently hear complaints of Labour's failure to further union interests, it is the converse which is perhaps more accurate: the unions appear to do little for the party. The relatively small amount paid in affiliation fees—I£22,238, or some 15 per cent of the party's income, in 1985—and the contributions to the election expenses of individual candidates constitute the bulk of what the unions offer Labour. There is no major effort to mobilise a working-class vote for the party, and their political contribution is in this sense marginal. Opinions in the party differ as to the reasons for this, with union officials claiming that it is impossible to mobilise Labour support through the unions, while some party members claim that the union leadership is simply not making sufficient effort. Whatever the reason, union membership remains a poor predictor of party choice in the Irish case.

The second major ancillary organisation is the youth movement, Labour Youth, which was established in 1978. As is the case with Ógra Fianna Fáil, members of Labour Youth must also be members of the party proper. Since 1984, however, senior figures in the party have indicated that Labour Youth may be pursuing a separate recruitment policy and that the organisation itself may be coming under the influence of the Militant Tendency (on the Militant Tendency in Britain, see Crick 1986). Organised by constituency, each youth section should have a minimum of ten members, which then entitles the section to four delegates on the constituency council. There is also a National Committee of Labour Youth and a National Youth Conference which elects two delegates to the Administrative Council. In 1985, membership of Labour Youth was reported to be 477.

Finally, Labour also organises a Women's National Council, established in 1978 to replace the Women's Advisory Council which, in turn, had been established in 1971. Since 1980, the National Council has been entitled to elect two delegates to the Administrative Council of the party.

Members and Branches

It has always proved particularly difficult to get an accurate figure for party membership in the Irish case. Fianna Fáil maintains no central register of members and individuals who join the party are not asked to pay a membership fee, although since 1982 an attempt has been made to establish a central computerised register which, in the event, has proved incomplete. Recruitment to the party is entirely a function of the local cumann, and while membership cards are sometimes distributed, this again is a matter for the local cumann. The problem is compounded even further by the party notion of associate membership for individuals who do not wish to join in a formal sense, but who nevertheless are obliged to contribute regularly to the local cumann funds. In theory, each cumann is obliged to have at least ten members, but even this rule gives little indication of the overall figures, since many cumainn have substantially more members than the minimum while others exist only on paper (see below).

However, when a cumann does complete its annual registration, the officers are asked to provide an indication of the number of members. In general, some 75 per cent of cumainn provide this information, and these figures do give some indication of overall membership strength. In 1982, for instance, a membership of 73,000 was reported by the cumainn, as against 79,000 in 1983, 77,000 in 1984 and 71,500 in 1985. While these figures are worth reporting, it must be emphasised that they are not very reliable, and that they are not guaranteed by the party itself. The sheer fluctuation in membership levels, for example, underlines their probable inaccuracy, since some cumainn may report their membership in one year but not in the next, and so substantially change the overall figure. Moreover, since membership reported in this way is entirely a function of cumann registration, any change in the number of cumainn will have a direct effect on the estimated number of members. Between 1982 and 1983, for instance, the number of cumainn in the constituency of Dublin South-Central fell from 37 to 19, with the result that there was a corresponding drop in the number of members in this constituency from 700 to 353. To the extent that the figures may be accurate, however, then a 75 per cent response rate from the cumainn, reporting an average of some 75,000 members, rounds to a figure of some 100,000 members in total.

Fine Gael has maintained a central register of members since 1970, but it is only since 1979 that it can be said to be reasonably accurate and effective. Estimates are available for 1977 and 1978, and these are reported in Table 3.1.

Labour has also maintained a central register of members since 1971, but reliable figures are available only since 1974, when the party introduced a membership fee payable directly to head office. These figures are reported in Table 3.1. As noted above, Labour also facilitates corporate or affiliated membership through the trade unions. In 1968, 145,000 members were so affiliated, rising to 160,000 in 1970 and to 175,000 in 1985.

As can be seen from the data in Table 3.1, both Fine Gael and Labour report increased membership in recent years. In the case of Labour, however, this reported increase runs counter to the declining trend in electoral support, which has fallen from 13.7 per cent in 1973 to just 6.4 per cent in 1987, while the reported increase of Fine Gael is matched by that party's electoral growth from 32.1 per cent to 39.2 per

Table 3.1 Individual membership figures for
Fine Gael and Labour, 1974–86

Year	Fine Gael*	Labour
1986	34,000	6,300
1985	31,000	6,200
1984	30,000	5,860
1983	31,000	5,377
1982	30,000	5,230
1981	32,000	5,375
1980	30,000	5,600
1979	27,000	5,100
1978	20,000	4,500
1977	20,000	4,500
1976	na	4,800
1975	na	4,100
1974	na	4,691

* Excludes Young Fine Gael
Source: Figures supplied by the parties.

cent through to November 1982, but fails to follow the sharp down-
ward trend apparent in 1987. The Fine Gael increase is also reflected in
a number of constituency reports. In the constituency of North
Tipperary, for instance, Fine Gael party organisers claimed an increase
in membership from 300 in 1977 to 1,000 in 1981 (*Magill*, February
1981, p. 17), while the Director of Elections in Limerick East also
reported a doubling of party membership over the same period
(interview with the author, 6 June 1981).

The real problem in effecting a systematic inter-party comparison,
however, is the lack of relevant data for Fianna Fáil. As noted above,
there are no reliable membership figures for the party, although
accurate details of the number of cumainn are available for the entire
post-war period, and these are reported in Table 3.2, together with
branch figures for both Fine Gael and Labour for available years.
Again, it is necessary to emphasise that one cannot really extrapolate
from the number of Fianna Fáil cumainn to a figure for individual
membership. First, some of the cumainn exist on paper only; second,
urban cumainn tend to have a larger number of members than those in
rural areas (see below), and third, individual membership in the party is
much less important to the party than is the cumann itself. In this sense,

Table 3.2 Numbers of branches of Irish parties, 1948–86

Year	Fianna Fáil	Fine Gael*	Labour
1986	2796	1700	486
1985	2771	1600	486
1984	2762	1500	497
1983	2818	1450	504
1982	2811	1500	470
1981	2750	1600	508
1980	2676	1500	510
1979	2475	1400	502
1978	2733	900	490
1977	2774	na	582
1976	2575	na	538
1975	2432	na	497
1974	2382	na	499
1973	2288	na	480
1972	2398	na	436
1971	2225	na	450
1970	2240	(1500)	479
1969	2003	na	501
1968	na	na	477
1967	2016	na	457
1966	1743	419	357
1965	1776	474	289
1964	1556	276	248
1963	1575	291 (1476)	na
1962	1581	363 (1464)	na
1961	1958	262	400
1960	1639	356	na
1959	1650	181	na
1958	1411	200	na
1957	1728	252 (1343)	na
1956	1645	365 (1335)	na
1955	1780	545	na
1954	1697	395	na
1953	1535	333 (1139)	na
1952	1556	308 (1058)	na
1951	1692	220	na
1950	1681	260†	na
1949	1530	260†	na
1948	1508	na	na

  * Figures refer to the number of *registered* branches; figures in brackets refer to the *total* number of branches
  † Average figure based on figure of 519 given for 1949 and 1950 combined
  Source: Fianna Fáil: Honorary Secretaries' Reports; Fine Gael: figures since 1977 are estimates supplied by the party; 1970 figure from Kenny (1972, p. 305); other figures from the Fine Gael archive in University College Dublin, p39, 6/12, 7/1, 1/6, bf38, 160); Labour: figures supplied by the party; 1961 figure from Desmond (1966).

the individual is a member of a Fianna Fáil cumann rather than a member of Fianna Fáil *per se*, such that when the number of cumainn declines—as in the case of Dublin South-Central cited above—the number of members also declines.

Despite such caveats, however, and to the extent that the cumann in Fianna Fáil—or the branch in Fine Gael or Labour—is the key unit in the mobilisation of electoral support at the local level, then the data in Table 3.2 are revealing. For the bulk of the post-war period, and allowing for the lack of comparative data in many years, Fianna Fáil evidences a much greater degree of organisational presence than does Fine Gael or, of course, Labour. The data from the 1950s suggest that Fianna Fáil cumainn outnumbered Fine Gael branches by as much as 50 per cent, and this figure increases almost fourfold if one only considers the registered branches of Fine Gael. Such data as are available for the 1960s suggest a more even balance, but the earlier bias is repeated in 1970. By the 1980s, however, in the wake of the organisational revitalisation of Fine Gael (see below), the parties had become almost comparable, while Fine Gael also appeared to be overcoming its problem with the lack of branch registration. It is also interesting to note the decline in the number of Labour branches from a peak of 582 in 1977 to lows of 470 in 1982 and 486 in 1985 and 1986, despite the reported increase in individual membership of the party (Table 3.1).

Finance and Staffing

Although the finances of Irish political parties are shrouded in secrecy, in that the parties and their financial backers are not obliged to publish details of their accounts, such data as are available suggest substantial growth over the past decade or so. Indeed, if head office finance were the only criterion, then the parties can be seen to have strengthened considerably in recent years, as can be seen in Table 3.3, which reports the available data concerning the expenditure of the three parties. The first thing to note about these data is that they do not include those election expenses incurred by the parties over and above any special income generated by specific appeals for election funds. In the case of Labour in 1981, for instance, the party accounts include a figure of I£93,528 for election expenses as against a specific election income of I£76,224, leaving a shortfall of I£17,034 to be drawn from other sources. In the case of Fine Gael the 1979 accounts include an item for I£49,435 which is listed as expenses for the árd fheis, meetings and

Table 3.3 Declared head office expenditure of Irish political parties, 1974–85

Year	Current prices (I£'000)			Constant (1975) prices (I£'000)		
	Fianna Fáil	Fine Gael	Labour	Fianna Fáil	Fine Gael	Labour
1985	701.0	574.2	137.1	209.8	171.9	41.0
1984	579.7	488.0	122.2	177.3	149.3	37.4
1983	503.6	541.8	95.9	167.3	180.0	31.9
1982	448.2	421.8	117.4	164.5	154.8	43.1
1981	446.9	295.1	91.5	192.1	126.9	39.3
1980	319.3	283.8	114.7	165.3	146.9	59.4
1979	204.7	208.9	79.7	125.3	127.8	48.8
1978	170.7	136.0	50.3	118.3	94.2	34.9
1977	188.8	78.4	38.2	140.8	58.5	28.5
1976	154.7	53.0	28.1	131.1	44.9	23.8
1975	109.5	na	25.3	109.5	na	25.3
1974	86.9	na	28.1	105.0	na	33.9

Source: Published accounts of the parties.

conferences, 'including deficit on Euro and local elections'. Since much of the increase in expenditure may be cancelled out by inflation, Table 3.3 also shows expenditure in constant (1975) figures, deflated by changes in the consumer price index.

The increased expenditure in current prices is striking in all three cases: the head office budget of Fianna Fáil has increased from just over I£85,000 in 1974 to over I£700,000 in 1985, while Labour has increased from I£28,000 to over I£137,000 over much the same period. The most striking increase is that of Fine Gael, however: for the years for which data are available, the head office budget of the party has increased from I£53,000 in 1976 to more than I£574,000 in 1985. In real terms the growth in Fine Gael expenditure vastly outstrips that of the other two parties, increasing by a staggering 280 per cent between 1976 and 1985, as against a 100 per cent increase for Fianna Fáil and a 21 per cent increase for Labour between 1974 and 1985 (note here, however, the erratic pattern of Labour expenditure: in real terms, Labour expenditure in 1980 was some 45 per cent higher than in 1985).

There is no single item in the parties' budgets which can account for this growth; on the contrary, expenditure on all budget items has registered an increase. As far as Fianna Fáil is concerned, however, expenditure on salaried personnel has shown a slightly disproportionate increase: salaries occupied just 21 per cent of head office budget in 1974, as against 27 per cent in 1985. In the case of Labour, salaries increased from 36 per cent of the budget in 1974 to just 40 per cent in 1985. In the Fine Gael case, on the other hand, expenditure on salaries fell from 62 per cent of total head office expenditure in 1976 to just 36 per cent in 1985. The expenditure on salaries is also clouded in that the parties often tend to use party group and individual MEP allowances from the Oireachtas and from the European Parliament to employ party personnel.

Nevertheless, the increase in the number of full-time party personnel is one of the most evident features of organisational growth, particularly in the cases of both Fianna Fáil and Fine Gael. In 1966, for instance, Fianna Fáil had a full-time headquarters staff of six, employed for a total salary bill of just I£5,000 per year. In 1973 the party added a full-time research director and a press officer, both of whom were at least partly financed through the Oireachtas grant. By 1977 there was a full-time staff of ten with a total annual salary bill of almost I£40,000, while by 1982 there was a full-time staff of thirteen, including a new youth officer, with a further five or six full-time research/publicity personnel in the party offices in the Dáil. In 1985 the party maintained a head office staff of 18, including the General Secretary, Deputy General Secretary, a national organiser and assistant organiser, a youth officer and a full-time accountant. They also employed a staff of 12 in the Oireachtas offices of the party, including a press officer and two assistants, with additional staff in the office of the party leader. In addition, between 1969 and 1982 the party maintained a permanent fund-raising committee with a salaried secretariat (Kennedy 1982).

Fine Gael has evidenced a similar trend. As recently as 1974 the party headquarters was staffed only by a General Secretary and seven secretarial assistants. In 1977 and 1978 the party appointed a new press officer and an assistant organiser with specific responsibilities for the youth section. In 1982 a research officer was also appointed, and by 1985 the staff had been augmented by two regional organisers, one for the Dublin area and one for the western constituencies, bringing the total head office staff to 17. As in the case of Fianna Fáil, much of the additional expenditure involved was funded through state support for the Oireachtas party. In 1985, a press officer and assistant press officer were employed in the Oireachtas offices of the party. In addition, and since at least the early 1960s, Fine Gael has also employed the services of two fund collectors/political organisers, whose duties kept them almost entirely in the constituencies. One of the two appears to have been primarily involved in fund-raising, and was largely paid through commission; the other was more of an organisational troubleshooter, and appears to have been salaried.

Largely due to its persistent shortage of funds, Labour is the only one of the three parties which has not experienced a steady increase in the number of full-time personnel. Moreover, it has regularly subsidised the salary of its General Secretary by arranging his/her election as a Senator, despite complaints that the extra duties involved detract from party organisational work. In 1951, in addition to the General Secretary, Labour employed two secretarial assistants and two full-time political organisers, the latter being fully engaged in constituency work. Since then the number of full-time personnel has fluctuated considerably. First one and then the other political organiser left the party, and neither was replaced. For a time the party employed a part-time organising secretary, and then a full-time political director who eventually succeeded to the post of General Secretary; then a new public relations officer, who later resigned and was not replaced, and finally an Assistant General Secretary. The current staff of the party thus now consists solely of the General Secretary, Assistant General Secretary, a youth education officer and two secretarial assistants, although additional personnel have been employed occasionally in the Oireachtas offices, currently including a press officer and a research officer.

Income and Fund-Raising

Figures concerning the declared incomes of the parties for available years and in constant (1975) prices are shown in Table 3.4. As was the case with expenditure levels, the pattern is one of substantial growth: Fianna Fáil income has more than doubled between 1974 and 1985, Fine Gael has increased by 262 per cent between 1976 and 1985, and Labour income by 78 per cent between 1974 and 1985. While these data cover the same period as the expenditure data in Table 3.3, different accounting practices make comparisons between the two particularly difficult. Certainly one can see immediately that the declared income of Fine Gael did not rise nearly so rapidly as its expenditure, and in 1981, an election year, the party recorded a deficit of some

How the Parties Organise

Table 3.4 Declared head office income of Irish political
parties, 1974–85 in constant (1975) prices

Year	Fianna Fáil* I£'000	Fine Gael I£'000	Labour I£'000
1985	217.2	209.7	45.7
1984	172.2	194.1	46.7
1983	170.4	132.8	39.5
1982	173.3	111.6	40.9
1981	201.7	105.1	44.4
1980	163.0	123.8	26.1
1979	125.3	127.8	31.0
1978	121.6	94.2	31.0
1977	140.8	58.5	30.3
1976	130.6	58.0	34.1
1975	110.9	na	34.1
1974	108.1	na	25.7

* In the case of Fianna Fáil, income is defined as the item in the party
accounts listed as 'amount received from the Trustees'.
Source: Published accounts of the parties.

£60,000 in current prices. In 1985, on the other hand, income *exceeded*
expenditure by some £126,000 in current prices.

The Fianna Fáil case is particularly problematic. The income of the
party is defined in the accounts as 'the amount received from the
Trustees', and more or less corresponds to the expenditure of the party
in any given year. The actual source of the Trustees' funds is not
specified, however, other than by the party's statement that the income
from the annual national collection is lodged in the Trustees' account.
The national collection is a major component of Fianna Fáil cumann
activities. Each cumann must take part in the collection, 60 per cent of
which goes to head office with the remaining 40 per cent being returned
to the constituencies. In 1985 the total national collection amounted to
I£468,000, of which head office retained I£281,000. Since 1979, the
increase in the national collection in real terms has failed to match the
corresponding increase in head office expenditure, with the result that
the party has had to place more reliance on alternative sources of
income. In early 1986, for example, the party leader arranged a four-
day fund-raising trip to the United States which was expected to net
I£60,000 (*Irish Times*, 28 February 1986). It is also worth noting that

whereas income from members and branches (i.e. the national collection) amounted to some 95 per cent of head office expenditure in 1974, in 1982 it has fallen to just 70 per cent. In 1983 the party initiated an additional source of popular fund-raising in the form of a 'members' draw', which is essentially a lottery organised by the constituencies. In 1985 the income from this source amounted to some I£730,000, 10 per cent of which was returned to the constituencies to cover local expenses.

Fianna Fáil has traditionally emphasised popular fund-raising, and the contributions—however small—of its members and supporters, and in recent years this emphasis has also been emulated by Fine Gael. Between 1976 and 1986, for example, the proportion of Fine Gael income deriving from members and branches (i.e. affiliation fees, subscriptions and levies, and the national collection) increased by some 38 per cent, reaching 89 per cent of total income. In this sense Fine Gael currently relies on grass-roots financial backing to an extent equivalent to that of Fianna Fáil in the late 1970s. Since 1984 Fine Gael has also adopted a similar lottery system to Fianna Fáil. Members contribute I£5 each month, and the income goes to head office.

There are also other interesting differences in the sources of income of the parties. In contrast to its two opponents, Fianna Fáil does not have a formal membership fee, and while members may be asked to contribute to their local cumann, any such income stays with the cumann. The cumainn do pay an annual registration fee (I£5 in 1985) to head office, but this is not listed as a separate item in the party accounts. In any case, a potential income of, say, I£13,500 from 2,700 cumainn in 1985, counts for little in the overall expenditure of £700,000 in the same year. Rather, the bulk of grass-roots financial support comes from the national collection and the lottery. By way of contrast, Fine Gael's national collection counts for relatively little—less than 2 per cent of total income in 1985. The bulk of Fine Gael grassroots financial support comes instead from branch affiliation fees (I£15 per branch in 1985), constituency levies and membership fees (I£2 per year), and the party lottery. In the case of Labour, membership fees (I£6 per year), account for the same proportion of its income as does the party's national collection (15 per cent for each in 1985), with a smaller contribution coming from branch (I£15 per year) and constituency council affiliation fees (I£4 per year), totalling 5 per cent of total income in 1985. A further source of income (15 per cent in 1985) comes from trade-union affiliation fees. Since 1984, Labour has lost a major source of income through the defeat of all its candidates in the European elections. MEPs' contributions to the party accounted for 21 per cent of total income in 1983 and 20 per cent in 1984. As in the case of the other parties, Labour has also come to rely heavily on a party lottery which, in 1985, accounted for 26 per cent of head office income.

All three parties also appear to enjoy alternative sources of income, ranging from contributions by the party's public representatives to the grants paid by the state to parties represented in the Oireachtas (see below). In addition, all three parties, but particularly Fianna Fáil and Fine Gael, receive undeclared income in the form of private donations from individuals and businesses.

Between 1969 and 1982 Fianna Fáil maintained a permanent fund-raising committee with a salaried secretary which met six times a year and which was quite autonomous of head office control. Indeed, the eventual disbandment of the committee came about as a result of a failed attempt to bring it under head office control (Kennedy 1982) when it was believed to be acting against the interests of the new party leadership. Since then a new fund-raising committee has been established, but staffed on a voluntary basis and responsible to head office. Prior to this, in the late 1950s, the party maintained a 'Business Election Committee' and the Dublin-based 'Cómhairle áth Cliath', both of which were designed to establish contacts with business people and to encourage contributions to the party. In the mid-1960s the party established a group called Taca, membership of which was by invitation only and cost I£100, and which generated some I£60,000 annually (Brady 1978). It seems likely, although this has been denied by Fianna Fáil, that such contributions were 'repaid' through government patronage.

Fine Gael also maintains a permanent fund-raising committee— known as the capital branch—which recently has attracted a considerable amount of business support (Crowley 1983, p. 29). Other sources of private financial aid for Fine Gael are less formalised: a senior Fine Gael figure in the North Tipperary constituency stated that during a visit to the constituency by the new party leader Garret FitzGerald in the late 1970s an informal meeting of some 30 local notables resulted in donations of some I£1,600 while 500 tickets for a fund-raising dinner, costing I£7 each, were also sold during the visit (interview with the author, 15 October 1980. For a general survey of private donations to the parties, see Crowley 1983).

Finally, since 1938, there has also been a degree of state financial aid provided to the parties—the Oireachtas grant. Originally this was restricted to the two main opposition parties and was designed to compensate for their lack of access to civil service back-up, and was extended in 1960 to include all qualified opposition parties and, in 1973, to all qualified governing parties. A 'qualified' party is one which has contested the previous election as an organised party, and has at least seven members elected to the Dáil. The grants are actually paid to the relevant party leaders, and the amounts as on 1 July 1985 are shown in Table 3.5. In the case of Fine Gael and Labour (the position with Fianna Fáil is unclear) this money goes directly into head office funds. The state also provides other aid to the parties in terms of personnel, financing a secretarial assistant for each TD and a number of administrative assistants for each party, the number varying according to the size of their Dáil representation.[1]

Table 3.5 State financial aid to parties, 1 July 1985 (annual sums payable to Dáil Éirann party leaders, in I£)

Government parties	
1. Where there is only one qualified* party:	77,103
2. Where there are two qualified* parties:	
larger party	53,972
smaller party	23,131
3. Where there are three or more qualified* parties:	
largest party	38,653
to be divided equally among other parties	38,653
Non-governing parties	
1. Where there is only one qualified* party:	192,757
2. Where there are two qualified* parties:	
larger party	153,086
smaller party	75,982
3. Where there are three or more qualified* parties:	
largest party	96,379
to be divided equally among other parties	96,379

* A qualified party is one which has contested the previous election as an organised party and which has at least seven members elected to the Dáil.
Source: Department of the Public Service.

Organisational Style

However useful it may be to document the general structure and the financial status of the parties, such bald information offers little insight into their actual organisational style and, in particular, fails to underline the very evident differences between the approach taken by Fianna Fáil, on the one hand, and that taken by Fine Gael and Labour, on the other.

First, from its inception, Fianna Fáil has been a self-consciously popular political movement, intent on spreading its organisational network as widely as possible and on involving its supporters—through the cumainn—in such a way that the party would become a real element in their everyday lives. Second, the original momentum of Fianna Fáil was provided by a crude alliance of small farmers and workers (see Chapter 1), who were not mobilised in terms of class as such, but rather as a coalition of the 'have nots' of Irish society. Third, despite its mass character, and despite its original radical appeal, Fianna Fáil never sought to emulate the organisational style of social democracy; that is, the party never sought to replicate the strategy of that larger, radical and necessarily class-based political mass-movement which had thrown open the boundaries of conventional politics throughout Europe around the turn of the century. Although this is not the place to begin to define the nature of Fianna Fáil's appeal (see Chapter 4), it nevertheless must be emphasised that the party's radicalism was always more populist than socialist. While sharing with social democracy an emphasis on the need to involve as many people in as many ways as possible, and while traditionally relying on the small contributions of countless supporters in order to finance its activities, even in its very early years Fianna Fáil never attempted the more classic social democratic strategy of mass incorporation and encapsulation. In short, it sought to penetrate civil society rather than attempting the complete integration of a defined constituency.

Fine Gael—or more properly, Cumann na nGaedheal—on the other hand, began as a much more cadre-style party, a loosely organised political movement which mobilised primarily through the influence of local notables who had achieved political as well as social prominence in the early years of the state. The party itself was formed from the top down by a political elite which felt the necessity to establish support networks throughout the country and, although it evolved quite a centralised system of control, it tended to rely on the work of paid organisers and placed little emphasis on mass involvement (Logan

1978, Chapters 10 and 11). Support for the party derived from its capacity to guarantee regime stability rather than from its activities on the ground. In short, and in sharp contradistinction to Fianna Fáil, it was not a grassroots party. Indeed, according to Garvin (1981a, p. 147), several of the early leaders appeared to have had 'a positive contempt for the whole business of grass-roots organisation . . . (and to have had) the ironic disadvantage of taking over government without having to fight an election of a truly competitive kind'. In Cumann na nGaedheal (and later Fine Gael) on the one hand, and Fianna Fáil, on the other, one could hardly have found two more contrasting styles of organisation.

The general organisational approach of Fianna Fáil is amply illustrated in its handbook *Bealach Bua* (literally 'Road to Victory'), an undated pamphlet which was probably published originally in the late 1920s or early 1930s and which is still available. The handbook deals with the activities of a Fianna Fáil cumann in inter-election periods, and it is worth quoting at some length, not least because it serves to underline the party emphasis on the cumann itself rather than the individual member as the key element in the organisation:

The most obvious [pre-election] preparatory activity for Cumann members is to make themselves familiar with the area for which they will be responsible during an election campaign. This knowledge should not merely include the geographical limits of the area, but all the economic and social problems arising in it. It should, as far as possible, extend to the political views of individual voters on the Electoral Register for the Cumann area . . .

It is a normal function of a Cumann to advise members of the public of the benefits available to them under existing schemes operated by Government Departments and Local Authorities . . . Members of Cumainn should let it be known that the Organisation is prepared to help individuals in their dealings with public authorities . . .

The aim of the Collection [the National Fund-Raising Collection] is not so much to get the largest possible amount subscribed in each area, although this is important, as to get the largest possible number of subscribers to give a contribution however small. The establishment of individual links with voters through the Collection is an important source of strength to the Organisation and also helps Cumann members to become familiar with the opinions of voters . . .

Cumann members should be encouraged to join, and take an active part in the work of other public organisations whose aims are in accord with those of Fianna Fáil . . . It has sometimes happened that local branches of organisations formed for worthy and non-political purposes have come under the control of political opponents of Fianna Fáil. It is the duty of each Cumann to counteract any such development in its area. If a local Trade Union Branch, for example, is being used to forward political interests hostile to Fianna Fáil, Cumann members of the Trade Union Branch concerned should be advised to attend regularly at the meetings and to counter such improper activities . . .

One of the main functions of Cumainn is to act as links of a nation-wide Intelligence Organisation to keep information on political events regularly supplied to the National Executive, and to Fianna Fáil Deputies and members of Local Authorities . . .

The effectiveness of Fianna Fáil as a National and Political Organisation is in direct relationship to the frequency and regularity of its contacts with the people. The aim of every Cumann should be to develop intimate contact with as many people as possible in the Cumann area. This cannot always be done by purely political activities, and Cumainn should consider as part of their normal working the organisation of other activities which will keep Fianna Fáil in the minds of the public and bring a larger number of people into association with it . . . [Social] functions in which the element of enjoyment is linked with the political significance of the event help the growth of membership. Aeriochta [i.e. outdoor entertainments], Céilithe [i.e. Irish dances], dances, card games and concerts should be organised regularly . . . At Aeriochta and concerts, a speech of a political character by a Deputy or other well-known person can usually be included in the programme, but political speeches are not always advisable at Céilithe and Dances . . . (*Bealach Bua*, pp. 3–9].

The logic of such a strategy is to combine a high party profile in a given area with an intimate knowlege of that area, favouring the formation of large numbers of small cumainn. Rather than emphasising organisational centralisation and, perhaps, organisational efficiency, the intention was to have a party presence in as many areas as possible, however small. This was particularly the case in rural areas, where small villages and townlands often maintained a sense of identity distinct from neighbouring villages and townlands. In this very parochial context, Fianna Fáil attempted to organise a cumann in every church or polling-booth area. In urban areas, on the other hand, where such a very localistic identity was less evident, the party tended towards larger cumainn with a brief for significantly larger sections of the electorate. In

Dublin in 1946, for example, when the area accounted for 23 Dáil seats, there were only 103 Fianna Fáil cumainn; in County Mayo, by contrast, where there were only eight Dáil seats, the party organised 131 cumainn. Nor was this simply a reflection of an electoral bias, since Fianna Fáil won 39 per cent of the Dublin vote in 1948 as against 42 per cent in Mayo. In addition, cumann organisation in rural areas tends to be less formal than in urban areas. In rural areas, the cumann meets on a formal basis on only two or three occasions during the year—to organise the national collection, to hold its annual general meeting and to meet with the local TD, and so on. Since the cumainn tend to be small and very local, however, the members do meet frequently on an informal basis. In urban areas, by contrast, with a larger and more dispersed membership, formal meetings take place approximately once a month, with correspondingly fewer informal gatherings.

Table 3.6 Number of electors and Fianna Fáil voters by cumann and by region

Region*	Number of cumainn			Number of electors per cumann			Number of FF voters per cumann		
	1948†	1965	1981	1948	1965	1981	1948	1965	1981
Dublin	103	190	301	2564	2381	1513	986	754	619
East & Midlands	519	852	1226	1140	839	618	460	301	275
West	499	505	907	650	689	381	288	261	198
Border	163	195	324	960	897	540	429	338	227

* Regions are those defined by Garvin (1977a).
† Cumann figures refer to 1946—a regional breakdown of the 1948 figure is unavailable.

The relatively strong organisational penetration of rural areas is shown in Table 3.6, which reports a breakdown of the number of electors and Fianna Fáil voters per cumann in different regions in 1946, 1965 and 1981. The regions are those defined by Garvin (1977a), and the contrast between the almost entirely urban Dublin area, the mixed urban/rural East and Midlands, and the overwhelmingly rural West is striking, with almost four times as many electors and Fianna Fáil voters per cumann in Dublin as against the West, a rural organisational bias which has persisted through to the 1980s.

Given the absence of individual membership figures for Fianna Fáil, and the absence of regional data concerning the branch network of Fine Gael, it is difficult to compare the relative organisational strength of the two major parties over the post-war period as a whole. At the same time, however, it is also difficult to avoid the intuitive conclusion that Fianna Fáil has traditionally enjoyed a greater organisational presence in rural areas, a conclusion which can be sustained by such limited local evidence as is available. In his study of local politics in Donegal, for instance, Sacks (1976, p. 105) noted a preference in Fianna Fáil for 'a close correspondence between the number of polling booths and established cumainn, while the Fine Gael party preferred fewer branches and larger domains, with 'key men or sub-directors (for elections) stationed at the different booths'. What is also interesting to note here is that, in addition to there being more Fianna Fáil cumainn than Fine Gael branches, Fianna Fáil also had a larger individual membership in Donegal, averaging 28 members per cumann as against an average of 15 members per branch in Fine Gael (ibid., p. 105). Gallagher (1985, p. 122), however, reports a regional breakdown of the parties' branches for 1983–4 which appears to reflect an extension of the Fine Gael branch network in rural areas. In Dublin, for example, Fianna Fáil cumainn outnumbered Fine Gael branches by some 66 per cent (256 versus 159), while in the heavily rural Connaught-Ulster area, Fianna Fáil cumainn outnumbered Fine Gael branches only by approximately 50 per cent (921 versus 658).

Nevertheless, one must be very cautious about using the branch network of any Irish party as an index of organisational strength or penetration. Since power within the parties rests firmly within the branches, which are the key weapons in the struggle for internal party influence, their proliferation may reflect the needs of local notables rather than organisational strength *per se*. In the Fianna Fáil case, for instance, and as noted above, each cumann has a postal vote in the election of members to the National Executive. At the same time, each cumann is also entitled to three delegates at the local constituency conventions which select candidates for nomination at general elections. An individual who is seeking power within the party will therefore attempt to control as many cumainn as possible. In addition, the rules which govern the establishment of a cumann are not onerous. First, each cumann must have a minimum of ten members but, since these are not registered with party headquarters, and since the actual names and addresses are known only at local level, such a membership need only be claimed rather than proven, a right jealously guarded by the cumainn themselves. In 1976, for instance, the party árd fheis rejected a motion calling for the names and addresses of members to be compulsorily registered with head office (*Iris Fianna Fáil*, 7, 1976, p. 20). Second, each cumann must pay a registration fee to head office, but since this was the equivalent of only 50p in 1946, and is only I£5 currently, this is not a serious obstacle. Finally, each cumann must contribute to the national collection, but again such money can be forthcoming without it necessarily requiring an active membership.

Given the political importance of the cumann and the relative ease with which it can be established, it is therefore not surprising to find that many exist on paper only, reflecting the tendency for local notables to accumulate as much intra-party voting strength as possible. Nor is it surprising to note an increase in cumann registration in election years as potential candidates attempt to secure their nomination. In the constituency of Mayo East, for example, 80 cumainn were registered in 1980, as against 140 in 1981, an election year. Following the un-expected defeat of Fianna Fáil in 1973, however, and the appointment of a new General Secretary, Seamus Brennan, attempts were made to improve organisational efficiency through the elimination of paper cumainn. Thus, in 1976, some 100 cumainn were closed down, while in Donegal alone, the number of cumainn was reduced from 200 to 120 between 1973 and 1977.

The problem of paper branches is not exclusive to Fianna Fáil. In 1965, for instance, a major row broke out in the Fine Gael constituency in Dun Laoghaire when one individual sought to affiliate a number of new branches in an effort to secure his nomination as a Dáil candidate. Labour has also been confronted with challenges to the legitimacy of certain branches. In the run-up to the 1977 election, for example, left-wing activists in the party accused three prominent Labour politicians of affiliating paper branches in order to secure their nominations.

In the Fine Gael case, however, the problem of paper branches always paled by comparison to the generally debilitated state of the organisation as a whole. One very evident indication of this are the figures from the 1950s and 1960s in Table 3.2 above, showing the difference between the total number of branches on the one hand and the number which actually registered on the other, the latter varying between a low of 19 per cent of the total in 1957 and a high of only 27 per cent in 1953. Certainly there was a Fine Gael branch network in this period, but the local organisations appear to have been largely autonomous of head office, preserving their attachment to the national organisation in name only. This picture is confirmed in the replies to a questionnaire sent to the constituency organisations by head office in 1957 (UCD Fine Gael archive, p39/2/5). The questionnaire sought details of the number of branches in each constituency, the number of these which were registered, and details of branch and constituency activities during the previous 12 months. In all, 44 constituencies were surveyed, but only 20 replies were received by head office. These reported a total of 625 branches, of which only 201 (32 per cent) were registered. Poor registration rates were reported primarily by Western constituencies. In County Clare, for example, there were 42 branches, but none were registered; in County Leitrim there were 17 branches, and only two were registered. But even the Dublin area was problematic: the five Dublin constituencies which replied to the questionnaire reported a total of only 30 branches, of which only 11 were registered.

Prior to the 1970s Fine Gael had also seemed remarkably aloof from any real notion of popular intra-party democracy. The árd fheis played little role in electing the executive of the party, and even within the árd fheis itself there were quite substantial limits to the level of branch representation. In short, the party appeared an essentially elite-dominated organisation, largely subject to the control and influence of the parliamentary party, and bore many of the characteristics of the early Cumann na nGaedheal. Within such an environment, it can hardly have been surprising that so few branches actually registered with head office, or that the central party units played such a small role in the affairs of the organisational periphery. In many cases, and particularly during the nadir in party fortunes in the mid-1940s, local Fine Gael TDs owed their election largely to their own personal appeal, while the party banner itself seemed of little import. This process went so far that, as Gallagher (1978, p. 6) points out, 'some candidates distanced themselves from the party label to the extent of not even mentioning Fine Gael in their election literature'. In general, Gallagher (1978, p. 5) also emphasises the lack of internal party solidarity as evidenced in a low (relative to Fianna Fáil) rate of lower-preference vote transfers between Fine Gael candidates which, he suggests, 'reflects the traditionally casual, amateurish approach which [the party] has always appeared to take towards organisational matters'.

Organisational problems appear to have persisted through the 1960s and 1970s. In the wake of the 1965 election an undated and unsigned report on the party campaign had been strongly critical of the local organisational performance, referring to the 'long delays in getting the election machine started in some constituencies because of poor organisation and slothful, negligent officials' (FG Archive, UCD (UCDFG) p.39/bf34(c)). A report on the organisation in Dublin in 1968 noted that in two of the seven constituencies there was 'virtually no organisation, with in each case only two branches and no [constituency] executive in existence, and in another constituency no meeting of the executive had taken place for nine months owing to internal disputes' (ibid., p39/218). It also noted that, prior to an attempt at reorganisation in 1968, clinics (that is, service centres established by TDs to receive constituents) had been organised in only two Dublin constituencies. Nevertheless, there were pockets of Fine Gael strength in the city, even if these were the exceptions: the constituency of Dublin North-East maintained 14 branches with a nominal membership of 300 and an estimated active membership of 150, while nine branches and 125 members were claimed in Dublin North-West and ten branches and 200 members in Dublin South-East. As against this, the Dublin North-Central constituency reported only one branch with ten members, and the constituency executive itself had last affiliated to the party in 1961 (ibid.). Yet despite this poor organisation, it is worth noting that this last constituency returned a Fine Gael TD to the Dáil in 1961 and 1965: organisational weakness does not seem to have wholly eroded electoral support.

The lack of a real sense of party is further confirmed in the response to the publication of Fine Gael's *Just Society* manifesto in 1965. In retrospect, the new policies in this election programme have been seen as marking a major watershed in the development of the party's appeal (see, Chapter 4) yet, at the time, they appear to have made little impact on the local parties. One party worker is quoted by Kenny (1972, p. 403) as stating that 'there was not always a clear Fine Gael position on some issues, so in writing speeches we would simply try to hammer out our own policy. When the belatedly issued copies of the *Just Society* reached us, we sometimes found that statements in it were in contradiction to positions our candidate, or other party candidates, had taken'.

The general conclusion to be drawn is of the long-term persistence of a poorly organised, cadre-style party, continuing to lay organisational emphasis on key notables or individuals, while eschewing mass involvement and tolerating a lax and sometimes even non-existent branch network. By contrast, Fianna Fáil has tended to play down the role of the individual notable as such, and to concentrate instead on the cumann. It is thus interesting to note that when Sacks conducted his study of the parties at local constituency level, the Fianna Fáil cadres

whom he interviewed tended to be cumann officers, whereas those in
Fine Gael tended to be 'key men' without a branch organisation.
Moreover, while the Fianna Fáil cadres tended to be small farmers,
county council workers, pensioners, and so on, those in Fine Gael
tended to represent the local community elite—teachers, publicans,
shopkeepers, contractors, and so on (Sacks 1976, pp. 105ff.).

In the public domain also Fine Gael has tended to give the impression of being a party of notables, one dominated by the professionally
qualified, moneyed, and socially sophisticated men (rarely women)
of good background, good education, good (or clean) money and often
good breeding. Even more so than is the case with Fianna Fáil, Fine
Gael appears to be dominated by particular families who hand down
power and a sense of national duty from one generation to the next,
from Desmond FitzGerald (Minister for External Affairs and for
Defence in the 1920s) to his own son Garret FitzGerald (Taoiseach in
1981–2 and 1982–7); from John A. Costello (Taoiseach in 1948–51
and 1954–7) to his son Declan Costello (Attorney General in 1973–
7); and from William T. Cosgrave (Prime Minister in the 1920s) to his
son Liam Cosgrave (Taoiseach in 1973–7), and eventually to his son
Liam T. Cosgrave, who held a Dáil seat until 1987. In terms of
educational background, the inter-party contrasts are also striking:
some 45 per cent of Fine Gael Cabinet ministers serving in the period
1973–82 had been educated at schools which now opt out of the
free education scheme (introduced in 1967) and which continue to
charge fees—the closest Irish equivalent to the British public schools—
while the figure for Fianna Fáil Cabinet ministers in the same period
is only 12 per cent (educational details from Nealon and Brennan
1981).

In this sense the post-war party appears to have retained many of the
features of Cumann na nGaedheal in the inter-war years, and to have
suffered many of the same disadvantages, particularly in the lack of
involvement in mass politics. Notables may be willing to take on
decisive jobs in government, but many also share with their predecessors 'a positive contempt for the whole business of grass-roots organisation' (Garvin 1981a, p. 147). 'It is hard to find suitable candidates',
wrote one Fine Gael organiser in 1967, 'most of the business and pro-
fessional people would not bother' (UCD Fine Gael archive p39/6/
12). James Dooge, a leading Fine Gael figure who was appointed to the
Senate and who became Minister for Foreign Affairs in the 1981–2
coalition government, reflected this view quite clearly when he stated
that his reluctance to stand for the Dáil in earlier elections resulted from

an unwillingness to sacrifice a private career for that of a full-time politician (McInerny 1975).

The contrasting styles of the two major parties were also evident in their respective attitudes to fund-raising. As noted above, the bulk of Fianna Fáil income traditionally derived from its national collection, which itself was seen as one method of integrating the cumann into the local community. According to *Bealach Bua* (p. 5), the party believes that 'the establishment of individual links with voters through the Collection is an important source of strength to the organisation and also helps the cumann members to become familiar with the opinions of voters'. The collection was also orientated to gaining contributions from as many individuals as possible, the funds being sent to head office with a proportion then being returned for use by the constituencies. Moreover, wherever possible, donors were formally thanked by head office, however small their contribution.

The convention in Fine Gael, on the other hand, was that the funds gathered through the national collection were retained by the local parties themselves, while head office income partially derived from the fund-raising activities of the two national organisations who were responsible to head office and quite independent of the local parties. In this sense, there were two distinct networks in operation, the one comprising head office and the organisers, the other involving the local parties which were independent of one another and of head office. Conflicts between the two did of course ensue, particularly in so far as the local parties often viewed funds collected by the organisers in their areas as being theirs by right. In 1968, for instance, one local TD wrote to head office claiming to have heard that the organiser had been collecting money in his area in preparation for the referendum campaign of that year, and demanding that the money be returned to the local party. The General Secretary then wrote to the organiser reprimanding him for contacting his TD in question: 'the moral of this is that you should keep away from the TDs and carry out your own collection separately' (UCDFG, p39/6/12). Later that same year, following a similar complaint, the General Secretary wrote again: 'I must emphasise to you that any collections you carry out on behalf of Headquarters are to be regarded as *strictly private and confidential*, and that you are not to discuss the amount with anybody, or to reveal names of subscribers. You have now put us in the same position as you did in ——, namely that the local organisation feel that monies collected by you should be offset against money due from their constituency' (ibid.). The impression is one of an essentially secretive organisation, as much in conflict with itself as with its opponents. The contrast with the very open, public and very self-confident style of Fianna Fáil could hardly be more evident.

Labour appears to have suffered from many of the same organisational debilities as did Fine Gael. Labour is the weakest of the three parties in organisational terms, and has been described by one observer as less a modern mass political party and more 'a loose coalition of like-minded but independent TDs' (Manning 1972, p. 80). A more recent and comprehensive study confirms this impression (Gallagher 1982). In 1957, for instance, the then party leader not only restricted his electioneering to his own constituency as opposed to organising a national campaign, but even in his election literature offered only a passing reference to the party as such (ibid., pp. 31–2). Nor was this exceptional. In many cases Labour nominated only a single candidate in the individual multi-member constituencies, and that candidate's campaign was often based on appeals to personality rather than party policy (ibid., p. 91). It was not until 1961 that individual Labour TDs were asked to concentrate their attention on specific policy areas, while the practice of appointing Labour spokespersons for the different areas of government activity did not begin until 1965 (ibid., pp. 44–5). Commenting on Labour's campaign in the 1965 election, the then Financial Secretary of the party remarked that 'when one compares our party ... with the other two parties we are still at the penny-farthing stage in a jet age' (Desmond 1966, p. 7).

This problem was to become particularly acute in 1969 when the party head office published a manifesto which reflected the leftward shift in party thinking (see Chapter 1), but which was judged to be too radical by some of the more conservative rural TDs and candidates. Some 10,000 'Notes for Speakers' were produced summarising the new policies, but only 5,000 of these were actually taken up by the local constituency organisations (Gallagher 1982, pp. 89–90). At the same time, the Administrative Council ruled that all outgoing TDs should have at least one running-mate in the 1969 election, a ruling which was rejected by three rural TDs, one of whom refused to contest his seat if obliged to share the party ticket with a second candidate (ibid., p. 102). The rule was later repealed in 1972.

These and other examples recounted by Gallagher serve to emphasise the lack of head office control over the party in the constituencies, a weakness which was probably at least as important as the general lack of resources in accounting for the party's general failure to break through to majority status. In terms of its degree of central head office control, Labour found itself in much the same position as pre-1979 Fine Gael. In 1968, for example, the party's potential income included I£1,200 in branch affiliation fees yet, by the end of the year, some I£650 was still outstanding, indicating that less than 50 per cent of branches had affiliated. The General Secretary recently complained that the full national collection had not been returned to head office since, it being an election year, the local parties had chosen to retain a proportion of the funds collected (interview with the author, 11 January 1982). A similar problem was indicated in the Annual Report for 1969, while in 1964 and 1965 the average national collection in the entire province of Munster was only I£26, seven of the 12 constituencies contributing nothing at all (Desmond 1966, pp. 5–6). This was despite the fact that in this period nine of the 16 Labour TDs represented Munster constituencies.

Desmond's 1966 report is a telling chronicle of organisational weakness. Over the period 1965–6, for instance, he noted that the officers of the party had met on only six occasions. Apart from the specific needs of the Dublin area, he observed that new branches needed to be established in at least ten other constituencies, noting that there had been a total of 500 branches in 1941 and 800 in 1943 as against fewer than 400 in 1961 (ibid., pp. 3–4). The poor state of the party was particularly evident in the Western part of the country, where only one of the 206 local council seats was held by Labour (ibid., p. 9). Desmond also criticised the operation of the 1965 general election campaign (ibid., p. 8–9).

> The full campaign committee met only briefly after the joint meeting of the Administrative Council and the Parliamentary Party. Details of the number of candidates were conflicting and the list of candidates notified was vague until late in the campaign; apart from press handouts, liaison with the Press seemed poor; the servicing of key constituencies with speakers for the meetings almost completely broke down; no prior panel of campaign speakers was arranged and circulated to branches; key marginals were not given special attention when it became obvious that they were in serious danger . . . the general election campaign fund was opened too late to accumulate and enable decisions to be taken on expenditure; the single telephone line at Head Office was constantly engaged and no extra clerical staff was employed for the campaign; only the bare minimum of the Election Manifesto was duplicated and no special election posters were produced.

Over and above these specific difficulties, and in common with its two opponents, Labour also experienced problems with paper branches which had been established by local notables. The incentive to form such branches is clear. Although the Administrative Council decides on the number of candidates to be nominated by any constituency, and although it retains the right to reject any of the candidates selected at local level, the local branches still retain a major role in selection conventions. Branches not only have the right to nominate candidates, but each branch—regardless of size—is entitled to four delegates at the convention itself. Given that there are so few branches to begin with, it is therefore relatively easy for a small group to win political control of the constituency. Moreover, the power which accrues to a branch may also be channelled in other directions, as, for example, at the national conference. While this is not a problem exclusive to Labour itself, the relatively small scale of the party organisation as a whole increases the rewards available, in that any one individual or constituency can affiliate sufficient branches to form an effective voting block at conference. In a case known to the author, for example, one rural TD hired a bus to ferry some fifty delegates to the party conference in Galway in 1974 with the intention of securing the election of a supporter to the Administrative Council. The TD in question had registered more than 20 branches in his constituency, each of which was then entitled to a minimum of two conference delegates. Those who travelled to Galway were told they could spend the weekend as they wished, and vote for the various resolutions as they thought fit, the only stipulation being that they voted as instructed in the Administrative Council election.

Tangentially, it should also be emphasised that the same forces which make for a proliferation of paper branches also help to ensure the survival of local parties. In many Western European countries, the local organisations of national parties appear to have waned in importance as election campaigning becomes increasingly nationalised (Daalder 1986). In the Irish case, however, despite a similar if not more pronounced level of national campaigning (Chapter 2), local organisations have thrived—the evidence in Table 3.2 is compelling. The explanation lies in the nature of the local organisations themselves, in that in many cases the local party is simply the party of the local notable. This is particularly evident in patterns of door-to-door canvassing, which might have been anticipated to have declined given the nationalisation of electioneering. In Ireland, however, canvassing remains important as a means of ensuring the election of the individual *candidate*, even if the national campaign may largely determine the overall support for the *party*. Many canvassers thus often approach voters not by saying 'I represent party X', but rather by saying 'I represent candidate A from party X'. They then ask for a first-preference vote for their favoured candidate and request lower-preference support for their candidate's running-mates. In this sense the party choice is often assumed to lie outside the canvasser's influence, the local branches efforts being devoted largely to achieving a particular rank-ordering from the party voter. Thus local parties, as the parties of local notables, survive. The contrast with Britain is striking: in 1979, for example, only some 15 per cent of respondents in a British MORI poll reported being visited by a representative of *any* of the competing parties. In Ireland in February 1982, by contrast, and allowing for differential constituency size, an IMS poll found that 54 per cent of respondents had been visited by a Fianna Fáil canvasser, 47 per cent by a Fine Gael canvasser, and 21 per cent by a Labour canvasser (McKee 1983, p. 185).

Revitalisation

Many of the contrasts in organisational style between Fianna Fáil and Fine Gael were to wane through the 1970s, as the latter initiated a major drive to revitalise and centralise the party machinery, and sought—quite successfully—to transform a party of notables into a modern mass organisation. The process of reform was relatively rapid, and began with the election of a new leader—Garrett FitzGerald—and the appointment of a new General Secretary in the wake of the unexpected defeat of the Fine Gael–Labour coalition government in 1977. The first stage in the transformation of the party was the appointment of a voluntary public relations officer and a constituency organiser in each of the constituencies, and while both were to be members of the local party, they were to be largely responsible to head office rather than to the local party *per se*; both were also obliged to declare in advance that they would not offer themselves as candidates at the next general election. In this way they could be seen to stand above local factional disputes, and at the same time they would provide a crucial link between head office and the local organisations, so curtailing the capacity of the latter to be reduced simply to the party of the local notables.

Branches were informed that in order to affiliate and to take part in candidate selection, they would not only have to pay their affiliation fee, but also take part in the party's national collection, supply details of their annual accounts to head office, and have a minimum of nine paid-up members who would be registered with head office. The changes proved to be effective. As recently as 1978 the Honorary Secretaries' report to the árd fheis had stated that some two-thirds of the branches were not registered with head office, while only one-third of constituency executives had responded to requests for information on the number of branches and their financial situation. Two years later, they were in a position to report a significant improvement: not only had the vast majority of branches affiliated, but they were also believed to be real and effective branches as opposed to simply paper branches: 'we have continued the process of weeding out ineffective branches and are now confident that the 1,849 branches which have affiliated for 1979 really exist and are largely effective' (Honorary Secretaries' Report to the 1980 Árd Fheis, p. 2).

The success in weeding out paper branches was largely due to the introduction of what the party called the new 'model system' for branches and for constituency or candidate-selection conventions. According to the new scheme, power no longer accrued to the branch simply as a result of its branch status *per se*, but rather according to the number of electors for which the branch had responsibility. Each constituency executive allocates a section of the constituency to each branch, notifying head office of the number of members in the branch and the section of the electoral register for which it has responsibility. Each branch which is responsible for up to 500 electors is then entitled to send three delegates to the constituency convention, with an additional delegate for every additional 250 electors. A further proviso states that a branch cannot send more than the equivalent of one-third of its members as delegates to conventions, so that a nine-member branch with a remit for 1,000 electors may still send only three delegates. In Dublin and Cork City, with more densely populated constituencies and fewer branches, responsibility for 1,000 electors entitles a branch to three delegates, with an additional delegate for every 500 additional electors.

The potential effects of such a reform are evident. First, by associating each branch with a specific number of electors, it discourages the proliferation of branches in one small area. Second, by giving each branch a specific remit, the party is able to maintain an external check on its activities and effectiveness—the absence of organisational activity in a given area can be traced back to the branch which is responsible for that area. Third, the reform facilitates a fairly proportionate representation of all areas in a given constituency. In situations where branches can be formed at will, and where sufficient power accrues to branches to encourage their proliferation, a constituency may be imbalanced in terms of the vast overrepresentation of areas where local notables have established their bases. Once again, Sacks (1976, p. 109) provides a suitable example of just such a pattern, this time in the case of Fianna Fáil. At the time of his study, there were 67 cumainn in the constituency of Donegal North-East, serving a total electorate of 37,371. Of these cumainn, as many as 25 (37 per cent) were concentrated in the Milford area of the constituency which included only 8,691 (23 per cent) of the electors, but which was at the same time the home base of Neil Blaney, then the leading Fianna Fáil politician in the constituency. As Sacks pointed out, these cumainn constituted the largest single block in the constituency conventions and, since intra-party power rested on the number of cumainn, Blaney thus maintained effective control over the nomination of candidates at local authority and Dáil constituency level. In the case of Fine Gael, the new model scheme is intended to prevent the emergence of such internal constituency imbalances (for a more general assessment of the Fine Gael case, see O'Byrnes 1986).

Despite its traditional organisational advantage, Fianna Fáil also initiated a process of revitalisation in the 1970s. In the wake of its unexpected defeat in 1973, the party appointed a new General Secretary and a new press officer, as well as a full-time research director with a brief to elaborate policy across a wide range of areas. As noted above, Fianna Fáil also initiated a major attempt to weed out paper branches and, to an extent, to subordinate local parties to head office interests. The new approach was to bear fruit in 1977, with the publication of a glossy and appealing party manifesto and with the mobilisation of an exceptionally well-orchestrated campaign, the groundwork for which had been laid months in advance. This was also the period when, as in the case of Fine Gael, the party launched its youth section, Ógra Fianna Fáil (see above), evidencing a new reliance on ancillary organisational efforts.

Labour has also attempted to revitalise its organisation in this period. Since 1980, for example, in an effort to weed out paper branches, the party has stipulated that each rural branch must have a minimum of five members and each urban branch a minimum of ten; each must participate in the national collection and pay the branch affiliation fee, and must be registered for at least six months before being eligible to participate in candidate selection conventions and the annual conference. Also since 1980, the number of delegates to conference varies according to the number of members, with each branch being entitled to send a minimum of two delegates and with one additional delegate for every five members over the minimum number necessary for affiliation.

To clean up its organisation is one thing, however; to make it more effective in terms of winning votes or seats is quite another, and whatever reforms have been introduced by Labour in the past decade or so seem to have done little to stem the general erosion of its electoral support. Indeed, as was evident in Table 3.2, this electoral erosion has been accompanied by a decline in the number of branches. In Dublin North-West in 1986, for example, formerly a strong Labour area, there were only two branches of the party, each with only some ten to 15 members. Moreover, head office still experiences difficulty in exerting its control over the local parties and local TDs. The party's leading vote-winner resigned in 1981, for example, when the Administrative Council insisted that he transfer to a new constituency in order not to split the Labour vote in his original constituency (*Irish Times*, 9 February 1981), and as recently as June 1986, a Labour TD and three local councillors resigned from the party due to what they claimed to be the unwarranted interference of the Administrative Council in local party affairs. The TD had earlier announced his intention of retiring at the next general election, and the Administrative Council had ratified in his stead a candidate who was opposed by the TD's own supporters. A number of branches in the area then disaffiliated from the party, and in a statement issued after following their resignation, the former Labour representatives complained that their local party had been 'taken over by Head Office and the Administrative Council ... This is not democracy when one is expected to pay membership fees, affiliations, etc, to an organisation and then to be told one cannot exercise any influence in deciding what one considers best for the party' (*Irish Times*, 11 June 1986). The mood was clearly similar to that of those TDs in 1969 who had opposed the head office ruling that they accept a running-mate at the forthcoming election (Gallagher 1982, p. 102), and in so far as it concerned the right of the local party to determine local electoral strategy, it reflected a conflict which has the potential to pervade all three parties, particularly given the centralising tendencies in party organisation in the 1970s and 1980s.

As far as all three parties are concerned, organisational revitalisation has led to a blurring of the traditional boundary between the national party and the local party. As the parties have faced the need to become more competitive, so the head offices have attempted to subordinate local interests to national needs (see Mair 1987a). There is a problem here, however, particularly in so far as the national party interest on the one hand and the self-interest of an already incumbent TD on the other need not coincide: what is good for the party may not be good for the incumbent, and vice versa. Thus conflicts of interest do ensue, particularly when a party is seeking to increase its support as opposed to simply accepting the status quo. Such might be the case if, say, Fine Gael holds two seats in a five-seat constituency and attempts to win a third. In order to win this extra seat, and recognising the importance of candidate appeal, the party will be required to nominate a strong third candidate to run with the two incumbent TDs. If Fine Gael were completely confident of winning three seats, such a nomination would present no problems; if, on the other hand, there was less certainty, and a strong possibility that despite the new strategy Fine Gael would still end up with only two seats, problems would inevitably arise. Which two seats would the party win? Would both incumbent Fine Gael TDs be re-elected or would one be displaced by the new nominee? Thus, while it might be in the *party* interest to nominate a strong third candidate— at worst they would still hold two seats—it may not be in the TDs' interest, as that candidate might well win one of the only two Fine Gael seats. It is in such circumstances that conflict ensues between the party and the TD and, since the local branches of the party are normally controlled by the local TD (see above), there is a conflict between the party at national level and the party at local level. At national level there is pressure for growth; at local level there may be pressure for maintenance of the status quo. Hence, for example, the opposition of a number of local parties to Labour's decision in 1969 that each outgoing TD should be accompanied by a running-mate.

Thus, while the increasingly competitive context of Irish party politics has emphasised the need to woo support, the parties themselves often find that their ambitions are thwarted by individual incumbent insecurity. As such, they have been forced to exert a greater and greater central control over the local parties and the local nomination processes. Part of this process has already been reviewed, and simply involves pressure to eliminate paper branches and to ensure that local notables are no longer able to pack selection conventions, and this can be seen in the new strictures on branch registration and in the new model system of Fine Gael in particular.

In addition, however, the party leaderships have also increasingly tended to exercise their right to impose additional candidates where the list of those nominated at local level is regarded as insufficiently representative in terms of either locality, gender, age, or whatever. In 1977, for instance, the Fianna Fáil leader imposed additional candidates in 16 constituencies in order to effect a more balanced list of nominees. Among these were six women, whom it was hoped would attract the growing women's vote. Of the 16, five were elected, two of whom displaced incumbent Fianna Fáil TDs. In 1981, the party also added names in some ten constituencies, while the Administrative Council of the Labour Party also added candidates in at least three Dublin constituencies in that election. Such instances offer a clear indication that the traditional boundary between the national campaign and the local campaign is being eroded. As party ambitions are seen to be vulnerable to the defensive strategies of insecure incumbents, so the competition for votes is being slowly taken over by the parties' head offices.

In common with its more pronounced attempt at organisational revitalisation, it is in Fine Gael—particularly in November 1982—that one finds the clearest evidence of this fusion of national and local strategy (Mair 1987a). Following the defeat of the Fine Gael–Labour coalition in February 1982, Fine Gael set up a 'Constituency Review Committee' which was asked to investigate 20 constituencies where the party felt it had a reasonable chance of winning an additional seat, and where it was felt that the list of candidates might be modified so as to ensure a maximum return of seats. The Wexford constituency affords perhaps the best example of the Committee's work. At the February election, this five-seat constituency had resulted in three seats for Fianna Fáil and two seats for Fine Gael, the third Fianna Fáil seat having been won from Labour. The two Fine Gael TDs were based in the north and centre of the constituency, and the Committee review recommended the nomination of a third candidate from the southern end, which included the towns of Wexford and New Ross where some 26,000 electors were registered. It was felt that if the two incumbents could let their personal vote drop slightly, the resultant surplus, when added to the additional southern vote produced by a strong third candidate, would ensure that candidate's election. In the event, the outcome went as planned. The overall vote for Fine Gael rose (partly in tandem with a national pro-Fine Gael swing and partly as a result of the attraction of new voters from the southern end of the constituency), the personal vote of the incumbents fell slightly, and the third candidate won sufficient first-preferences to remain in the running as the counts progressed, and to remain ahead of the Labour candidate whose transfers she received when he was eliminated, until she was eventually deemed elected.

Similar examples of the successful Fine Gael strategy could be cited for other constituencies in the November 1982 election, most notably in the case of the Galway West constituency where the strategy was aimed at winning a seat from Labour (Mair 1987a). On a less ambitious scale, there was already evidence in 1977 that Fianna Fáil was also beginning to attempt the more effective management of its vote. In the Sligo-Leitrim constituency in 1977, for example, the party attempted a more equitable and more effective distribution of its first-preferences by issuing posters which urged its supporters in the northern half of the constituency to rank the Fianna Fáil candidates in one way, and in the southern half to rank them in a different way, and a similar strategy was adopted by Fine Gael in the different wards of the constituency of Dublin South-Central in November 1982. The idea here is that one candidate should not accumulate so many of the party's first preferences that it will result in the early elimination of his or her running-mates; rather, with a more equitable distribution, all of the party's candidates would remain in the running throughout the various counts and would thus be in a position to receive additional transfers from other eliminated candidates.

Such strategies demand a certain degree of self-sacrifice on the part of incumbent TDs. In essence, the TDs are being asked to forfeit a proportion of their first-preferences in order to assist a non-incumbent running-mate. Yet there is not necessarily a great deal of incentive for incumbents to be so altruistic. Not only are they under threat from their running-mates to begin with, but this threat has actually increased since the national parties have begun to intervene more effectively in local nomination strategies: between 1977 and 1982, for example, 42 per cent of all incumbent losses resulted from intra-party displacement, as against just 28 per cent between 1951 and 1973 (Mair 1987a).

In this battle to win new votes, what can the parties offer in return for incumbent self-sacrifice? If the party is doing well, then one possibility is preferment, with the prospect of those TDs who have placed party-interest before self-interest being rewarded with government office. Indeed, if the party's prospects are good, then it will enjoy a double advantage: the party candidates should benefit from an overall swing in favour of the party and this in turn should encourage a more altruistic approach. If the party is not likely to win office, however, then not only does head office have little to offer self-sacrificing incumbent TDs, but the TDs themselves are likely to feel even more vulnerable and so will expend an even greater effort in resisting head office overtures. Thus, when Fine Gael was appearing particularly vulnerable to the PD challenge in 1987, head office capacity to ensure the subordination of incumbent self-interest proved limited. The constituency of Wexford, for example, where the vote management strategy had proved so successful in 1982, was riven with intra-party rivalry in 1987, as each of the Fine Gael TDs attempted to ensure their own survival in the face of an almost inevitable swing away from the party (O'Higgins 1987). In the wake of the election, the *Irish Times* (18 February 1987) reported similar intra-party Fine Gael wrangles in five other constituencies.

To the extent that the party head offices can weed out paper branches, and to the extent that it becomes increasingly apparent that the candidates' fortunes depend on the national campaign at least as much as on the local campaign (see Chapter 2), then it is likely that the head offices will gradually gain the upper hand in this enduring conflict between organisational centre and organisational periphery. If the party is suffering a secular decline, on the other hand, then it will prove more difficult to defeat incumbent self-interest and, as such, the party's capacity to compete will clearly be curtailed.

Does Organisation Matter?

Political parties constrain voter choice in a variety of ways: through the formulation of governing alternatives, through the specification of electoral appeals, and, of course, through their organisational strategy and style. Indeed, it can be argued that the organisational intervention of parties is a constituent part of any 'freezing' process, while the converse also clearly holds true, in that organisational decline can lead to a 'thawing' of party systems, and a process of de- or realignment. Thus it is the historical dimension which is perhaps the most relevant when assessing the importance of Fianna Fáil's organisational advantage for, as has been argued here as elsewhere (e.g., by Logan 1978; see also Garvin 1981a), Fianna Fáil/Sinn Fein was the first genuinely mass party in the new Irish state, setting down strong roots in local communities, and establishing a pervasive organisational network which completely overshadowed its more cadre-style opponent, Cumann na nGaedheal. In this sense, and in competition with Cumann na nGaedheal/Fine Gael in the 1920s and 1930s, Fianna Fáil enjoyed advantages similar to those enjoyed by certain of the mass continental socialist parties in their struggle against the right.

The importance of such an organisational advantage cannot be overestimated. For example, Lipset and Rokkan (1967) speak of the early mass organisations 'narrowing the "support market" and so constraining the possibilities for the future mobilisation of an alternative politics.' Yet, as they also point out, this process occurred unevenly in certain party systems, with the French case in particular being characterised by the early growth and consolidation of mass organisations on the left of the political spectrum, but not on the right. The result was that while the left 'support market' was narrowed, that on the right remained relatively open, and thus while the left was characterised by relative organisational persistence, there remained substantial scope for organisational change and discontinuity within bourgeois French politics (Lipset and Rokkan 1967). Applying this perspective to the Irish case, it is indeed tempting to suggest that the long-term success of Fianna Fáil may have been due in part to its capacity to build up an extensive mass organisation in the early years of the state and so narrow its particular 'support market', while the relative failure of the other parties may have derived from an incapacity to effect a similar closure of any potential constituency. Thus, while the support market may have been narrowed on one side of the political divide, it remained broad and open on the other, an imbalance which may account for the relative stability of the Fianna Fáil 'side' of the party system, and the relative instability within the block of opposing parties (cf. Chapter 2). In a sense, this is a defence of the freezing hypothesis, in that the early organisational advantage of Fianna Fáil is seen to account for its later persistence, stability and success. What must be emphasised yet again, however, is that such freezing as has occurred has been uneven, with the non-Fianna Fáil 'side' of the party system remaining electorally fluid and organisationally volatile. If anything, the Irish experience points to the importance of the *organisational* variable in accounting for the persistence of party systems—or at least certain parts of party systems (cf. Rokkan 1977).

It is also clear from this general survey that Fianna Fáil continued to enjoy a clear organisational superiority long after the initial formation of the party system. The party maintained a more extensive branch network and established a substantially greater degree of organisational presence than has been the case in either Fine Gael or Labour. To judge by what partial figures do exist, it also appears to have enjoyed a substantially larger membership. If we take the crude figure of 75,000 members as reasonably valid, for example, then even in the 1980s party membership has been almost double that of Fine Gael. Finally, Fianna

Fáil has also commanded significantly more resources than the other two parties, both in terms of finance and in terms of party personnel, or at least did so until Fine Gael began to close the gap in the late 1970s.

But to what extent does organisation continue to matter? Of necessity, any attempt to understand the configuration of the contemporary party system must emphasise the sheer organisational acumen of Fianna Fáil as a major factor contributing to its relative position of dominance. By comparison with Fine Gael, and particularly with Labour, the degree of organisational cohesion and penetration enjoyed by Fianna Fáil remains one of its most distinctive characteristics. Against this, however, it must be emphasised that in the medium to long term, it may be difficult to distinguish the independent effects of organisational strength and electoral popularity. To the extent that the former is measured simply in terms of membership or popular financial support, then it is likely to ebb and flow in tandem with a party's electoral following. When the party is gaining support, it will also tend to gain members and to enjoy greater success in its fund-raising activities. Equally, as the membership and resources of a party increase, so also will its capacity to persuade voters to its side. In a sense, therefore, both measures of party support are reciprocal, and while each affects the other, their mutual variation is more likely to be the result of other, more exogenous factors (for a discussion of these themes, see McAllister 1981).

On the other hand, however, certain measures of organisational strength are more readily subject to enquiry, and can be said to have had a relatively independent impact on electoral support. The sheer organisational presence of a party, for example, is likely to affect its campaigning potential, and is also likely to have an impact on general electoral predisposition and affective attitudes. The more closely a party is integrated into the local community, for instance, the more likely it is to be capable of riding out short-term disaffection and electoral volatility. Organisational cohesion and authority are also clearly important, particularly in so far as the central party organisation can develop and co-ordinate local electoral strategy which, given the STV electoral system, can prove so crucial to a party's fortunes.

Even in these terms, however, Fianna Fáil may be in danger of losing its crucial edge. Since 1979 in particular, the party has experienced severe internal faction-fighting (e.g., Garvin 1981b; Walsh 1986, pp. 145–52) which necessarily undermines its organisational cohesion. To be sure, faction-fighting is nothing new in Fianna Fáil—in the 1950s, for example, there was quite a sharp radical–conservative division within the party (Bew and Patterson 1982)—but on previous occasions these disputes were largely contained within the party and, as Gallager (1985, p. 29) remarks, 'no cracks appeared in the public façade'. The split which gave rise to the Progressive Democrats proved much more public, however, and the eventual defection of the dissident TDs was also accompanied by a wave of defections from local cumainn (cf. *Sunday Tribune*, 26 January 1986).

Moreover, as Farrell (1986) makes clear, and as is also shown by the hi-tech PD campaign in 1987 (e.g., O'Reilly 1987), conditions are now such that a capital-intensive, marketing-orientated party can make substantial advances in the newly competitive arena of Irish politics, almost regardless of the strength and coherence of its local machine. As campaigning becomes increasingly nationalised (Chapter 2), and as media presence becomes at least as important as organisational presence, even those traditional advantages which have been retained by Fianna Fáil may not count for a great deal. To the extent that *party*— as opposed to *candidate*—preference is dictated by national perform-ance and national appeals, then even 75,000 members may not make any difference. To be sure, these local members may prove crucial in the ordering of candidates *within* the party, but overall party perform-ance may itself owe much more to what is actually said at national level.

The key question then becomes whether the parties actually can be distinguished in terms of their national policies: this will be the topic of the following chapter.

Note

1. State-funded personnel assistance was first made available in 1975, when one secretarial assistant was provided for each ten non-office holding TDs. In 1978, the ratio was improved to one secretarial assistant for each seven non-office holding TDs, and thereafter progressively improved until 1982, when the ratio became one secretarial assistant for each non-office holding TD. Further, in October 1981, an additional 17 posts were made available to the *parties* (as opposed to the TDs *per se*) for general administrative and research purposes. The distribution of these appointments (as in June 1986) was as follows: Fianna Fáil, 7; Fine Gael, 5; Labour 4; Workers Party, 1. In the case of the three larger parties, one of these appointees acts as a general administrator, with the remaining appointees working as research assistants or as assistants in the press offices of the parties (information supplied by the Department of the Public Service).

4

WHAT DIVIDES THE PARTIES?

The 'end of ideology' debate in the 1960s, together with the literature documenting the emergence of catch-all politics in Western Europe, has already provoked quite frequent debates about what—if anything—divides competing parties in contemporary democracies. In the Irish case the question seems especially apposite, particularly given the tendency in the present Irish literature to suggest that there are virtually *no* programmatic or ideological divisions underlying contemporary political oppositions. Fianna Fáil and Fine Gael, according to one recent analyst, 'provide no real alternatives to Irish voters on substantive issues'. The same author goes on to argue that this is yet one more deviant characteristic marking off the Irish case, for 'in no other European polity does a small number of programmatically indistinguishable parties constitute the entire party system' (Carty 1981, pp. 43, 85). Nor is this an eccentric view. According to Gallagher, both major parties offer 'pragmatic images . . . frequently not backed up by policies at all', with Fine Gael simply looking 'like a less-well-packaged version of Fianna Fáil, with the same basically pragmatic, problem-solving approach' (Gallagher 1981, pp. 279, 282). Yet other interpretations find the lack of ideological conflict confirmed by the pattern of coalition formation, which joins the traditionally moderate left (Labour) with the traditionally moderate right (Fine Gael) in opposition to the traditionally dominant centre (Fianna Fáil). While such a coalition of the 'extremes' against the centre might cause raised eyebrows in other party systems, in Ireland it can be readily understood, since the very limited range of the overall political spectrum means that even 'the "extremes" are not very far apart' (Cohan 1979, p. 325). In sum, ideological divisions, even in a very loose sense, are absent, and such competition as is involved in national election campaigns 'inevitably revolve[s] almost entirely around valence issues' (Carty 1981, p. 118).

A dull and dreary picture, to be sure. Indeed, despairing of finding substance in contemporary inter-party divisions, many commentators on the Irish party system find themselves reverting to historical explanations. Traditional differences on the national question and relations with Britain are thus ushered forth again and again as providing the continuing key to the puzzle. Since Fianna Fáil carried the banner of more militant nationalism in the 1920s and early 1930s, this is then seen to provide the basis of its post-war success. Fine Gael, on the other hand, ended up in an ambiguous and compromising position on the national question, and this ambiguity is still seen to account for its failure to displace Fianna Fáil in the contemporary period. The emphasis on the legacy of history is also seen to account for the persistent weakness of Labour, since its attempts to inculcate a social democratic outlook in Irish politics could not have been expected to do anything else but founder on the rocks of primarily territorial concerns.

As far as ideological competition is concerned, therefore, the conclusion is that in the beginning was the Treaty, and that thereafter everything has been frozen. In this sense it is not the legacy of history *per se*, but rather the legacy of a particular history—that of the 1920s and 1930s—for developments are seen to come more or less to a stop with the advent of Fianna Fáil to power in 1932 or, at a pinch, with the adoption of the new Constitution in 1937. As argued above (Chapter 1), the autonomous impact of events and developments from the 1940s onwards is often ignored, and contemporary political divisions are seen to be simply the aged and rather tired expression of those crucial conflicts in the early years of the state. Thus, for example, it is interesting to note that a study of the electorate in the general election of 1977 (Sinnott 1978) began by devoting a substantial proportion of the analysis to the nature of alignments in the 1920s and 1930s, and then dived more or less immediately into opinion poll evidence from 1977. Nothing of note seems to have happened in between.

A similar reversion to history can be seen in Cohan's (1982, p. 269) largely intuitive attempt to define the cleavages underlying contemporary Irish politics, where he suggests that the primary conflict remains one of 'strong vs weak' nationalism (dividing Fianna Fáil and Fine Gael), with a 'planned vs market economy' conflict (and dividing Labour and Fine Gael) playing a secondary role. Basil Chubb (1970, pp. 58–60), in his pioneering study of the Irish political system, also identified a version of the nationalist cleavage as the basic underlying dimension, with secondary conflicts revolving around left versus right and town versus country. Yet another study, this time based on an attitude survey of party activists, found that a 'territorial-nationalism' dimension was particularly important, although in this case the dominant dimension was 'clericalism vs pluralism', while a third 'anti-capitalist radicalism' dimension also proved important (Garvin 1974, pp. 321–2). The emphasis on the traditional ideological alignment is, of course, understandable. If divisions on contemporary issues are so slight, and if competition revolves entirely around valence issues, then the inevitable conclusion is that Irish politics is either 'about' territorial nationalism or it is 'about' nothing at all, and few observers would be willing to concede the latter (although see Gallagher 1981).

But while such an emphasis may be understandable, the thesis itself is hardly plausible. If, as argued above (Chapter 1), the political alternatives themselves were not frozen into place in the 1920s and 1930s, why should one expect that the ideological conflicts have proved immutable? On the face of it, one can anticipate that the relevance of territorial nationalism would have declined as the new state cemented its independence from Britain with the adoption of the 1937 Constitution and with the declaration of a republic in 1948. To be sure, the persistence of partition has acted to keep 'the national question' alive to a certain extent but, at least until very recently (Cox 1985; Mair 1987c), this was a problem far removed from the forefront of political debate, and lacked the immediacy and relevance of such earlier issues as dominion status, the oath of allegiance, and the economic war. Indeed, as politics in the post-war period has developed, the parties have inevitably become increasingly enmeshed in the more conventional concerns for economic growth, industrial management and the establishment and maintenance of a modern welfare state. But if it can be argued that territorial nationalism is no longer so relevant to inter-party divisions, what then has emerged to the fore? If Irish politics is no longer about nationalism, is it then not about anything at all?

On the basis of an analysis of the policies of the three main parties between 1961 and 1982, I will contend that Irish politics in that period has indeed been about certain substantive issues and ideologies, and that these issues and ideologies go far beyond disputes simply about territorial nationalism. In essence, I will argue that the basic ideological division underlying the competition between Irish parties in this period, and which separated Fianna Fáil from Fine Gael *and* Labour, was that of corporatist ideology versus social democracy. To be sure, the ideologies involved are rather moderate examples of what is found in a more intense, cogent and coherent version in other countries. Nevertheless, the conflict is there, it is real, and it makes sense not only of inter-party divisions in general, but also of the pattern of coalition formation in particular.

Following Bew and Patterson (1982), I will argue that the post-war period has seen a conscious attempt by Fianna Fáil to reconstruct its dominant political appeal through means other than simply an emphasis on its nationalist pedigree. Through a combination of economic expansionism, a commitment to welfare, and a persistent opposition to the politicisation of social conflict, the party developed what might be termed a corporatist ideology, congruent with but also at quite a remove from its traditional appeal to territorial nationalism. Against this, both Fine Gael and Labour mobilised a more social democratic appeal, emphasising notions of social justice and redistribution, and advocating the merits of economic planning and control.

The route which I have chosen to follow in elaborating this argument is not to assume the ideological positions of the parties, but rather to look at what they actually say, and to analyse the actual policies which they advocate in the competitive arena of national election campaigns. In other words, I am looking at what Sani and Sartori (1983) refer to as the dimensions of competition rather than at the domains of identification, and it is perhaps for this reason that territorial nationalism receives less emphasis (see below). The chapter reports an emphatically empirical enquiry, based on a content analysis of party programmes and election speeches.[1] The contents of these programmes were coded according to a scheme originally devised by Robertson (1976) for an analysis of British party manifestos, and subsequently modified by a research group of the European Consortium for Political Research (ECPR) for cross-national application. The coding categories used in this present analysis represent a further modification of the scheme,[2] and are listed in Table 4.1. In all, 38 coding categories were used, ranging from economic themes such as *enterprise* and *controlled economy*, to governmental themes such as *government authority* and *government efficiency*, and themes relating to the social fabric, such as *defence of the Irish way of life* and *national effort* and *social harmony*. Each of the 34 election programmes or surrogates (12 Fianna Fáil, ten Fine Gael, ten Labour, and two Fine Gael–Labour coalition programmes) issued between 1948 and 1982 was broken down into these categories, counting each sentence or complete phrase as the relevant unit of analysis. Sentences or phrases with no particular reference were treated as 'empty' and were not coded (the subsequent analysis excludes these empty sentences, the average proportion of which is also shown in Table 4.1). The result is a unique profile of each of the programmes which, in turn, can be aggregated by party to provide a more generalised profile of each of the major protagonists. Table 4.1 reports the result of this breakdown, listing the average proportion of sentences in each category for the period 1961 to 1982.

As can be seen from the list of election programmes in the bibliography (see pp. 230–1), the type of document used in this analysis varies substantially from party to party and from election to election, and includes formal election manifestos, party leaders' speeches, radio broadcasts, newspaper reports, and so on. More recent elections have tended to be characterised by a genuine manifesto politics, and formal statements of the parties' policies have tended to receive a greater emphasis. Fine Gael and Labour, for instance, which have always had a more directly competitive orientation than Fianna Fáil (see Chapter 2), have both published proper manifestos for virtually each of the elections since 1961, while Fianna Fáil itself did not publish a formal manifesto prior to 1977, earlier statements of election policy being largely restricted to speeches by the party leader or radio broadcasts. Partly for this reason, although also as a result of more substantive considerations (see below), the bulk of the subsequent analysis focuses on the 1961–82 period, with only slight reference to the policies proposed between 1948 and 1957.

Dimensions of Competition and Domains of Identification

The first and most obvious thing to note about Irish manifestos and election programmes is that virtually none pays any significant attention to territorial nationalism in general, nor to the Northern Ireland problem in particular. As can be seen from Table 4.1 (below), for instance, the *Irish unity* category counts for an average of little more than 2 per cent of the contents of all party manifestos during the 1961–82 period. The case of Fianna Fáil is of particular interest here since it is the party which is generally regarded as being the most militantly nationalist of the three parties, but even here statements in favour of Irish unity account for less than 3 per cent of the contents of the programmes, although the category does rank in tenth position in the party's leading priorities (Table 4.2). An appeal to traditional nationalism may be seen in the relatively high ranking for the category *defence of the Irish way of life*, which accounts for an average of just less than 6 per cent of the Fianna Fáil programmes, and which ranks in sixth position in the list of priorities, but even this category pales by comparison to the emphasis on more mundane social and economic issues.

This relative paucity of direct appeals to territorial nationalism is particularly striking given that, as noted above, such a concern is still seen as the basis of contemporary inter-party competition. One possible explanation for this dissonance may be found in the nature of election programmes themselves. These are essentially expressions of short-term policy intent, committing the parties to programmes which can be implemented in the lifetime of the incoming government. Nationalist appeals, on the other hand, may be seen as of more long-term import, reflecting a basically timeless 'aspiration' to Irish unity which few politicians believe can be realised in the forseeable future (e.g. Cohan 1977). As such, there is little of relevance that can be said in the context of an election programme. In a related sense, one can argue that territorial nationalist demands are devoid of policy content. Short of sponsoring a militant anti-partitionist campaign, there is little that any party or government can do to advance the cause of unity in any practical sense. To be sure, the protracted violence which began in Northern Ireland in 1969 has increased the salience of nationalist issues in the Irish Republic, and has placed a particular onus on the various governments to develop policies concerning the constitutional future of the province, but even now manifesto rhetoric remains simply rhetoric. In the context of its lengthy 1977 manifesto, for instance, Fianna Fáil was content to allocate Northern Ireland just a small paragraph, asserting that a central aim of the party

> is to secure by peaceful means the unity and independence of Ireland as a democratic Republic. We totally reject the use of force as a means of achieving this aim. Any progress on the lines suggested in Fianna Fáil's policy statement on the North, published in 1975, would add greatly to the impact of our economic strategy by promoting confidence both north and south and facilitating a return to a normal economic and tourist environment (p. 44)

Even by the standard of conventional election programmes, this statement is striking for its sheer banality.

An alternative explanation might be that the issue of territorial nationalism is essentially consensual, and therefore plays no role in the competitive electoral arena. All three parties pay homage to the principle of Irish unity to the extent that it is reflected in their party constitutions and/or even their names (Fianna Fáil—the Republican Party; Fine Gael—the United Ireland Party). The claim to Northern Ireland is also enshrined in Articles 2 and 3 of the 1937 Constitution, a factor which has long been a source of irritation to Ulster Unionists. The appeal of territorial nationalism is in this sense a given: as Charles

Haughey, the leader of Fianna Fáil, observed at a press conference during the 1981 campaign, 'the issue of a united Ireland is always in the consciousness of the Irish electorate' (noted by the author, 10 June 1981). Fine Gael is perhaps the exception here, given its ambivalence on the constitutional question in the 1920s and 1930s, and given that it contained a significant strand of opinion hostile to the policy of neutrality adopted by the Fianna Fáil government during World War II. Hence, I feel, the *relative* emphasis accorded by the party to the Irish unity category in the early post-war elections: between 1948 and 1957, an average of some 3.3 per cent of Fine Gael manifestos concerned Irish unity, as against just 0.2 per cent in the case of Fianna Fáil and just over 1 per cent in the case of Labour.

Yet whatever the explanation, the reality of the election programmes shows that appeals to territorial nationalism have played an insignificant role in competitive inter-party politics in the post-war period. However important territorial nationalism may be in understanding the *historical* differences between the parties, and however important it may be in the establishment of *affective loyalties* to the parties, it is not an issue *in competition* between the parties.

The distinction between the identity of a party, on the one hand, and the dimension(s) along which it competes, on the other, is central to this analysis, and has been emphasised at some length by Giacomo Sani and Giovanni Sartori (1983) in their analysis of patterns of polarisation and fragmentation in Western democracies (for an earlier application of this distinction, see Chapter 2 above). Differentiating between domains of identification and dimensions of competition, Sani and Sartori (1983, p. 330) argue that

> The *domain of identification* addresses the query, which electors are identified with a given party in, or under, whatever dimension? Here we discriminate between identified and non-identified partisans; we sort out the former, and the likely finding is that most if not all polities obtain many dimensions of partisan identification (ideological, religious, ethnic, linguistic, sub-cultural, centre-periphery, etc.). By way of contrast, the *space of competition* ultimately addresses the query, along which dimensions lie the non-identified partisans or floating voters for which it is rewarding to compete? To be sure, the two questions are complementary, yet they diverge in that the competition that is perceived as being rewarding (by the party leaders) is unlikely to occur along the dimensions in which voters are assumed to be—precisely because identified—out of reach.

Sani and Sartori were concerned to show that despite the potential existence of a multiplicity of domains of identification, competition could—and often does—occur along a single left–right dimension. Within the context of this present analysis, however, the distinction is also crucial in helping to resolve the apparent dissonance between what election programmes actually say and what commentators commonly regard as the mainspring of the party system. In this sense, territorial nationalism can be seen as primarily a domain of identification, cementing long-term partisan loyalties on one side or the other of the Fianna Fáil–Fine Gael divide. At the same time, however, it need play only a minimal role in the election programmes of the parties since, as can be assumed, these are primarily orientated to those voters *in competition* (Chapter 2). Territorial nationalism may well be the basis for partisan loyalism, while more mundane social and economic concerns may determine how partisan pragmatists cast their ballots, although this will remain to be proven when suitable survey data become available.

In the context of this particular analysis, the distinction between domains of identification and dimensions of competition cannot be overemphasised. The analysis concerns election programmes, that is statements of policy designed to win electoral support in a highly competitive arena, and will inevitably emphasise those issues which are in competition rather than those which may form the basis of party identification. To be sure, the programmes will not be orientated solely to those voters in competition, in that the parties will also be obliged to expend some effort on the mobilisation of its existing loyalists. The assumption, however, building on the arguments above (Chapter 2), is that the primary purpose of the election programme is to win voters in competition rather than to mobilise existing identifiers. In the Fianna Fáil case, for example, electoral strategy over much of the post-war period was not primarily orientated to winning new votes but rather at ensuring the mobilisation of its core support—hence the long-term eschewal of manifesto politics and the necessity to look at party leaders' speeches, radio broadcasts, or whatever, in order to assess its pre-1977 election policies. Although such data do of course provide a clear insight into the policy strategy of Fianna Fáil, nevertheless they also indicate the long-term absence of a genuinely competitive orientation.

As Sani and Sartori emphasise, it is also necessary to underline the essential complementarity of the two notions since, for example, a particular conjuncture of circumstances may carry issues associated with the domain of identification into the forefront of competitive politics. Such was the case in Norway when the EEC referendum reawakened latent centre–periphery tensions (e.g. Valen 1976), and such has also been the case in Ireland in the mid-1980s, when the New Ireland Forum and later the Anglo-Irish Agreement thrust the question of degrees of commitment to Irish unity to the centre of the political stage (e.g. Cox 1985). Both notions may also be related in another looser sense, through the absorption of issues in competition into the language of identification. Just such a confluence is evident in the West German case where, according to Pappi (1984), the grand coalition of the CDU/CSU and the SPD was facilitated by a communality of interests between the Catholic corporatism of the former and the trade-unionist commitment of the latter. In the Irish case, such a confluence is even more evident and even more important, in that the appeals of *social* nationalism inherent in Fianna Fáil's corporatist ideology gelled neatly with the party's residual commitment to *territorial* nationalism (see below). As the parties competed to stress their respective capacities in social and economic policy making, and as they emphasised the need for the nation to advance, they often found themselves employing a language which tapped into more traditional appeals to territorial nationalism. This situation differed from that in the 1920s and 1930s, however, in that the key motif was an emphasis on social rather than primarily territorial nationalism; the appeal was for social and economic rather than strictly constitutional self-respect.

But this is to anticipate the general conclusions of the analysis. For now, suffice it to note once again that the emphasis in this study is on the dimension(s) of competition rather than on the domains of identification, even if these remain complementary notions. It must also be emphasised that the bulk of the analysis focuses on the 1961–82 period, with only passing reference to the earlier post-war elections. While, as noted above, this decision is partly motivated by the availability of sources, there is also a more important consideration. Given that election programmes tap specific policy proposals in a highly competitive arena, it can be anticipated that the concerns which they reveal will themselves change as the pattern of competition changes. This is particularly likely given that the *format* of a party system, that is the number of relevant parties in the system, appears to be related to the level of ideological polarisation (Sartori 1976, Chapter 6). As such, one might anticipate that the Irish party mosaic in the late 1940s and 1950s, when Clann na Talmhan, Clann na Poblachta and—briefly—National Labour also competed, would throw up quite a different complex of dimensions of competition than would the later period, when the party system was virtually wholly dominated by Fianna Fáil, Fine Gael and Labour. Equally, one can anticipate a substantial shift in 1987, with the emergence of the Progressive Democrats. It is primarily for this reason that the bulk of the subsequent analysis will focus on the 1961–82 pattern which, in terms of format, represents a reasonably 'steady-state' period in Irish politics. But enough of preamble; let us now look at the data.

An Overview of the Data

A breakdown of the contents of the party programmes according to the coding categories used in this analysis is shown in Table 4.1, which lists the average proportion of the individual party's programmes devoted to the particular issues for the period 1961 to 1982. The 38 categories have been grouped into six broad issue areas: external relations, democratic procedures, government, economy, welfare and social fabric. Table 4.1 also indicates the average proportion of the programmes which could not be coded into any specific categories, this proportion varying from just over 8 per cent in the two coalition programmes to less than 2 per cent in the case of the Labour programmes.

The first point to note about the data in Table 4.1 is the relative importance of economic concerns. Taking all 22 programmes together, the economic content averages almost 30 per cent. Welfare concerns are also particularly important, accounting for almost 21 per cent of all the programmes taken together and for almost 28 per cent and 26 per cent in the cases of Labour and the coalition respectively. Social fabric concerns also figure prominently, averaging almost 20 per cent over all the programmes, and over 26 per cent in the case of Fianna Fáil. This is followed by concerns with government, registering an overall average of almost 17 per cent, and then by references to external relations and democratic procedures, each of which averages just less than 5 per cent.

These general patterns mask more explicit emphases, however. In the relatively minor external relations area, for example, the majority of references fall into just one category—*Irish unity*: 2.96 per cent in the case of Fianna Fáil, 2.02 per cent in the case of Fine Gael, 1.72 per cent for Labour, 3.17 per cent for the coalition (both of the coalition programmes postdate the outbreak of violence in Northern Ireland and the prorogation of the Stormont Parliament), and 2.38 per cent in the case of all the programmes taken together. Similarly, in the area of democratic procedures, virtually all the references fall into the category

Table 4.1 Coding categories used in the analysis of Irish party programmes, and mean percentage of references to each category by party, 1961–82

Coding category*	Description	Mean percentage of references by:				
		Fianna Fáil	Fine Gael	Labour	FG–Lab coalition	All parties
External relations						
1. Relationship with Britain	Favourable mention of Ireland's relationship with Britain	0.07	0.13	0	0	0.06
2. Irish unity	Favourable references to uniting Ireland and/or severing of links between Northern Ireland and the rest of the UK	2.96	2.02	1.72	3.17	2.38
3. Decolonisation	Favourable mention of decolonisation	0	0.12	0	0	0.03
4. Military—positive	Favourable mention of need to maintain self-defence and military expenditure	0.38	0	0.16	0	0.18
5. Military—negative	Unfavourable mention of above	0	0	0	0	0
6. Peace	Favourable reference to peaceful means of solving crises. Favourable reference to disarmament	2.17	0	0.62	0	0.96
7. Internationalism—positive	Support for UN international co-operation, international courts, etc.	0.86	0.22	0.57	0.31	0.56

8. Internationalism—negative	Unfavourable reference to above	0	0	0	0	0
9. EC—positive	Specific support for EC	1.20	0	0.23	0	0.50
10. EC—negative	Specific opposition to EC	0	0	0.31	0	0.08
Total: external relations		7.64	2.49	3.61	3.48	4.75
Democratic procedures						
11. Freedom and democracy	Favourable mention of democracy as method or goal; support for worker participation; favourable mention of importance of personal freedom, civil rights, freedom of speech, freedom from coercion, etc.	2.86	3.10	6.36	8.90	4.43
12. Constitutionalism—positive	Support for specified aspects of a formal constitution, use of constitutionalism as an argument for policy as well as generalised approval of 'constitutional' ways of doing things	0.10	0	0	0.87	0.12
13. Constitutionalism—negative	Unfavourable mention of above	0.27	0	0	0	0.10
Total: democratic procedures		3.23	3.10	6.36	9.77	4.65
Government						
14. Decentralisation—positive	Support for regional or local administration of politics or economy; deference to local expertise	1.58	1.57	1.42	1.18	1.49

Table 4.1 Cont.

Coding category*	Description	Mean percentage of references by:			
		Fianna Fáil	Fine Gael	Labour	FG–Lab coalition	All parties
15. Decentralisation—negative	Unfavourable mention of above	0	0	0	0.56	0.05
16. Government efficiency	Need for efficiency in government, economy in government, etc. Need for improvement in governmental procedures	5.74	11.13	9.30	5.63	8.17
17. Government corruption	Need to eliminate corruption in government; need to oppose pandering to selfish interests	0	1.85	0.48	0	0.36
18. Government authority	Need for strong, effective and stable government	8.19	7.54	3.98	4.60	6.54
Total: government		15.51	21.09	15.18	11.97	16.61
Economy						
19. Enterprise	Favourable mention of private property rights, personal enterprise and initiative, etc.; favourable mention of free enterprise over state; need for					

financial and other incentives; need for wage and tax policies designed to induce enterprise, favourable reference to home ownership	4.03	8.33	2.80	6.61	5.10
20. Controlled economy — Favourable reference to need for government control of economy, prices, incomes, etc. Favourable mention of central planning, regulation of capitalism, etc.; action against monopolies and in defence of consumers	2.91	6.57	13.88	10.90	7.63
21. Protectionism—positive — Favourable reference to imposition, maintenance of extension of tariffs to protect internal market, or other domestic economic protectionism	0.98	1.26	1.89	1.64	1.36
22. Protectionism—negative — Unfavourable reference to above	0.37	0	0.03	0	0.14
23. Non-specific economic goals — General statement of intent to pursue economic goals that are policy non-specific	0.66	0.61	0.96	1.59	0.81
24. Keynesian demand management — Adjusting government expenditure to prevailing levels of employment and inflation	0.05	0	0	0	0.02
25. Productivity — Need to encourage or facilitate greater production, increase foreign trade, etc. Need to increase employment, need for economic growth, aid to agriculture, tourism, industry, etc.	12.74	5.71	5.96	6.10	8.37
26. Technology and infrastructure — Importance of modernising industrial administration, importance of science and technological development in industry; need for training and					

Table 4.1 Cont.

Coding category*	Description	Mean percentage of references by:				
		Fianna Fáil	Fine Gael	Labour	FG–Lab coalition	All parties
	government sponsored research; improvements in communication and transport; development of nuclear energy	2.62	2.14	2.17	2.51	2.36
27. Nationalisation	Favourable reference to government ownership or control of industry or land	0.05	0	2.09	0	0.59
28. Economic orthodoxy	Favourable reference to need for traditional economic orthodoxy, balanced budget, low taxation, reduced borrowing, fiscal rectitude, etc.	0.91	7.79	2.10	0.31	3.06
Total: economy		25.32	32.41	31.88	29.64	29.44
Welfare						
29. Quality of life	Favourable reference to environmental protection, preservation of natural resources, etc; need for expenditure on arts, leisure, media, sport, etc.	2.33	2.13	5.28	3.69	3.21
30. Social justice	Need for fair treatment of all; protection for exploited and underprivileged; fair treatment in tax					

	Description					
	system; need for equality of opportunity, fair distribution of resources, and for removal of class barriers, discrimination, etc.	2.42	8.55	11.17	7.05	6.90
31. Expansion of social services	Need to maintain or expand any basic service or welfare scheme, health, education, housing, etc. Support for free basic social services	10.81	8.73	11.29	15.11	10.77
Total: Welfare		15.56	19.41	27.74	25.84	20.88

Social fabric

	Description					
32. Defence of Irish way of life—positive	Support for national ideas, traditions and institutions. Support for Irish language and Gaeltacht, etc.	5.66	2.14	3.23	1.18	3.63
33. Defence of Irish way of life—negative	Unfavourable reference to above	0	1.08	0.28	0	0.37
34. Traditional morality—positive	Favourable mention of suppression of immorality; favourable mention of Catholic Church, censorship etc.; opposition to divorce, abortion, contraception, etc.; favourable reference to the family	0.13	0.07	0	0	0.06
35. Traditional morality—negative	Unfavourable mention of above	0	0	0	0	0
36. Law and order	Favourable mention of need to maintain law and order; action against crime and terrorism; support					

Table 4.1 Cont.

Coding category*	Description	Mean percentage of references by:				
		Fianna Fáil	Fine Gael	Labour	FG–Lab coalition	All parties
	for police and need for internal security; tougher attitudes in courts, etc.	3.19	1.02	0.59	0.31	1.63
37. National effort and social harmony	Appeal for national effort and solidarity; need for nation to see itself as united; appeal for public spiritedness; decrying anti-social attitudes in times of crisis; support for public interest, bipartisanship, etc.	3.93	3.29	0.81	1.64	2.70
38. Social group interests	Favourable reference to particular social groups such as the working class, farmers, women, young people, etc.	13.38	10.22	8.74	7.99	10.76
Total: social fabric		26.29	17.82	13.65	11.12	19.15
Total coded contents		93.55	96.32	98.42	91.82	95.48
Total uncoded contents		6.48	3.70	1.59	8.19	4.51
Total		100.0	100.0	100.0	100.0	100.0

* These coding categories represent a modification of those originally devised by Robertson (1976) for an analysis of British party programmes, and later extended by a research group of the European Consortium of Political Research for a wider, cross-national application (Budge *et al.*, 1987). The major differences between the categories listed above and those employed by the ECPR group are as follows: the collapsing of the two ECPR categories of *freedom* and *democracy* into a single new category (11 above); the collapsing of the three ECPR categories of *regulation of capitalism, economic planning* and *controlled economy* into a single new category, *controlled economy* (20 above); the collapsing of the two ECPR categories of *enterprise* and *incentives* into the new single category of *enterprise* (19 above); the collapsing of the two ECPR categories of *environmental protection* and *art, sport, leisure, media* into the new single category of *quality of life* (29 above); and the collapsing of five different social group categories into a single social group interests category (38 above). Finally a number of the ECPR categories which were not applicable to the Irish case were simply excluded from the list. For a full discussion of the application of all the ECPR categories to the Irish case, see Mair (1987b).

of *freedom and democracy*, with only Fianna Fáil and the coalition including any references to constitutionalism. In the area of government, the bulk of references fall into the categories of *government efficiency* and *government authority*. *Government corruption* is clearly not an issue—at least as far as the election programmes are concerned—and questions relating to the pros and cons of decentralisation also play only a minor role.

Concerns with the economy are more evenly spread. All three parties accord substantial emphasis to *productivity*, reflecting a general commitment to economic growth and increased employment. All three parties also share a lesser concern with *technology and infrastructure*, reflecting a generalised commitment to the improvement of roads, communications and training. *Enterprise* and *controlled economy* prove more contentious, the former being emphasised by Fianna Fáil and by Fine Gael, and much less so by Labour, with the latter being emphasised by Labour and Fine Gael, and much less so by Fianna Fáil. There is greater consensus on welfare issues. All three parties emphasise *expansion of the social services* and *quality of life*, although here Labour lays particular stress. *Social justice* proves slightly more contentious, receiving quite significant emphasis from Fine Gael and from Labour, and less so from Fianna Fáil.

Finally, the social fabric area also reveals interesting contrasts, with Fianna Fáil laying substantial emphasis on *defence of Irish way of life— positive, social group interests, national effort and social harmony* and *law and order*. While concern with *social group interests* is also shared, albeit to a lesser extent, with Fine Gael and Labour, the other three categories vary significantly. *Law and order* is virtually an exclusive Fianna Fáil concern, while *national effort and social harmony* is also emphasised by Fine Gael but not by Labour. What is also interesting to note is that Labour lies more or less midway between the relative level of concerns shown by Fianna Fáil and Fine Gael for *defence of Irish way of life—positive*. None of the parties evinces any substantial concern either for or against *traditional morality*, while Fine Gael is the only party to have evinced any 'objections' to *defence of Irish way of life*, reflecting the party's traditional opposition to the compulsory teaching or examination of Irish language proficiency in secondary schools.

What the Parties Emphasise

1948–57 and 1961–82 Contrasted

A first test of what divides the parties, and a first real indication of the extent of conflict and consensus in the Irish party system can be seen in the differing issue priorities. Tables 4.2 and 4.3 report these emphases, listing in order of frequency the most mentioned categories in the programmes of each party. Table 4.2 reports the results for the 1961–82 period, and Table 4.3 those for 1948–57. While the contrasts between the two sets of data are interesting, it must also be emphasised that the relative unreliability of the 1948–57 sources necessitates a somewhat cautious approach to these particular findings.

The most evident contrast between the two periods can be seen in the relative emphasis attached to *government authority* in the earlier period. Taking all three parties together, this category ranks in third position, accounting for more than 11 per cent of the contents of the twelve programmes. In party specific terms, *government authority* ranks highest in the case of Fine Gael, with an average of 20 per cent, and second highest in the case of Fianna Fáil; by way of contrast, the category barely figures in the Labour programmes.

It seems hardly surprising that the bigger parties should devote so much of their programmes to the theme of government authority during this period. Party competition in the first post-war decade was structured around the opposition of Fianna Fáil to a broad, multi-party coalition led by Fine Gael, and within such an environment much of the debate naturally focused on the relative merits of single party as against multi-party administrations (Mair 1979). Fianna Fáil continually stressed its long-term experience of government and the essential political coherence which derived from monocolore cabinets, employing appeals built around these notions as a key element in its election campaigns. In 1954, for example, the characteristic appeal was couched as follows:

> All our cards are on the table, face upwards. If Fianna Fáil gets an overall majority in the new Dáil, the Government will consist of members of our party chosen, by the Taoiseach, for their personal suitability for the Departments to which they are appointed and for their capacity to work together as a team. In all democracies, in normal times, this is how effective governments are formed . . . As an alternative, you are offered some kind of coalition. Every coalition

Table 4.2 What the parties emphasise: the leading categories, 1961–82

Rank	Parties (number of programmes)				
	Fianna Fáil (8)	Fine Gael (6)	Labour (6)	FG–Labour coalition (2)	All (22)
1.	38. Social group interests	16. Government efficiency	20. Controlled economy	31. Expansion of social services	31. Expansion of social services
Mean %	13.38	11.3	13.88	15.11	10.77
2.	25. Productivity	38. Social group interests	31. Expansion of social services	20. Controlled economy	38. Social group interests
Mean %	12.74	10.22	11.29	10.90	10.76
3.	31. Expansion of social services	31. Expansion of social services	30. Social justice	11. Freedom and democracy	25. Productivity
Mean %	10.81	8.73	11.17	8.90	8.37
4.	18. Government authority	30. Social justice	16. Government efficiency	38. Social group interests	16. Government efficiency
Mean %	8.19	8.55	9.30	7.99	8.17
5.	16. Government efficiency	19. Enterprise	38. Social group interests	30. Social justice	20. Controlled economy
Mean %	5.74	8.33	8.74	7.05	7.63

6.	32. Defence of Irish way of life—positive	28. Economic orthodoxy	11. Freedom and democracy	19. Enterprise	30. Social justice
Mean %	5.66	7.79	6.36	6.61	6.90
7.	19. Enterprise	18. Government authority	25. Productivity	25. Productivity	18. Government authority
Mean %	4.03	7.54	5.96	6.10	6.54
8.	37. National effort and social harmony	20. Controlled economy	29. Quality of life	16. Government efficiency	19. Enterprise
Mean %	3.93	6.57	5.28	5.63	5.10
9.	36. Law and order	25. Productivity	18. Government authority	18. Government authority	11. Freedom and democracy
Mean %	3.19	5.71	3.98	4.60	4.43
10.	2. Irish unity	37. National effort and social harmony	32. Defence of Irish way of life—positive	29. Quality of life	32. Defence of Irish way of life—positive
Mean %	2.96	3.29	3.23	3.69	3.63

Table 4.3 What the parties emphasise: the leading categories, 1948–57

Rank	Parties (number of programmes)			
	Fianna Fáil (4)	Fine Gael (4)	Labour (4)	All (12)
1.	38. Social group interests	18. Government authority	38. Social group interests	38. Social group interests
Mean %	17.74	19.72	27.14	17.52
2.	18. Government authority	19. Enterprise	25. Productivity	25. Productivity
Mean %	13.55	16.30	15.08	11.90
3.	25. Productivity	25. Productivity	31. Expansion of social services	18. Government authority
Mean %	11.67	8.96	13.06	11.33
4.	31. Expansion of social services	38. Social group interests	30. Social justice	31. Expansion of social services
Mean %	10.22	7.67	10.86	9.63
5.	26. Technology and infrastructure	28. Economic orthodoxy	20. Controlled economy	19. Enterprise
Mean %	9.39	7.37	9.26	7.99

6.	19. Enterprise	37. National effort and social harmony	26. Technology and infrastructure	27. Technology and infrastructure
Mean %	5.26	6.11	5.44	5.41
7.	11. Freedom and democracy	11. Freedom and democracy	16. Government efficiency	30. Social justice
Mean %	3.55	6.07	4.11	4.81
8.	37. National effort and social harmony	31. Expansion of social services	37. National effort and social harmony	37. National effort and social harmony
Mean %	3.05	5.61	3.38	4.18
9.	16. Government efficiency	2. Irish unity	19. Enterprise	26. Controlled economy
Mean %	2.59	3.33	2.46	3.94
10.	32. Defence of Irish way of life positive	36. Law and order	11. Freedom and democracy	11. Freedom and democracy
Mean %	1.97	2.70	1.23	3.62

government—irrespective of the quality of its members—is bad
government (Transcript of Lemass broadcast, 11 May 1954)

In the same vein, Lemass had earlier emphasised that

every coalition government is bad government. It is incapable of
giving effective leadership or of applying a consistent policy ...
Whether Fianna Fáil was a good government or a bad government it
is better than any coalition could be. The Fianna Fáil team will work
together for a known and sensible programme and that is the type of
government which the country needs (Transcript of Lemass broadcast, 5 May 1954)

The 1957 programme went even further, emphasising the need for
'the adult manly determination to succeed—to advance together as a
community in a steady, ordered, disciplined manner towards the ends
we have in view', and insisting in block capitals that 'nothing can be
accomplished by men who are reconciled to defeat before they start, or
who are so intimidated by the magnitude of the task that they have not
the heart to tackle it'.

In response, Fine Gael tended to argue that coalition government
meant better government since it necessitated co-operation, while the
pursuit of power by a single party militated against the likelihood that
policies would be devised in the national interest. The statement of the
outgoing Fine Gael Taoiseach in 1957 is typical of this reasoning:

The parties in government stood for cooperation and only through
cooperation could the nation be saved ... [It is] desirable to weaken
that party which stood aloof demanding an overall majority for itself,
and so, through seeking what it is impossible to obtain, confused
public life and made only for instability of government (*Irish Times*,
1 March 1957).

As in the case of Fianna Fáil, the key emphasis here is the need for
stable and effective administration. To adopt Fanning's (1984, p. 43)
phrase, government had become not a means to an end but an end in
itself. And although Fianna Fáil couched its appeal for stability in terms
of an emphasis on political coherence and administrative experience,
and Fine Gael couched its appeal in terms of the benefits of inter-party
co-operation, the appeal itself was none the less essentially consensual.
Stable and effective government was necessary for the good of the
nation.

Such a stress has not played an equivalent role in the parties' programmes between 1961 and 1982. The category itself ranks fourth in the Fianna Fáil list of priorities and seventh in that of Fine Gael (Table 4.2). What is also interesting to note, however, is that in this latter period the category also figures among Labour's priorities, albeit only in ninth position. Taking all three parties together, *government authority* is the seventh most-mentioned category, averaging just over 6.5 per cent.

This relative decline reflects the changing dynamic of party competition and, in particular, the long-term abeyance of the coalition question. The defeat of the inter-party government in 1957 and the subsequent eclipse of Clann na Talmhan and Clann na Poblachta pushed Fine Gael and Labour into separate strategies in which each aimed at maximum party growth, and in which each hoped to reach a position of governing alone. In such a contest, Fianna Fáil proved much less able to play the coalition card. The persistent inability of either Fine Gael or Labour to win through to majority party status, however, induced a reversion to a coalition strategy in 1973, a shift which prompted a relatively strong emphasis on *government authority* in the 1973 Fianna Fáil programme. But even then, the value of the anti-coalition appeal was limited. The 1973 coalition involved simply two parties, as against the five and later four parties in the coalition governments of 1948 and 1954. In such circumstances, the traditional Fianna Fáil attack on the dangers of politically heterogeneous governments proved much less plausible. Moreover, the 1973 campaign was accompanied by the publication of a joint Fine Gael–Labour election manifesto which indicated prior agreement on policy areas and which also further underlined the potential political coherence of the coalition. One of the means by which Fianna Fáil had traditionally sought to undermine the appeal of a potential coalition was to emphasise what it referred to as the 'undemocratic' and 'ad hoc' nature of inter-party, post-election bargaining. The pre-election publication of the joint Labour–Fine Gael 'Statement of Intent' in 1973 did much to head off this potential criticism, thereby obliging Fianna Fáil to seek alternative angles of attack.

Interestingly enough, the emergence of the Progressive Democrats prompted Fianna Fáil to resurrect this traditional appeal for government authority and stability. In a radio interview (reported in the *Irish Times*, 13 January 1986) following the formation of the new party, Charles Haughey emphasised the apparent dangers associated with a 'further splintering of the body politic through the formation of new parties'. Harking back to the Lemass emphases of 1954, he stressed that 'I believe what is really needed is for a party—I hope it is our party—to get an overall majority in the next general election'. The same theme was emphasised again and again during the 1987 campaign, achieving a particular resonance in the wake of the break-up of the Fine Gael–Labour coalition. At the Fianna Fáil press conference which launched the 1987 election programme, Haughey stated that 'I look with horror at the prospect of another coalition government, and the instability, bargaining, and so on', and argued that 'only a single party government which is united' could restore the public confidence necessary to ensure an upturn in the economy. For Haughey, the business community needed a government which 'knows what had to be done and is prepared to do it ... we have in Fianna Fáil the confidence and the experience' (noted by the author, 29 January 1987; see also Chapter 5).

In general, however, the 1961–82 period witnessed a general decline in the relative emphasis on *government authority* and a commensur-ately greater concern with *government efficiency*. This latter category received such little attention in the first post-war decade that it is excluded from the ten priority issues for all the parties taken together (Table 4.3), and also falls outside the priority issues of Fine Gael. In the case of Fianna Fáil, it ranked only in ninth position with an average of less than 3 per cent, although it did receive a greater prominence in the Labour case, ranking seventh with an average of more than 4 per cent. In 1961–82, by contrast, *government efficiency* is the fourth ranking priority issue of all the parties taken together (Table 4.2), occupying the highest position in the case of Fine Gael with an average of more than 11 per cent, and fourth and fifth positions in the case of Labour and Fianna Fáil respectively.

Again, the shift between the two periods is hardly surprising. The publication of the Department of Finance document *Economic Development* in 1958, and the subsequent adoption of the *First Programme for Economic Expansion* in the same year marked the beginning of an era of economic planning and programming which was to do much to modernise Irish politics and society. Hailed by one commentator as 'a landmark in modern Irish history' (Fanning 1983, p. 192), and by another as marking 'the major revolution in Irish administrative history' (Lee 1982, p. 1), the two documents were to demand a major shake-up in the machinery of government in the post-war state (e.g., Chubb 1982, pp. 240–7). These new conerns were also reflected in the programmes of the parties, which brimmed over with strident calls for administrative modernisation and for the creation of new agencies for the monitoring and implementation of public policy. As the argument over the merits of single party or coalition government waned, and as the new age of programming and planning dawned, so the parties proved less concerned with the authority and effectiveness of government and commensurately more concerned with its operational efficiency.

This shift in priorities is also reflected in other issues of concern to the parties. The enthusiastic embrace of planning and programming also ushered in an emphasis on the need to control the different elements within the economy, be it the need to control prices and incomes, the need to regulate private enterprise or simply the need to plan effectively. These new concerns are clearly reflected in the increased emphasis on the category of *controlled economy* which, taking all the parties together, figured only in ninth position with an average of less than 4 per cent in 1948–57, but which proved the fifth most-mentioned category in 1961–82, with an average of almost 8 per cent. The contrast is particularly marked in the case of Labour, where emphases on economic control ranked first in the party's priorities in 1961–82 as against fifth in 1948–57. In the Fine Gael case, the contrast is also noteworthy: *controlled economy* barely figured in the party's programmes in the earlier period, yet ranks eighth in the list of 1961– 82 priorities, as well as second in the coalition priorities in 1973 and 1977.

The final point in contrast which needs to be underlined is the general increase in concerns for welfare and democratic rights. The three relevant categories here are *expansion of the social services, social justice*, and *freedom and democracy*. Together these emphases accounted for an average of 18 per cent of the party programmes in 1948–57, as against 22 per cent in 1961–82. The contrast is particularly marked in the case of Fine Gael, which registers an increase from less than 14 per cent in 1948–57 to more than 20 per cent in 1961–82. This shift in Fine Gael concerns is of crucial importance. The increased stress on *social justice*—which is the fourth most-mentioned category in 1961–82—and on *expansion of the social services*, together with the increased emphasis on *controlled economy*, undoubtedly indicate a leftward push from the party and a greater opening-up to more social democratic concerns. This impression is further sustained by noting the relative decline in the emphasis on the classic conservative themes of *enterprise* and *economic orthodoxy*. These latter two themes ranked in second and fifth place respectively in 1948–57, and in fifth and sixth place respectively in 1961–82. Together, they accounted for an average of 24 per cent of the content of Fine Gael programmes in the earlier period, as against 16 per cent in the later period. To be sure, they remain prominent in the party's list of concerns, and in this sense there has been no wholesale shift towards a distinctly social democratic appeal, but elements of such a move are evident and do appear to mark a sea-change in the party's competitive orientations (see below).

1961–1982: Consensual and Party-Specific Themes

As noted above, commentaries on the Irish party system tend to suggest that there is no real difference between the parties and that, in the words of one author, national election campaigns 'inevitably revolve almost entirely around valence issues' (Carty 1981, p. 118). In essence, the picture is one of catch-all parties *par excellence* (e.g., Gallagher 1981), with little more than a choice of personnel being offered to voters, and with a policy agenda foreshortened to a degree almost without parallel in contemporary Western Europe.

Evidence both to counter and to sustain this thesis can be seen in the data in Table 4.2. On the one hand, the parties tend to emphasise valence issues, that is issues on which there is really only one position. Themes such as *social group interests* and *productivity* figure prominently in all the parties' lists of most-mentioned issues. On the other hand, the relative emphasis on these issues does vary across the parties. Thus while Fianna Fáil devotes an average of some 26 per cent of its programmes to both the themes cited above, the comparable figures for Fine Gael and Labour are just 16 per cent and 15 per cent respectively. In addition, each party also emphasises what might be termed *party-specific issues*, that is issues which figure among the ten most-mentioned categories of one or two parties, but not of all; *defence of the Irish way of life*, for example, figures in the Fianna Fáil list and in that of Labour, but not in that of Fine Gael. Fine Gael in its turn emphasises the classic conservative theme of *economic orthodoxy*, an emphasis which is not shared by either of the other two parties. Finally, *controlled economy* is the most-mentioned issue in the Labour repertory, ranks eighth in the case of Fine Gael, and is not included among the ten most-mentioned issues in the case of Fianna Fáil.

This suggests that a more accurate picture of inter-party differences can be obtained through a reorganisation of the data in Table 4.2 into two groups: *consensual* themes and *party-specific* themes. Consensual themes are here defined as those issues which figure among the ten most-mentioned issues in the programmes of each of the parties, including those of the coalition. Five of the categories fulfil this requirement: *social group interests*, *productivity*, *expansion of the social services*, *government authority* and *government efficiency*. Together they amount to a plea for an effective and efficient administration which aims at catering for group interests in the context of a wider commitment to growth and development, and provide a basic and readily comprehensible set of commitments which would be appropriate to almost any government in contemporary Western Europe. The average proportion of each party's programmes devoted to these themes is shown in Table 4.4.

What is most revealing about the data in Table 4.4, however, is not so much the categories which are included, but rather the relative emphasis which these categories receive across the different parties. Fianna Fáil devotes an average of slightly more than 50 per cent of its programmes' contents to these consensual themes, as against 43 per cent in the case of Fine Gael and 40 per cent in the cases of Labour and the coalition. The image can be substantiated even further by reference to the rankings of each of the themes in the repertories of the individual parties. The five consensual themes occupy the five leading positions in the Fianna Fáil list, as against the leading three positions and the seventh and ninth position in the Fine Gael list, while they are dispersed fairly evenly among the ten leading issues of Labour. Fianna Fáil clearly emerges as the party with the most consensual appeal. In effect, and to recall the words of Éamon de Valera, 'Fianna Fáil . . . is in the middle of the road. Our social objectives are also in the middle of the road' (*Irish Times*, 18 May 1954).

The emphasis on *party-specific* themes is also revealing. *Law and order* and *Irish unity* are the only two issues specific to Fianna Fáil, and together rank only in ninth and tenth position with a combined average of 6 per cent (Table 4.2). The party shares emphases on *enterprise* and *national effort and social harmony* with Fine Gael, and *defence of the Irish way of life* with Labour. With the possible exception of *enterprise*, each of these themes taps into a more generalised appeal to the nation, either in terms of pursuing national goals (*National effort, defence of Irish way of life* and *Irish unity*—together occupying an average of almost 13 per cent of Fianna Fáil programmes), or in terms of protecting the society against crime or subversion (*law and order*).

There is only one issue specific to Fine Gael, *economic orthodoxy* (occupying an average of almost 8 per cent), which does perhaps reflect the traditional concern of the party with fiscal rectitude and which, in many ways, appears to sit uneasily alongside the more recent commitment to social justice and welfarism. Reflecting this latter commitment,

Table 4.4 Consensual issues, 1961–82*

Category	Average percentage of contents of programmes of				
	Fianna Fáil (rank)	Fine Gael (rank)	Labour (rank)	Coalition (rank)	All Parties (rank)
16. Government efficiency	5.74 (5)	11.13 (1)	9.30 (4)	5.63 (8)	8.17 (4)
18. Government authority	8.19 (4)	7.54 (7)	3.98 (9)	4.60 (9)	6.54 (7)
25. Productivity	12.74 (2)	5.71 (9)	5.96 (7)	6.10 (7)	8.37 (3)
31. Expansion of social services	10.81 (3)	8.73 (3)	11.29 (2)	15.11 (1)	10.77 (1)
38. Social group interests	13.38 (1)	10.22 (2)	8.74 (5)	7.99 (4)	10.76 (2)
Total (average rank)	50.86 (3.0)	43.33 (4.4)	39.27 (5.4)	39.43 (5.8)	44.61 (3.4)

* Consensual issues are those figuring in the list of the ten most-mentioned categories (of Table 4.2) of *each* of the parties, including the coalition.

Fine Gael shares with Labour an emphasis on *social justice* and *controlled economy* and, given that these themes figure so prominently in the Labour agenda, this suggests a potential policy rationale behind the 1973 coalition (see below). The only issues specific to Labour itself are *freedom and democracy* and *quality of life*, which together account for an average of almost 12 per cent of the party's programmes. Over and above the Labour appeal to more straightforward social democratic concerns (e.g. *controlled economy, expansion of the social services* and *social justice*, together accounting for an average of more than 30 per cent of the programmes and which rank in the top three positions in the Labour agenda), these specific emphases suggest a more contemporary concern for the 'new politics' issues which have already encroached on the agenda of parties elsewhere in Western Europe (e.g. Hildebrandt and Dalton 1978).

The final point to note here is the agenda involved in the two Fine Gael–Labour coalition programmes of 1973 and 1977 (Table 4.2). The ten leading issues comprise the five consensual themes, both of the issues shared by Labour and Fine Gael but not by Fianna Fáil (i.e. *controlled economy* and *social justice*), *enterprise*, which is shared by both Fianna Fáil and Fine Gael, but not by Labour, and the two party-specific issues of Labour, *freedom and democracy* and *quality of life*. The presence of these latter two issues, and the absence of the single party-specific Fine Gael issue of *economic orthodoxy*, suggest that Labour achieved a greater influence on the joint programmes than did Fine Gael, a degree of influence quite disproportionate to its relatively smaller electoral following. However, more of this later.

In general, therefore, this brief analysis indicates that there is more of a policy divide in the Irish party system than is normally acknowledged. Although much of the debate focuses on consensual issues, the variation in the relative party emphases on these issues, together with the pattern of party-specific themes, casts doubt on the notion that the parties are programmatically indistinguishable. If election programmes do provide a valid picture of a party's competitive stance, and if they or the speeches which are based on them do offer voters a genuine guide to electoral choice, then these data imply the existence of meaningful policy options. In other words parties in Ireland—as elsewhere—offer alternative cues to voters. The next step is therefore to see if the issues which are in competition vary in a systematic way, and to see whether there is any evidence of a more generalised ideological opposition.

The Dimensions of Competition

Having looked at the different patterns evident in the election programmes it is now necessary to subject the data to a more rigorous
statistical analysis in order to identify the underlying dimensions of
competition. This will be done through a factor analysis of the data,
taking the individual programmes as the cases and the percentage of
references to the individual categories as the variables. Factor analysis
is a familiar statistical technique, and the value of its application to the
study of election programmes is ably argued in Budge *et al.* (1987,
Chapter 2), in that it allows a spatial representation of the dimensions
of competition and enables one to locate the individual programmes,
and therefore the parties, within that space. Two possible patterns can
be anticipated to emerge. First, the factor analysis may reveal that two
or more of the categories (that is, the variables) are systematically
related in the sense that a high percentage of references to one is
accompanied by a high percentage of references to the other(s), and a
low percentage of references to one is accompanied by a low percentage of references to the other(s). These variables would therefore be
seen to 'load' onto the same factor or dimension, which in turn implies
that they are related in some underlying way which is tapped by the
dimension or factor. Categories such as *social justice* or *controlled
economy*, for example, could load onto the same dimension or factor,
and this would suggest that the dimension reflects a more generalised
social democratic appeal. The location of the individual cases or
programmes along this dimension can then be determined, so enabling
one to rank them in terms of their relative degrees of social democratic-
ness (see Robertson 1976).

Second, the analysis may reveal that two or more variables are
associated with one another in a systematic but *opposing* sense, such
that a high percentage of references to one would be associated with a
low percentage of references to the other(s), and vice versa. Following
from the example in the previous paragraph, it seems plausible to
suggest that a high percentage of references to *social jusice* and
controlled economy might be associated with a low percentage of reference to, say, *enterprise* and/or *economic orthodoxy*. The dimension
tapping this oppositional association would therefore be bipolar, confronting social democratic emphases, on the one hand, to more orthodox bourgeois concerns, on the other. And again, the various cases or
programmes can be located along this bipolar dimension according to
their relative social democratic-ness or bourgeois-ness.

This particular analysis will be confined only to the programmes issued between 1961 and November 1982, a period in which the format of the party system has remained more or less unchanged, and in which the dimensions of competition might be expected to have remained reasonably stable. More preliminary analyses have been reported using a two-stage factor analysis of the 1948–81 data (Mair 1987b), and also using only the economic policy issues for the period 1948–82 (Mair 1986a). It should also be noted that this analysis also includes only those categories which register an average of more than 1 per cent of the content of all the programmes taken together.[3]

The results of the factor analysis are reported in Table 4.5, the analysis having revealed seven factors or dimensions with an eigenvalue greater than 1.0. For present purposes however, attention will be focused on the first four dimensions, each of which records an eigenvalue greater than 2.0, and which together account for 58.5 per cent of the total variance.

At first sight, the patterns in Table 4.5 appear confusing and difficult. If a loading of ±0.5 is taken as an intuitively meaningful cut-off point, however, the dimensions appear more readily interpretable. With the exceptions of *protectionism—positive*, which loads on dimensions 4 and 6, each of the categories loads substantially on only one dimension. Moreover, a number of the dimensions are clearly unipolar, that is to say that the categories which do load substantially on these dimensions all load in the same direction, either positively or negatively. The two categories which load onto dimension 6, for example, *enterprise* and *protectionism—positive*, both load positively, as do the two categories loading onto dimensions 2 and 5 and the three categories loading onto dimension 3. On the other hand, both dimensions 1 and 4 are bipolar, registering substantial loadings in both the positive and negative directions. Finally, dimension 7 is also unipolar, registering only one substantial—and negative—loading. However, before going on to a more extensive analysis of these dimensions, and of the first four in particular, it seems useful at this stage to present a brief synopsis of the different dimensions, taking them in reverse order of statistical importance.

Dimension 7 is clearly the least problematic of the dimensions, registering only one, albeit very substantial and negative loading from the *quality of life* category. While this clearly reflects Labour's virtually exclusive emphasis on the 'new politics', the dimension itself contributes very little to the overall analysis, accounting for less than 7 per

Table 4.5 Factor analysis of the manifesto data, 1961–82

Rotated solution	Dimensions and loadings*						
Category	Factor 1	Factor 2	Factor 3	Factor 4	Factor 5	Factor 6	Factor 7
2. Irish unity	.135	.397	*.656*	-.207	-.193	.238	-.023
11. Freedom and democracy	.211	-.238	-.011	*.784*	.039	.052	.114
14. Decentralisation—positive	.161	.362	-.264	.395	-.055	*.537*	.245
16. Government efficiency	.419	.059	-.128	-.030	*.728*	-.022	.184
18. Government authority	*-.505*	.174	-.438	-.135	-.436	-.183	.230
19. Enterprise	-.033	.029	.174	-.163	.164	*.856*	-.098
20. Controlled economy	*.709*	-.353	-.171	.339	-.208	-.100	-.142
21. Protectionism—positive	.031	-.136	-.166	*.501*	.098	.626	.054
25. Productivity	*-.844*	-.109	-.241	-.049	-.039	-.284	.102
26. Technology and infrastructure	-.099	.067	-.123	.118	*.890*	.184	-.057
28. Economic orthodoxy	.244	-.300	-.266	*-.718*	-.105	.070	.388
29. Quality of life	.057	-.115	-.101	-.003	-.057	.009	*-.959*
30. Social justice	*.706*	-.108	-.125	-.248	.194	-.267	.238
31. Expansion of social services	.130	.102	*.679*	.158	-.092	-.048	.343
32. Defence of Irish way of life	-.139	-.174	*.851*	-.006	-.050	-.056	-.078
36. Law and order	-.065	*.916*	-.102	-.072	.006	-.175	.092
37. National effort and social harmony	*-.640*	-.431	.006	-.466	-.282	-.009	-.080
38. Social group interests	-.023	*.919*	.127	-.011	.084	.200	.028
Eigenvalue (unrotated solution)	*3.483*	*2.801*	*2.206*	*2.031*	*1.549*	*1.315*	*1.215*
Percent of variance (unrotated solution)	*19.3*	*15.6*	*12.3*	*11.3*	*8.6*	*7.3*	*6.7*
Cumulative percentage of variance	*19.3*	*34.9*	*47.2*	*58.5*	*67.1*	*74.4*	*81.1*

Number of cases: 22   Number of variables: 18   * Loadings with an absolute value greater than .5 are in italics.

cent of total variance. Dimension 6 also plays a relatively marginal role, accounting for just more than 7 per cent of total variance, and with substantial (and positive) loadings from the categories of *enterprise* (.865) and *protectionism—positive* (.626). This particular dimension therefore appears to tap into a more generalised commitment to foster the growth of private capital. Dimension 5 accounts for almost 9 per cent of the total variance, and again is unipolar, registering positive and substantial loadings from the categories of *government efficiency* (.728) and *technology and infrastructure* (.890). Both of these themes fit well together, and appear to tap into a more generalised concern for infrastructural adaptation and modernisation—emphasising both an improvement of the administrative machinery, and a commitment to modernising communication and training. Both emphasise the need to adapt to the demands of a modern economy and society. It is also interesting to note the relatively high negative loading from *government authority* (−.436) on this dimension, suggesting that there is a potential opposition between emphases on governmental effectiveness, on the one hand, and government efficiency, on the other—an opposition which is also reflected in the respective loadings of both governing categories on dimension 1.

Dimension 4 accounts for more than 11 per cent of the total variance and is also strongly bipolar: positive loadings are registered by *freedom and democracy* (.784) and *protectionism—positive* (.501), and a negative loading by *economy orthodoxy* (−.718); it is also worth noting that *national effort and social harmony* (−.466) also records quite a high negative loading on this dimension. The opposition reflected by dimension 4 is certainly confusing. In one sense, the negative loadings can be seen to reflect a loose conservative impetus—the combination of an appeal for fiscal rectitude and an appeal for the citizenry to work together in the national interest. But while the positively loading appeal in favour of freedom and democracy may be seen to counter elements of this loose conservativism, any potential symmetry in the equation is confounded by the positive loading from the pro-protectionism appeal. In short, this dimension does not make a great deal of overall ideo-logical sense, and simply seems to tap the conflicting partisan appeals of Fine Gael and Labour. In this sense, it appears to be virtually a wholly party-structured dimension, pitting the Fine Gael emphases on *economic orthodoxy* and *national effort and social harmony* against the relative Labour emphases on *freedom and democracy* and *protectionism—positive* (cf. Table 4.1). But even this may be to overinterpret the results.

Dimension 3 is at once more interesting and more easily interpreted, and accounts for more than 12 per cent of the total variance. This is essentially the Irish Nationalism dimension, being effectively unipolar and registering loadings from *defence of the Irish way of life* (.851) and *Irish unity* (.656), as well as from *expansion of the social services* (.679). The combination suggests the traditional Fianna Fáil appeal of strong nationalism and welfarism, a package of concerns which strongly characterised the party in its early phase of electoral mobilisation (Chapter 1). The only incongruous component in this dimension is the relatively high negative loading registered by *government authority* (−.438), the stress on which also played a crucial role in the Fianna Fáil package—albeit at a slightly later period.

Dimension 2 is also effectively unipolar, and accounts for almost 16 per cent of total variance. The loadings in this case are particularly strong, and come from *social group interests* (.919) and *law and order* (.916), the one tapping into a traditional brokerage appeal based on the incorporation and representation of various sectoral and social interests, and the other tapping into an emphasis on the strong state. The combination itself is not untypical: interests will be respected, but the law will be enforced; the state is strong, but it is also representative. Indeed, the combination of concerns gells rather neatly with those reflected in dimension 1, and this is something which will be addressed shortly.

Dimension 1 itself is clearly the most interesting and the most important of the various dimensions, accounting for more than 19 per cent of total variance. It is strongly bipolar, with positive loadings from *controlled economy* (.709) and *social justice* (.706), and with negative loadings from *productivity* (−.844), *national effort and social harmony* (−.640) and *government authority* (−.505). There is also quite a high positive loading from *government efficiency* (.419). The positive loadings in this case clearly reflect classic social democratic concerns with egalitarianism and interventionism. The negative loadings, how-ever, may appear less immediately penetrable. Certainly they do not represent the typical conservative appeals which one might anticipate to be countering those of social democracy. What does seem to hold them together, however, is the particular conjuncture emphasising the need for economic growth, on the one hand (*productivity*), and the effective government of a united society (*government authority* and *national effort*), on the other. It is in this sense that this side of the dimension gells with the pattern shown in dimension 2, with its emphasis on the strong but benign or representative state.

The general nature of dimension 1 will be discussed at greater length below, and it will be argued that it holds the key to much of what is in competition in the contemporary Irish party system. Before going on to this, however, it is perhaps useful to get a preliminary indication of the mean party positions along these seven dimensions. Reference has already been made to the likelihood that the different dimensions tap different patterns of opposition, such that dimension 7 opposes Labour to both other parties, while dimension 4 pits Fine Gael versus Labour, with Fianna Fáil somewhere in between. Party positions along the dimensions can be extracted relatively easily. Since factor analysis allows us to compute a numerical score or value for each of the cases, that is for each of the programmes, in relation to each dimension, these scores can be aggregated by party and thus a mean party score can be derived. These mean scores for each dimension are reported in Table 4.6.

A first indication of the relative positioning of the parties can be seen in the fourth column of Table 4.6, and the pattern here is indeed striking. The first three dimensions, accounting for almost 47 per cent of total variance, divide Fianna Fáil from Labour, with Fine Gael in the middle. The remaining four factors, on the other hand, accounting for just 34 per cent of the variance, divide Fine Gael from Labour, with Fianna Fáil in the middle. The dimensions with the greatest *spread* of values are 1, ranging from −.847 (FF) to .737 (Lab); 4, ranging from −.902 (FG) to .533 (Lab), and 6, ranging from −.458 (Lab) to .673 (FG). In effect, two of the three most polarised dimensions separate Fine Gael and Labour, while only the first puts both coalition parties on the same side *vis-à-vis* Fianna Fáil. This pattern would therefore appear to confound the coalition strategy of the smaller parties. Nevertheless, if the relative importance of the seven factors is considered, that is the relative percentage of variance explained by each, then the coalition strategy appears to make some ideological sense: given that the first three dimensions put Fine Gael and Labour on the same side of Fianna Fáil, and given also that the first and most important of these dimensions is also the most *polarised*, the alliance of Fine Gael and Labour appears eminently appropriate. Both smaller parties register positive scores on the first dimension as against a negative score for Fianna Fáil, while both register negative scores on dimensions 2 and 3, as against a positive score for Fianna Fáil. But what exactly does dimension 1 signify? What is the nature of the opposition which it reflects and which is so central to this analysis?

At one end, the dimension is readily interpretable. The combination of high positive loadings from *controlled economy* and *social justice*

Table 4.6 Mean scores of parties* and level of polarisation†

Dimension	Mean scores of			Order of parties (ascending)	Level of polarisation
	Fianna Fáil	Fine Gael	Labour		
1	−.847	.304	.737	FF–FG–Lab	1.584
2	.495	−.222	−.326	Lab–FG–FF	.829
3	.301	−.378	−.120	FG–Lab–FF	.679
4	.077	−.902	.533	FG–FF–Lab	1.435
5	.003	.096	−.027	Lab–FF–FG	.126
6	−.194	.673	−.458	Lab–FF–FG	1.131
7	−.050	.333	−.242	Lab–FF–FG	.575
No. of programmes	8	6	6		

* Mean scores are calculated by taking the average of the factor scores for each party's programmes.
† Polarisation is defined as the distance between the two extreme cases. For dimension 1, for example, it is .737 − (−.847), which is 1.584. Thus the larger the value, the greater the polarisation and the wider the spread of positions. This is a variation of the method applied by Sani and Sartori (1983) to survey data on left–right positioning.

indicates that it is bounded on one side by a more generalised social democratic appeal. Moreover, the fact that both Fine Gael and Labour also score positively on this dimension (Table 4.6) lends credence to this interpretation—but more of that later. The negative end of the dimension, where the mean Fianna Fáil position is located, is more problematic, however, and less immediately decipherable. For present purposes, I have chosen to define this combination of appeals as reflecting a *corporatist ideology*, but clearly such a definition requires further elaboration, as well as some justification.

Corporatist Ideology

The first point to emphasise here is the distinction between corporatism as ideology and corporatism as practice (Schmitter 1974, pp. 86–7), a distinction which is also reflected in the writings of Malloy (1974; 1977) on Latin America and of Winkler (1976) on the various meanings of corporatism. As far as the Irish case is concerned, the relevant focus is corporatism as ideology rather than as practice *per se*. Second, it should also be emphasised that the Irish case represents an essentially moderate and loosely defined version of this ideology, which lies at a far remove from that quasi-fascistic variety discussed by Malloy in the Latin American context, and which was founded on the explicit rejection of a competitive party system and of legislative representation based on territorial divisions. While such a pattern is clearly inappropriate to the Irish case, it can be noted tangentially that a tendency in this direction was evident in the 1930s and 1940s. Then, in the wake of the papal encyclical *Quadragesimo Anno*, the notion of a corporate state was taken up by leading Cumann na nGaedheal/Fine Gael intellectuals and was espoused by ideologues of the Blueshirt movement (Manning 1970). In addition, a form of vocational representation was introduced into the electoral system of the new Senate which was set up under the 1937 Constitution. Finally, in 1939 the then Fianna Fáil government established a Commission on Vocational Representation in order to report on the practicalities of establishing functional or vocational organisations and to assess their likely relations with the Dáil and Senate (Lee 1979).

In the event, and despite the appeal of corporatist practices to Catholic thinking at the time, these various moves came to nothing. The vocational panels in the Senate continued in name only as the chamber itself came under the effective control of the political parties (e.g., Garvin 1969) while in 1943 the eventual report of the Commission on Vocational Representation was effectively ignored by the government

(Lee 1979). The partisan character of Irish politics, together with an emphasis on *party* government which can be traced back to the very early years of the state (Malone 1929), left little real incentive to cede any representational political authority to corporatist or vocational associations. It is in this sense that the concern of this analysis lies with corporatism as ideology rather than with corporatist practice *per se*, at least in the extreme form, for, as some recent literature emphasises, there remains substantial scope for enquiry into the practice of *neo*-coporatism in the Irish case (e.g., Hardiman and Lalor 1984; Roche 1982).

What is the essence of this corporatist ideology? There are three basic components, the first of which can be defined as an opposition to the politicisation of social conflict and an appeal to the national interest which, in terms of this present analysis, is reflected in the category *national effort and social harmony*. This appeal, which emphasises the need for social solidarity, is more or less common to all three Irish parties, each of which at various stages has laid claim to the representation of national as opposed to sectional interests. But it is in the Fianna Fáil case that the emphasis is both more pronounced and more enduring. As early as 1933, for instance, de Valera had insisted that Fianna Fáil was a 'National Party, representing all sections of the community' (*Irish Press*, 20 January 1933), while on the eve of his retirement as party leader his message was that 'Fianna Fáil is a national movement rather than a political party organisation' (*Irish Times*, 18 May 1954). More recently, Jack Lynch began a review of party policy in 1969 by emphasising his pride in being leader of

> this great democratic organisation, of this broadly based national movement representative as it is of all the people—and I mean all sections of the people—farmers, workers, businessmen and employers. Representing such a broad spectrum of Irish life, Fianna Fáil is in a unique position to produce and put into effect the policies best suited to the needs of the Irish people (Lynch 1969, p. 1).

His successor, Charles Haughey, has spoken in similar terms. In 1983, for example, he insisted that 'our hopes, our beliefs, and aspirations are not sectional. They are national. They are not confined or limited by any regional boundaries or attitudes' (Haughey 1983, p. 1). Examples such as this are legion. A Fianna Fáil recruitment leaflet of 1969 heads the possible reasons for joining the party by emphasising that it is 'a nationalist party—which welds men and women of all classes and creeds into a great and effective national movement to serve the welfare of the nation as a whole'. In 1977, a canvasser's manual issued by the party stressed that 'Fianna Fáil is a national movement attracting support from all sections of the community'. And so on.

In general, as was seen in Chapter 1, these Fianna Fáil claims were not without foundation. The party did consistently win support from farmers and from workers, from professionals and employers, from young and old, etc., such that its enduring constituency seemed like a microcosm of Irish society as a whole. Nor was Fianna Fáil averse to employing this cross-class appeal to its advantage, and in this sense the emphasis on social solidarity came easily. Given its constituency, Fianna Fáil could more credibly claim a national political project than could its more sectionally-based opponents. In 1943, for example, when the notion was mooted of replacing a single-party Fianna Fáil government with an inter-party national government, Fianna Fáil leaders argued that 'a government which came from a party representing all sections of the community was much more entitled to be called a national government than would a government composed of the odds and ends of little sectional groups' (*Irish Press*, 16 June 1943).

Precisely because Fianna Fáil drew substantial support from all the major social groups, such promotion of social solidarity served its electoral interest. In the first place, and to the extent that the general interest was perceived by the electorate as being of greater importance than any specific sectional interest, then, one could anticipate a general drift towards Fianna Fáil as the most broadly representative 'national' party. More specifically, however, in so far as the promotion of social solidarity militated against the politicisation of social conflict, it also acted against any possible break-up of the party's broad, cross-class coalition. To set one group against another would be to divide the party against itself. To mobilise town against country, or worker against employer, would be to undermine the very social solidarity on which the party depended. It was in just such a context that Séan Lemass urged the incorporation of working-class interests in party policy in the 1950s and 1960s (Bew and Patterson 1982): no single social group could be excluded from the remit of the party.

The emphasis on the national interest which accompanied this appeal for social solidarity is also crucial to an understanding of the Fianna Fáil appeal. As Haughey (1981, p. 33) once stated in one of his more memorable rhetorical flourishes, 'in the broad sweep of [Fianna Fáil] membership and their faith and devotion to their country, there resides what one might well call "the Spirit of the Nation"'. Indeed, the promotion of the national interest is such that one rather acerbic commentator, Conor Cruise O'Brien (1972, p. 197), was led to suggest that 'in Ireland there is only one condition that is decidedly more frowned upon than being a bad Catholic, and that is the condition of being anti-national'.[4]

But it is also important to emphasise that this particular appeal to the nation finds expression in *social* rather than in strictly *territorial* terms. The nation must be united, but it is a unity which derives from social solidarity. Of course, the appeal may also be accompanied by an emphasis on territorial nationalism *per se*, but, as can be seen in the contrasting weights of the categories *Irish unity* and *national effort and social harmony* in Table 4.1, it is the social rather than the strictly territorial element which receives greater attention. What can be argued, however, is that the two appeals do reinforce one another, in that it is precisely a record of militancy in terms of territorial national-ism which lends credibility to appeals to social solidarity and the national interest. Conversely, a party seen to be lukewarm if not hostile to national territorial interests may find it difficult to mobilise con-vincingly around appeals to the national interest in the more mundane social and economic sense. In strict party political terms, therefore, these considerations suggest that it is again Fianna Fáil which is more likely to emphasise a social solidarity/national interest appeal. Not only is such an appeal necessary for the maintenance of its broad, cross-class coalition, but it is also ideologically compatible with the more tradi-tional emphasis on strictly territorial nationalism. The link between the two was perhaps most clearly expressed by Jack Lynch in an interview with the *Irish Times* (28 June 1975): 'the soul of Fianna Fáil is still anti-Partition', he argued. 'To be in Fianna Fáil you must have a Republican outlook in its broadest conception. One must also have a very strong social sense, the desire to represent the broadest political spectrum of the Irish people.'

So far, I have argued that the appeal for social solidarity and the emphasis on the national interest constitute a key component of corporatist ideology in general, and of Fianna Fáil ideology in particular. But this begs the question: towards what end are these princ-iples evoked? What specific goals are being set? The answer can be found in the two remaining components of corporatist ideology, a stress on economic growth and development, on the one hand, and a stress on strong and effective government, on the other. In terms of this particular analysis, these emphases are tapped by the categories of *productivity* and *government authority* respectively, both of which also load onto the negative end of dimension 1 (Table 4.5). Corporatist ideology is, above all, an ideology of development which shies away from strict capitalist or socialist orthodoxies, emphasising a 'humanistic' appeal which finds particular resonance in dependent or economically underdeveloped environments (Malloy 1974, p. 54). Moreover, this particular emphasis on development and growth goes hand in hand with the appeal for social solidarity for, as in the populist regimes discussed by Malloy (1977, p. 11), it stresses 'the possibility of achieving development with a minimum of social conflict. The key to achieving this goal was to construct society around a set of principles that would foster interdependence and cooperation'. In the Irish case also the key principle evoked was that of the national good, while the pursuit of sectional goals—by unions, farmers, employers or whoever—was seen to counter this principle and was decried as anti-national. Finally, a concentration of national effort behind the goals of economic growth and development was seen to require strong and effective government, the third major component of corporatist ideology and one which has been justly underlined by Winkler (1976, p. 108), who emphasises the *ends-orientated* character of corporatism, with the concomitant stress on effectiveness and success rather than on efficiency and justice.

It seems hardly necessary to point to the relevance to the Irish case of both these appeals. A stress on the strength and stability of government has occupied much of Irish political rhetoric since at least the 1940s (Mair 1979), while post-war public policy, particularly in the 1950s and 1960s, was concerned with the promotion of economic growth to the virtual exclusion of all other considerations (e.g., Bew and Patterson 1982). At a time when much of continental Europe was prospering, the Irish economy remained stagnant: GNP in the 1950s grew by only 1 per cent per annum, agriculture still accounted for a large proportion of national output and exports, and the welfare state remained essentially underdeveloped. The adoption of the *First Programme for Economic Expansion* in 1958, an opening up of the economy and the attraction of foreign capital, and a major shift to export-led growth, were to effect a transformation in the 1960s, a period which was also to witness a massive expansion of the welfare state (Litton 1982; Maguire 1985).

The elaboration of the policies which led to such a sea-change dominated party attention throughout the first post-war decades, and it was in this context that the language of Fianna Fáil, focusing as it did on the concern for development, effective government, and the pursuit of the national interest, revealed many of the characteristics of a more generalised corporatist ideology. Yet it must be emphasised again that such an emphasis was not inconsistent with the party's traditional appeal to territorial nationalism. In so far as appeals for social solidarity, strong government and economic growth are couched in such a way as to emphasise the national interest, they seek to tap a similar response to that sought by the more traditional emphasis on territorial integrity and independence. Indeed, as early as 1948 both elements were specifically linked by Séan Lemass when he argued that

> our national welfare depends almost entirely upon the success of plans made to increase national productivity and to expand the range of our economy. Let us not have any doubt that the development of our economic policy must proceed step by step with the realisation of our political objectives [i.e. Irish unity and the restoration of the Irish language]. Anything which tends to restrict, to limit or to discourage our economic development is directly opposed to our political objectives (*Irish Press*, 24 June 1948).

This linkage also offers the key to what otherwise seems a puzzle of Irish political development: how was it that Fianna Fáil managed to retain its nationalist credentials and its popular support, given that it underwent a major policy reversal between the early 1930s and the late 1950s? Fianna Fáil had come to power on a strong nationalist platform which, *inter alia*, pledged a policy of economic autarchy: the erection of tariff barriers, the discouragement of foreign investment, and the fostering of native industry behind a broad protective shield. By the late 1950s and early 1960s, the same party, with more or less the same leadership, had opened up the economy, was offering massive incentives to foreign capital, and was laying the ground for an Anglo-Irish Free Trade Agreement and membership of the European Economic Community. The hallmarks of its earlier nationalist platform had been discarded entirely, yet the party remained as powerful as before and still claimed a monopoly of the nationalist credentials. How was this achieved?

The answer lies, I believe, in an effective and fundamental recasting of nationalist discourse. Whereas in the earlier period the national interest had been seen to demand political, cultural and economic isolation, in the later period it came to imply the achievement of material prosperity. Independence *per se* was no longer sufficient, rather economic and social self-respect were necessary if, in the frequently cited aspiration of nationalist ideologues, Ireland was to take its place among the nations of the world. Nationalism remained a key motif, but by the 1960s the success of the nationalist endeavour was to

be measured in wealth and economic growth rather than in cultural or
territorial integrity. Indeed, the displacement of the territorial component of nationalism was such that Lemass felt able to attempt a
rapprochement with Northern Ireland and to afford Northern Ireland a
degree of pragmatic recognition which would have been inconceivable
in the earlier years. In 1964 he travelled to Northern Ireland to take
part in what was the first official meeting between the Prime Ministers
of Northern Ireland and the Republic. In 1967, as a leading member of
the Oireachtas Committee on the Constitution, he recommended a
modification of those Articles which laid claim to Northern Ireland,
urging their replacement by an Article expressing simply an aspiration
to unity. Fianna Fáil remained in the forefront of Irish nationalist
politics, but by the 1960s its credentials were to be measured in terms
of the success of its economic and social programme and in the broad
range of its electoral support. Nationalist discourse remained important, even if its terms of reference had been fundamentally recast.
Indeed, the entire process offers a clear example of the phenomenon
noted above, whereby *issues in competition* (such as economic and
social policy) can be absorbed into the *language of identification*
(traditional nationalism). Nevertheless, despite the linkage, it is necessary to maintain the analytic distinction between traditional territorial
nationalism, on the one hand, and—to employ perhaps an unfortunate
if useful term—the more recent social nationalism on the other.

This, then, is the conjuncture which gives meaning to the negative end
of dimension 1: the specific combination of appeals to the national
interest and social solidarity (*national effort and social harmony*),
towards the enduring goal of economic growth and development
(*productivity*), under the directive hand of a strong and effective
administration (*government authority*). And what is also important
here is that this combination of appeals catches the stance of Fianna
Fáil in particular. It is not the case that Fianna Fáil is the only party to
adopt these emphases: indeed, both   *productivity* and *government
authority* are consensual categories which are included among the ten
leading themes of each of the parties between 1961 and 1982 (Table
4.4), while Fine Gael also emphasises the *national effort* appeal. What
is important, however, is that Fianna Fáil stresses each of the categories
and accords them a combined emphasis which far outweighs that of the
other two parties. Taken together, the three categories account for
almost 25 per cent of the content of Fianna Fáil programmes, as against
less than 17 per cent in the case of Fine Gael and less than 11 per cent in
the case of Labour (Table 4.1). Taken individually, each of these

categories is not exclusively associated with Fianna Fáil. In combination, however, and in terms of their collective degree of emphasis, they begin to define the otherwise rather amorphous character of post-war Fianna Fáil ideology.

Corporatist Ideology versus Social Democratic Ideology

The conflict tapped by dimension 1 now becomes clear: corporatist ideology versus social democracy, the latter constituted by the high positive loadings from *social justice* and *controlled economy*. Given that we already know that Fianna Fáil lays the greatest substantive emphasis on the corporatist ideology categories, followed by Fine Gael and then by Labour, it is perhaps now interesting to note the relative rankings in terms of the two social democratic categories. The figures in Table 4.1 reveal that the ordering of the parties is exactly the same *but in the opposite direction*. Labour lays most emphasis on the social democratic categories, which account for 25 per cent of the contents of its programmes. Fine Gael then follows with just over 15 per cent, and Fianna Fáil comes third with just over 5 per cent. In short, not only does this bipolar dimension make 'ideological' sense, but it also orders the parties in the same way, with Fianna Fáil as the most corporatist, Labour as the most social democratic, and with Fine Gael in the centre. This ordering is based, of course, on a simple count of programmatic emphases, and reflects a mean party position for the 1961–82 period as a whole. A more precise location can be derived from the factor scores, which will also allow us to trace the movements of the parties along the dimension and from election to election (see Figure 4.1 below). The mean value of these factor scores has already been reported in Table 4.6, and this confirms the relative ordering based on the simple count of programmatic emphases.

In so far as the social-democratic appeal represents a conventional political alternative which is found in varying degrees throughout Western Europe, it does not require substantial specification in this particular study. What is necessary, however, is an elaboration of the Fine Gael position, given that—as can be seen in Figure 4.1 below—the party has often tended towards quite a strong emphasis on the social democratic end of the dimension, a stance which appears quite at odds with the party's original conservative approach.

Fine Gael's social democratic emphasis is at its most apparent in the elections of 1965 and 1969, the first two elections to be fought on the basis of the *Just Society* proposals which, in turn, can be seen to mark a major watershed in the general political approach of the party. Pressure from within the party to abandon its traditional conservatism had already been apparent since the late 1950s, however, in the wake of the defeat of the second inter-party government and well before the publication of the *Just Society* programme in 1965. In 1959 Declan Costello, a young Fine Gael TD who was later to play a crucial role in formulating the *Just Society* programme, argued that

> we should not be afraid to use techniques traditionally associated with the parties of the left ... we should be prepared to jettison motives and concepts which belong to the heyday of nineteenth-century liberalism ... we [should] try to bring about conditions where there is a genuine equality for all, irrespective of the level of society in which they have been born ... I believe that Fine Gael should move openly and firmly to the left (quoted by Gallagher 1982, p. 39)

The contrast between this approach and that which still dominated the party leadership in the late 1950s could hardly be more striking. Enunciating 'thirteen principles' of Fine Gael policy in 1954, the then Taoiseach John A. Costello (father of Declan) continually stressed the need for a minimum of state interference in civil society. Among these 13 principles were

> That all classes in the community be equally treated and that no-one goes in want or suffers from disease which can be alleviated, through defects in organisation. That, where possible, any assistance be stimulated and supported by state activity but not supplanted or coerced ...
>
> That a careful watch be kept on the development of the Central Government and the expenditure in its hands to administer, and that the electorate be encouraged to a recognition that any promises or benefits are, in effect, promises by politicians to take more money from the people and spend it for them ...
>
> That the financial policy of the Government be primarily concerned to foster incomes instead of merely providing relief schemes for those for whom deficient prosperity has failed to provide. That this policy of increased incomes can be done less well by direct Government activity than by the stimulation of the activity of private enterprise ...
>
> That in all directions, whether in the fields of culture, industry or agriculture, a positive approach of encouragement replaces a negative policy of control (*Irish Press*, 3 May 1954).

These principles were to be fundamentally changed by the middle of the 1960s, in part as a result of the pressures of a younger generation in the party, and in part as a result of changes in the external economic and political environment. Almost exactly ten years after John A. Costello's elaboration of the Fine Gael principles, the Fine Gael parliamentary party unanimously adopted a resolution which was explicitly based on the belief that 'there is an urgent need for economic and social reform in order to produce a more just social order . . . [and] that such reform can best be brought about by a more effective management of our economy and a more equitable distribution of the nation's wealth'. The resolution itself asserted that 'sufficient economic progress cannot be achieved by economic "programming". Full-scale economic planning is necessary'. Further, this planning would 'involve not only detailed targets for the public sector, but for the private sector as well'. In conclusion, the resolution stated that 'the Government must undertake direct investment in the industrial field where desirable and in the public interest' (Fine Gael Archive, p. 39/169(d)).

This resolution was to lead to the drafting of the *Just Society* manifesto in the 1965 election, and was to push Fine Gael towards the social democratic end of the crucial dimension identified above. Thus by 1981, in his address to the Fine Gael árd fheis, Garret FitzGerald could confidently claim that 'the single great issue that makes us different from Fianna Fáil as any two parties could be is our commitment to social justice' (*Irish Times*, 30 March 1981). By way of contrast, when John A. Costello complained to the 1954 Fine Gael árd fheis that 'one of the more irritating questions raised by political commentators concerning the political position in Ireland at the moment was—what was the difference between the parties?', he could only respond by emphasising contrasts in competence and personnel (*Irish Independent*, 18 February 1954).

Thus we find Fine Gael joining Labour in a shared emphasis on a social democratic appeal, and both parties confronting the corporatist emphases of Fianna Fáil. The mobilisation of a social democratic opposition to corporatist ideology is not in itself surprising. As Winkler (1976, p. 107) notes, corporatism is by no means egalitarian, and contains 'no principle favouring redistribution or equality'. Moreover, he also emphasises that the ideology contains no inherent sense of justice: given that the national interest is the supreme interest, and that the national good overrides any other collective or individual good, any alternative criteria of justice must necessarily achieve only secondary status. In the words of Manoilesco, who he cites (ibid., p. 108), 'all that conforms to the national interest is just; all that is contrary to that interest is unjust'. That opposition to the corporatism of Fianna Fáil should therefore take the form of an appeal to the egalitarianism and social justice of social democracy was not unexpected. To be sure, the opposition in the Irish case represents an essentially lukewarm version of what has occurred elsewhere. In Ireland, to use Sartori's (1976, p. 137) term, ideological fever does not run high: the ideologies concerned are neither intense nor very coherent, and to a certain extent they do also share a common discourse. Nevertheless, real differences exist, and these can be seen to separate the protagonists in a meaningful way.

The emergence of a social democratic opposition can also be seen to be in part a consequence of the very success of Fianna Fáil governance in increasing national wealth and resources, and hence inculcating a mild revolution of rising expectations. Resources had grown enormously in the 1960s—between 1961 and 1973, when Fianna Fáil was eventually displaced by the Fine Gael–Labour coalition, GDP grew by an annual average of 4.4 per cent (Maguire 1985)—and demands for the more egalitarian distribution of these resources also grew apace. The differing attitudes to redistribution are therefore revealing. For Fianna Fáil, increased social expenditure was dependent on economic growth: in the words of Séan Lemass, 'without economic progress there could be no social progress' (quoted in Bew and Patterson 1982, p. 160). From the social democratic side, on the other hand, there was a call for more immediate redistribution, and the assertion that pressure for the remedying of social grievances was such that the country could no longer afford to wait for further economic progress. In the more graphic language of day-to-day political debate, the opposition often took the form of claiming—from the corporatist side—that 'a rising tide lifts all boats', only to be countered—from the social democratic side—by the assertion that not all boats could 'afford to wait for the rising tide.[5]

This is not to deny the very crucial role played by welfarism in corporatist thinking. Indeed, as Bew and Patterson (1982, Chapter 6) ably demonstrate, a commitment to building the welfare state was essential to the post-war strategy of Fianna Fáil. Between 1961 and 1973, for example, social expenditure grew from 14.3 per cent of GDP to 22.1 per cent, and from 46.7 per cent of total public expenditure to 55.8 per cent (Maguire 1985). But the Fianna Fáil approach to welfare was articulated in quite a different fashion to that of Fine Gael or Labour. For the latter, welfare was a matter of right, an essential component of what has been defined as 'social citizenship'. For Fianna Fáil, on the other hand, the commitment to welfare was much more contingent, tending to be viewed as a function of munificence or Christian charity, rather than a matter of right *per se*. Thus, as early as 1939, justifying increased expenditure on pensions, de Valera had asserted that 'we regard it as a social obligation on us to maintain these people' (quoted in Moynihan 1980, p. 407). Much later, in an election broadcast in 1954, the then Fianna Fáil Minister for Health and Social Welfare, James Ryan, defended increased expenditure in the following terms: 'Do you really grudge this help to those who are less fortunate than you? ... You know you are bound to love your neighbour; you know that in conscience you cannot be really said to love him if you fail to come to his help when misfortune overtakes him and his children' (6 May 1954, manuscript). It is in this sense that corporatism is not a simple right-wing appeal: there is a commitment to welfare, but it is necessarily contingent, and as such runs counter to the rights-emphasising appeal of social democracy. Moreover, as a contingent commitment, it will inevitably falter when confronted by a social democratic opposition, particularly if and when economic growth itself begins to slow. By the time Fianna Fáil faced the increasingly radical assault from Fine Gael and Labour in the late 1960s, it seemed that 'the populist movement ... had become a party of privilege ... A rising tide, Lemass had said, lifts all boats. In the 1960s, it lifted Fianna Fáil boats more than most, and left others beached in relative poverty' (Walsh 1976).

There are clear similarities here to the dynamics of party competition in France in the 1950s and 1960s, at least as analysed by McHale and Shaber (1976), who define the appeal of Gaullism by distinguishing two phases, aggressive Gaullism and defensive Gaullism. The former characterised the modernistic ethos of the party in the late 1950s and early 1960s, with an emphasis 'on national goals, on the need for political stability, and on the effective management of a complex and expanding economy' (ibid., p. 295). The appeal proved largely successful, but as a result of the rapid growth of the French economy, distributional issues were reawakened which, in turn, damaged the party's capacity to appeal for the subordination of sectional demands to the national good, and forced Gaullism into a more defensive stance in which it reverted to more traditional appeals. The parallel with the Irish case is tempting:[6] a shift away from traditional appeals such as nation, church and family to a more corporatist emphasis, stressing the national interest in order to achieve economic growth and the subordination of sectional demands; the growth in resources then stimulating demands for redistribution and leading to the politicisation of social conflict which, in turn, worked to undermine the attraction of the corporatist appeal. In the French case, McHale and Shaber argue that defensive Gaullism led to a revival of more traditional emphases and appeals. To the extent that the parallel is valid, then, it might be expected that defensive Fianna Fáilism would lead to a revival of traditional republicanism and traditional Catholicism. Certainly, the new Fianna Fáil emphasis on territorial nationalism (Cox 1985; Mair 1987c), together with its opposition to the moves towards a more pluralist society (e.g., Cooney 1986; Girvin 1986), suggest that this is the case. Indeed, it was precisely such a reversion to traditional appeals which was largely responsible for the significant intra-party tension in Fianna Fáil which helped give rise to the Progressive Democrats (see Chapter 5).

Plotting the Parties

Figure 4.1 plots the factor scores derived from dimension 1, that is it locates each of the individual election programmes in terms of the factor itself. The pattern shown by these data is striking. Although all three parties lie on the corporatist ideology side of the dimension in 1961, the base year, there nevertheless remains a basic dichotomy between Fianna Fáil on the one hand and both Fine Gael and Labour on the other. This dichotomy becomes even more evident in 1965, as Fine Gael and Labour move firmly to the social democratic side of the dimension, a position which they retain in 1969 as well as in 1981. Fine Gael moves to the corporatist side in February 1982, and finally moves back to rejoin Labour on the social democratic side in November 1982.

A number of other features of these alignments should also be noted. First, despite Labour's own leftward shift in the mid-1960s, the dimension records Fine Gael adopting a more social democratic appeal than Labour in both 1965 and 1969, although the positions are reversed thereafter. Second, the Fianna Fáil scores reveal a consistently *declining* trend in the emphasis on corporatist ideology from 1961 through to February 1982. Third, the pattern of the data reveals a sharp shift in the Fine Gael–Labour coalition position between 1973 and 1977, the former being clearly located at the social democratic end of the dimension, while the latter is clearly corporatist in character. What is interesting to note here is that the 1973 programme was drafted when both parties were at the end of a period of 16 years in opposition and were undoubtedly full of reformist zeal. In 1977, by contrast, they were defending a record of four years in government and attempting to recover from the crisis created by the 'oil shock' of the early 1970s.

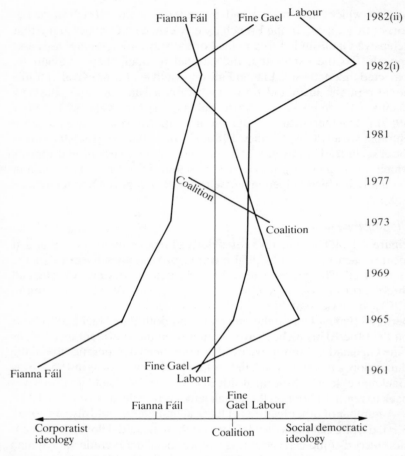

Figure 4.1. Party movements along dimension 1, 1961–82

Fourth, it is interesting to note the 'disruption' in the general trends in February 1982 when, in the wake of the defeat of the short-lived coalition government, Labour competed on the basis of a decidedly social democratic programme, while Fine Gael adopted its most corporatist stance for the entire period, exceeding even that of Fianna Fáil. Labour had been somewhat of a reluctant partner in the 1981–2 government, and the immense gap which separated the coalition parties' programmes in February 1982 is perhaps indicative of the general increase in Labour scepticism about the value of future alliances. In the wake of the February election, the Administrative Council of the Labour Party voted not to form a coalition in the new Dáil but, if necessary, simply to support a minority Fine Gael administration (Gallagher 1982, pp. 247–52). In the event, Fianna Fáil managed to win sufficient external support to form its own minority government and, when it in turn was defeated in November 1982, it was again replaced by a coalition of Labour and Fine Gael which, judging from the data in Table 4.1, had by then enjoyed a new *rapprochement*. In the event, the camaraderie was to evaporate as increasing left–right tensions drove the parties further and further apart, a process which eventually culminated in Labour's withdrawal from government in January 1987.

Finally, the base line in Figure 4.1 also shows the mean positions of the parties for the entire period (cf. also Table 4.6), as well as the mean position of the two coalition programmes. Fianna Fáil is clearly on the corporatist side of the dimension, with Labour clearly on the social democratic side, and with Fine Gael also on the social democratic side, albeit less pronouncedly so than Labour. The coalition position is more centrist again, although it also emerges on the social democratic side of the dimension.

Noting these mean positions serves once again to underline an earlier and important observation, and that is that in reality the overall space of competition is quite limited. To be sure, the dimension itself offers a very real insight into contemporary competition in Ireland and, as can be seen from Figure 4.1, it does separate the parties in a meaningful way. Nevertheless there is little 'ideological stretching' (Sartori 1976, Chapter 6) in the Irish case: the overall space of competition is limited, the mean positions of the parties are reasonably close to one another and to the centre, and competition itself appears essentially centripetal. In short, the contemporary Irish party system bears all the hallmarks of a system of 'moderate pluralism' (Sartori 1976). While I have identified an opposition between corporatist ideology, on the one hand, and social democratic ideology on the other, it must be emphasised yet again that the Irish case is characterised by an essentially moderate version of this opposition.

The moderacy of the opposition has already been underlined with respect to the corporatist stance (see, p. 177). And much the same can be said of the social democratic position. Labour's socialist turn in the 1960s, for example, was largely rhetorical, and in practical terms many of the policies remained unchanged. The moderacy of the Fine Gael position is even more evident.[7] To be sure, the party evinced a genuine commitment to social justice in the 1960s and 1970s, and it also emphasised the need for a degree of state control of the economy. Nevertheless, voices within the party have also continued to assert the more traditional party view. Thus, in a 1977 pamphlet entitled *The Role of Fine Gael*, the newly-elected party leader, Garret FitzGerald, echoed the earlier principles of John A. Costello, arguing that

> while Fine Gael is not inhibited about the State playing its role where the needs of society require it do so, it is conscious of the desirability of maintaining in these areas as high a degree of independence of state intervention as possible and—in practice often more important—of ensuring that aid is provided in a way that does not undermine the independence of the individual or the economic unit involved (FitzGerald 1977, p. 10).

In short, there is competition along this dimension, and there is a fairly consistent division between the parties over time, but the overall space of competition is quite abbreviated.

Other Dimensions of Competition

So far the discussion has focused on the dynamic revealed by the first dimension of competition which, though significant, is hardly the whole story. What of the other dimensions, particularly dimensions 2 and 3 which also serve to separate Fianna Fáil from the other two parties (cf. Table 4.6)?

It is my contention that these second two dimensions simply tap other reinforcing aspects of corporatist ideology. It will be recalled that dimension 2 reflects a view of the state as essentially benign or representative (the high loading from *social group interests*) but also strong (the high loading from *law and order*). Seen in this light, dimension 2 represents a variation of the strong government component of corporatist ideology, as well as the natural corollary of the appeal for social solidarity. The emphasis on social solidarity in dimension 1 is paralleled by the willingness to cater for group interests in dimension 2, while the stress on government authority in dimension 1 is also paralleled by the stress on law and order in dimension 2. Dimension 3 also appears to reflect an understandable corollary to dimension 1, given that here the high loadings emphasise a more traditional version of the national interest, that is *Irish unity* and *defence of the Irish way of life*. This dimension also records high loadings from *expansion of the social services* (but not *social justice*), a commitment to welfarism which again fits easily into the 'humanistic' appeals of corporatism. The picture is not wholly uncluttered, of course: dimension 3 also records quite a high negative loading from *government authority*, which runs counter to the pattern evinced by dimensions 1 and 2. Nevertheless, in general, and without wishing to engage in further lengthy elaborations, the image presented by dimensions 2 and 3 seems to reinforce the importance of a wider corporatist appeal, and so helps to complete an understanding of the overall dynamic of post-war party competition.

Finally, it should also be noted that the categories involved in the high loadings on dimensions 2 and 3 do not account for such a high proportion of the contents of the parties' programmes as those involved in dimension 1. The combination of *social group interests* and *law and order*, which load on dimension 2, account for an average of less than 17 per cent of Fianna Fáil programmes, just over 11 per cent of Fine Gael programmes, and just over 9 per cent of Labour programmes (cf. Table 4.1). The categories with major loadings on dimension 3—*Irish unity*, *defence of the Irish way of life* and *expansion of the social services*—together account for 19 per cent in the case of Fianna Fáil, 13 per cent in the case of Fine Gael, and 16 per cent in the case of Labour. These are not negligible proportions by any means; nevertheless, they are clearly of less central concern to the parties than are the corporatist *and* social democratic categories loading on dimension 1, and which together account for some 30 per cent of the contents of Fianna Fáil programmes, 32 per cent in the case of Fine Gael, and 36 per cent in the case of Labour.

Dimensions 2 and 3 are also *unipolar*. They load substantially in only one direction and so involve only the opposition of more versus less emphasis, rather than that of one appeal versus another. Dimension 2 defies easy summary under a single rubric, and for the sake of simplicity can be labelled *emphasis on law and order/group interests*. Dimension 3 is more easily defined, however, and can be labelled simply *emphasis on traditional nationalism*.

In the interests of brevity, the graphical presentation of these two dimensions will be restricted simply to recording the mean positions of the parties and the coalition, setting these against the mean positions of the parties on dimension 1. The results are shown in Figures 4.2 and 4.3, both of which underline the basic division between Fianna Fáil, on the one hand, and Fine Gael and Labour, on the other. Joining dimensions 2 and 3—emphasis on law and order/group interests and emphasis on traditional nationalism—to dimension 1, which opposes corporatist ideology to social democratic ideology, reveals a clear

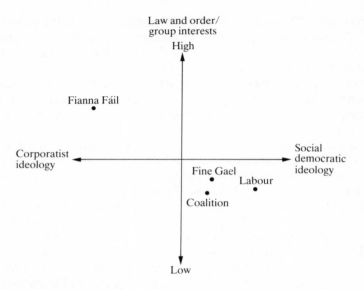

Figure 4.2. Mean positions on dimensions 1 and 2

spatial distinction between Fianna Fáil and the other two parties. In both cases Fianna Fáil is in the upper left-hand quadrant, emphasising corporatism and either law and order/group interests (Figure 4.2) or traditional nationalism (Figure 4.3), while both Fine Gael and Labour lie in the lower right-hand quadrant, emphasising social democratic ideology, and evidencing a weaker concern for both of the other sets of issues. To be sure, there are distinctions between the two smaller parties. On the traditional nationalist dimension, Labour tends to be more centrist than Fine Gael, while Fine Gael tends towards a more centrist position on the law and order/group interests dimension. Nevertheless, these differences are slight relative to those separating both parties from Fianna Fáil and, more importantly, it must be underlined that the two smaller parties are always on the same side of each dimension with Fianna Fáil on the opposing side.

It is also interesting to note the location of the coalition programmes. The combination of dimensions 1 and 2 (Figure 4.2) places the coalition programmes firmly within the Fine Gael–Labour space, evincing a log-rolling pattern whereby they are less social democratic than is Labour, but less emphatic on law and order/group interests than is Fine Gael. By way of contrast, the combination of dimensions 1 and 3

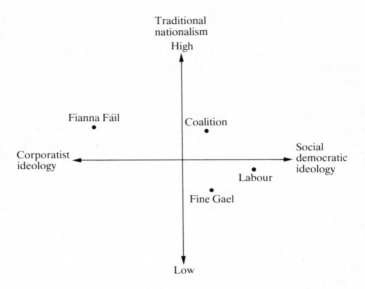

Figure 4.3. Mean positions on dimensions 1 and 3

(Figure 4.3) places the coalition programmes on the Fianna Fáil side of dimension 3, reflecting a greater emphasis on traditional nationalism than is usually the case with either of the coalition parties taken on their own. But these are very rough measures: the coalition position is based on the mean of the 1973 and 1977 programmes, while the positions of the individual parties are based on the mean for the entire period from 1961 to 1982. A more meaningful understanding of the coalition position with respect to the individual parties would seem to necessitate a comparison of the coalition programme of 1973 with the positions of the individual parties in 1969, the last election prior to the formation of the coalition, and this enquiry will be addressed below (p. 197).

This raises the final point in this section, which is the pattern of party positions shown by the bipolar dimension 4 which, as noted earlier, appears to involve two overlapping oppositions: *interventionism* versus *economic orthodoxy* in the economy domain, and *freedom and democracy* versus *national effort and social harmony*. The overlap between the two is certainly confusing, and it is difficult to identify any single underlying opposition which can account for the dual set of conflicting emphases. At one end, there is undoubtedly a conservative imperative reflected in the emphases on fiscal rectitude and social solidarity. The other end is more problematic, but for the sake of simplicity it can be seen as expressing a more generalised appeal for protectionism—safeguarding individual rights, on the one hand, and incipient economic interests, on the other. But even this may be to push the interpretability of the dimensions too far. In practice, this actual coincidence of appeals is largely a function of party-specific concerns: Labour tends to emphasise both *protectionism* and *freedom and democracy*, while Fine Gael has tended to emphasise *economic orthodoxy* and *national effort*. Fianna Fáil is ambivalent. While the larger party also emphasises *national effort*, it pays less attention to each of the three remaining categories. In addition, it should be noted that the combination of these high-loading categories does not contribute substantially to the actual content of the respective party programmes, accounting for less than 9 per cent in the case of Fianna Fáil, some 11 per cent in the case of Labour, and some 15 per cent in the case of Fine Gael.

Figure 4.4 reports the mean positions of the parties with respect to the combination of dimensions 1 and 4. Dimension 4 clearly separates Fine Gael and Labour, the former at the 'conservative' end of the dimension, the latter at the 'protectionist' end. Fianna Fáil lies in a

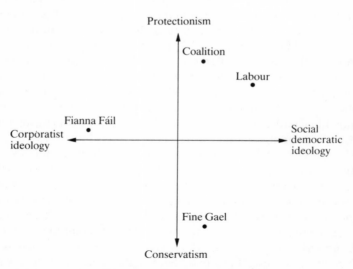

Figure 4.4. Mean positions on dimensions 1 and 4

virtually neutral position along this dimension. What is interesting about dimension 4, therefore, is that it is the first of the major dimensions to place Labour and Fine Gael on different sides *vis-à-vis* Fianna Fáil. It is also interesting to note the mean coalition position, since it is clearly at the Labour end of the dimension and is almost as distant from Fine Gael as is possible. This may of course reflect the different time period involved, given that the coalition position derives only from the elections of 1973 and 1977. A clearer idea of the relative proximities therefore necessitates a closer analysis of party positions in the period immediately before the formation of the coalition in 1973.

Dimensions of Competition and Coalition Formation

As was underlined above (Chapter 1), the governing alternatives in post-war Ireland have been single-party Fianna Fáil administrations, on the one hand, or anti-Fianna Fáil coalitions on the other. Within this context, there has been a major variation in that anti-Fianna Fáil alliance, which involved five parties at the beginning of the post-war period (Fine Gael, Labour, National Labour, Clann na Poblachta and Clann na Talmhan) and only two during the most recent periods of coalition (Fine Gael and Labour). This change was due simply to the consolidation of the party system in the 1950s and 1960s, and to the elimination of the smaller parties. Thus, when Fine Gael joined Labour in coalition in 1973, it was as much the alliance of 'all' non-Fianna Fáil Dáil parties as were the earlier, more broadly based coalitions of 1948 and 1954. In addition, however, it is also important to recognise that the willingness of the non-Fianna Fáil parties to form an alliance has also varied over the post-war period. Following the Fianna Fáil success in 1957, both Labour and Fine Gael determined to 'go it alone', each aspiring to majority-party status and hoping to accumulate a sufficient electoral following to allow the formation of an alternative single-party administration. This situation persisted through three successive Fianna Fáil victories in 1961, 1965 and 1969 until, in 1973, the two opposition parties forsook their independent strategies and reverted to coalition, an alliance which persisted until 1987. The parties campaigned on a joint programme in 1977 as they had done in 1973, and while they developed independent programmes thereafter, the coalition option was always kept alive. The two parties returned to office in 1981 and again in November 1982.

In effect, therefore, while the governing alternatives have remained those of Fianna Fáil versus the rest (Mair 1979), the period from 1961

to 1969 was characterised by the practical absence of an alternative to
Fianna Fáil. Neither of the smaller parties seemed in a position to
challenge for government on its own, while both also rejected the
possibility of an alliance against Fianna Fáil. Throughout the post-war
period Fianna Fáil also remained stubbornly opposed to the idea that it,
too, might—if necessary—form a coalition alliance. If the party lacked
the Dáil strength to govern alone, the preferred policy was to go into
opposition. In other words, Fianna Fáil remained aloof from the
possibility of a coalition alliance with any party, thus obliging Fine Gael
and Labour to either ally with one another or forego any opportunity
for office.

Given this pattern, and given also the very heterogeneous and ad hoc
nature of the first post-war coalition in 1948, it is then not surprising to
note that coalition formation in Ireland has been characterised as
essentially *opportunistic*, with the desire for office outweighing any
considerations of potential policy compatibility. This conclusion is
further reinforced by the popular and historically derived perception of
Fine Gael and Labour as being on opposite sides *vis-à-vis* Fianna Fáil,
and that coalition formation is effectively the unity of left and right
against the centre. This certainly is the conclusion of Cohan (1979;
1982), who locates Labour on the left and Fine Gael on the right with
Fianna Fáil in the centre, and who then emphasises opportunistic,
circumstantial or 'situational' variables as the key explanatory factors in
Irish coalition formation. To be sure, Cohan also argues that the
essential homogeneity of Irish society and the political culture act to
contract the political spectrum in such a way that even the 'extremes' of
left and right are not very far apart. Although Labour and Fine Gael
may be on opposite sides of the left–right spectrum, the distance which
separates them is minimal, and certainly insufficient to *prevent* coalition. Thus, for Cohan (1979), Ireland offers an example of what he
defines as an open coalition in a closed society.

While it is always difficult to assess the extent of opportunism
or sheer circumstance in the process of alliance formation, an analysis
of party programmes such as this does permit a more rigorous analysis
of the coalition option, in that it allows a systematic comparison
of policy differences between the parties, and of the relative distances
which separate them along the various dimensions of competition.
In addition, the analysis allows us to locate the coalition programmes
themselves along these dimensions, and to assess the relative distances
between these programmes and those of the individual parties. To
the extent that the most proximate parties are also those which form

the coalition alliance, and to the extent that the coalition programme is also more proximate to the positions of these individual parties than to those outside the coalition, then it can be assumed that opportunism and circumstance were not the only factors accounting for the alliance. To the extent that the coalition programme more closely reflects that of a party outside the coalition, however, or to the extent that the parties which do ally are also the least proximate, then opportunism or circumstance can be assumed to have played an important role.

The formation of the 1973 coalition offers a crucial test of this approach. First, this was a coalition which was formed by parties which had spent some 16 years in opposition, and therefore occurred when opportunistic or situational factors can be expected to have played a major role. Second, 1973 affords a more appropriate test than 1977 in that the decision by Labour and Fine Gael to campaign once again on a joint programme in this second election partly derived from the success of the first alliance, and came within a context in which experience of office was likely to have predisposed the two parties to further collaboration. In other words, after 1973 the crucial elements of 'inertia' and 'familiarity' came into play, variables which have proved of particular relevance to an understanding of coalition formation in other party systems (Franklin and Mackie 1983).

The preceding discussion of the major dimensions of competition already suggest that there was a far greater policy rationale underlying the 1973 coalition than is normally taken to have been the case (see also Mair 1986a). In terms of their mean locations for the entire period, Fine Gael and Labour lie on the same side of key dimensions and on the opposite side to Fianna Fáil. This is certainly the case for dimensions 1, 2 and 3, although it is not the case for the other, less significant dimensions. But even this may be misleading, since the mean positions involve averaging scores for Fine Gael and Labour in 1981 and 1982, as well as between 1961 and 1969. In other words, they include the programmes which postdate the joint programmes of 1973 and 1977 as well as those which predated these programmes.

Accordingly, Table 4.7 presents the more restricted picture of a comparison of party scores in 1969—the last election preceding the coalition—and the coalition programme of 1973. This allows a clear test of the policy rationale, if any, of the 1973 alliance, given that Table 4.7 also reports the various inter-party distances—between Fianna Fáil and Fine Gael, Fianna Fáil and Labour, and Fine Gael and Labour—as well as the distances between each of the individual parties and the

Table 4.7 Inter-party distances*, 1969 and 1973

Dimensions	Party positions				Inter-party distances					
	Fianna Fáil (1969)	Fine Gael (1969)	Labour (1969)	FG–Labour coalition (1969)	FF 69–FG 69	FF 69–Lab 69	FG 69–Lab 69	FF 69–Coal 73	FG 69–Coal 73	Lab 69–Coal 73
1	−0.95	0.81	0.47	0.93	.86	.52	.34	1.88	.12	.46
2	−0.38	−0.25	−0.38	−0.40	.13	0	.13	.02	.15	.02
3	3.42	−0.07	−0.98	0.05	3.49	4.40	.91	3.37	.12	1.03
4	−0.14	0.02	2.08	1.11	.16	2.22	2.06	1.25	1.09	.97
5	−0.63	−0.16	−1.31	−0.59	.47	.68	1.15	.04	.43	.74
6	0.52	0.39	1.47	−0.39	.13	.92	1.08	.91	.78	1.86
7	0.09	1.06	0.97	−0.09	.97	.88	.09	.18	1.15	1.06

* Absolute difference between factor scores

coalition. *Ceteris paribus*, the smaller the distance between a pair of parties (that is, the smaller the difference between their respective factor scores) the more likely they are to be the parties which form a coalition alliance. In this sense, if there is a policy rationale, we can expect to find the distance separating Fine Gael and Labour to be smaller than that separating either party from Fianna Fáil. Conversely, to the extent that either party is closer to Fianna Fáil than to its coalition ally, it can be assumed that factors other than policy were more important in determining the alliance.

The data in Table 4.7 clearly confirm the presence of policy rationale. The distance which separates Fine Gael from Labour is smaller than that involved in any other combination of parties on dimensions 1, 3 and 7. The smallest gap on dimensions 4, 5 and 6 are those between Fianna Fáil and Fine Gael, while Labour and Fianna Fáil are closest, being in identical positions, on dimension 2. In sum, the relative positions on the most important dimension, corporatist ideology versus social democratic ideololoogy, predict the formation of a Fine Gael–Labour coalition. This is also the case for dimension 3, emphasis on traditional nationalism, largely due to the sheer extremity of the Fianna Fáil position. On the other hand, relative positions on dimension 2, emphasis on law and order/group interests, predict a Fianna Fáil–Labour coalition, while relative positions on dimension 4, 'protectionism' versus 'conservativism', clearly predict a Fianna Fáil–Fine Gael alliance.

In policy terms, therefore, all three coalition arrangements are possible: Fianna Fáil–Fine Gael, Fianna Fáil–Labour and Fine Gael–Labour. In practice, however, the data confirm the plausibility of the Fine Gael–Labour alliance. First, this is the option predicted by the most significant of the dimensions; second, it is also predicted by dimension 3; and third, it is countered primarily by dimension 2, but here the relative inter-party differences are so slight, and the dimension itself so lacking in polarisation, that it could not be envisaged as outweighing relative agreement on other more important, or more polarised dimensions.

The plausibility of the Fine Gael–Labour alliance is further under-lined by the data showing the relative distance between the individual parties, on the one hand, and the actual coalition programme, on the other. Again, on the first and most significant dimension, the coalition position is substantially closer to both Fine Gael and Labour than it is to Fianna Fáil, and while this is not the case for dimension 2, the distances involved are again so slight that they barely register. Finally,

on dimension 3, the coalition position is also found to be closer to both
Fine Gael and Labour and at quite a remove from the rather extraneous
position of Fianna Fáil.

In short, taking account of both the relative significance of the dimensions, as well as relative inter-party distances, the analysis of the 1969
programmes predicts the formation of a Fine Gael–Labour coalition in
1973. Far from opportunistic, circumstantial or situational factors
being so important as to outweigh policy differences, these data suggest
an essential policy compatibility pulling the two coalition parties
together, and a degree of ideological proximity which can only have
served to reinforce rather than to challenge any situational and office-
seeking incentives.

Finally, the analysis allows us to assess the relative impact of each of
the coalition parties on the joint programmes. Assessing the relative
distances between the 1973 coalition and the programmes of Labour,
on the one hand, and Fine Gael, on the other, allows us to assess the
parties' relative contributions to the joint policy. In other words, does
the coalition programme bear a greater Fine Gael stamp or a greater
Labour stamp? As far as dimensions 1 and 3 are concerned, the answer
is unequivocal: the coalition programme of 1973 bears much more
evidence of Fine Gael influence than it does that of Labour. On
dimension 1, the relative distance separating the 1973 coalition
programme from the 1969 Fine Gael programme is .12; in the Labour
case, it is .46. The respective figures for dimension 3 are .12 and 1.03.
The balance itself is not unexpected: given that Fine Gael was by far the
largest party in 1969, as it remains today, it is not surprising to find that
its policy concerns also have a commensurately greater weight. Thus,
not only does the analysis predict the formation of the Fine Gael–
Labour coalition in 1973, and so demonstrate the policy rationale of
that coalition, it also indicates a stronger Fine Gael voice in the content
of the joint programme, a bias proportionate to that party's greater
electoral and political weight. If coalition pay-offs are as meaningful to
policy as they are to the distribution of Cabinet seats, then the policy
pay-offs in the coalition in 1973 appear as the eminently rational
outcome of inter-party bargaining.

Conclusion

At the beginning of this analysis of the party programmes it was
suggested that prevailing views of the substance of Irish party competition appeared to imply that politics was either about nationalism or

about nothing at all. A nationalist opposition had structured the original formation of the party system and, for many observers, such an opposition was still the only substantive way of making sense of the contemporary alignment. Little else could be seen to divide the parties. The conservative roots of Fine Gael, as well as the party's enduring support among more well-to-do middle-class voters (cf. Chapter 1), did seem to indicate the possible maintenance of a more generalised radical-conservative opposition, but even this was belied by the coalition strategy adopted by Fine Gael, and by its enduring alliance with the Labour Party. An emphasis on the nationalist opposition also helped to account for the continued marginalisation of Labour itself, given that the party might have been expected to make greater electoral headway if inter-party divisions concerned such more conventional issues as welfare, distribution and class.

On the other hand, to the extent that nationalism was advanced as the key to an understanding of the contemporary alignment, other problems then arose: how, for instance, could one account for the sheer absence of references to traditional nationalism in the campaigns and appeals of the competing parties? How could one account for those opinion polls which evidenced a general popular indifference to issues which lay at the heart of nationalist concerns—such as the Northern Ireland problem—and which clearly showed that the voters were almost exclusively concerned with the more mundane issues of inflation, unemployment and economic growth (cf. Rose *et al.* 1978)?

Finally, and as was emphasised in Chapter 2, the growth of government in Ireland would seem to imply the immense relevance to many citizens of domestic economic policy and thus the immense relevance of what the parties have done in the past or are promising to do in the future *vis-à-vis* the economy. In such a context, it is not implausible to assume that at least some voters choose between the competing domestic appeals of the governing alternatives and, if that is the case, it should be possible for the analyst to distinguish these appeals. In short, there is an expectation that there are real differences between the parties, that these differences go beyond simply a historically defined nationalist opposition, and that they relate to and directly concern those economic and social options which face government on an everyday basis.

Hence the empirical analysis of election programmes. If there are differences between the parties, then the best way of ascertaining the nature of these differences is to look at what the parties themselves say and, in particular, to look at what they say in the intensely competitive arena of general election campaigns. Moreover, precisely because it is this arena which provides the context for the analysis, the focus of concern rests with the dimension(s) of competition rather than with the domain(s) of identification (cf. Sani and Sartori 1983). This distinction has been crucial to the overall analysis, particularly in so far as it has permitted a more discriminating approach to the role of traditional nationalism in party competition. Thus I have argued that although traditional nationalism may have remained an important element in contemporary Irish politics, its significance has lain mainly in the domain(s) of identification, and it has not played a crucial role in terms of the post-war dimension(s) of competition. Traditional nationalism may well provide the basis for the long-term generation of affective loyalties for particular parties, but it does not provide the basis for their strategy of competition or their electoral appeals. To judge from the election programmes at any rate, the parties do not appear to emphasise traditional nationalism as a means of attracting the support of those voters who actually choose between the parties. If election programmes do influence voting choice, then they do so on the basis of competing emphases on the economy, on welfare and on the style of government.

That said, the analytic distinction between domains of identification, on the one hand, and dimensions of competition, on the other, is often blurred in practice. In the Irish case, for instance, there is no doubt but that the principal dimension of competition, that between corporatist ideology and social democratic ideology, relates indirectly to the historical emphasis on traditional nationalism. Corporatist ideology is emphatic in its stress on social solidarity and the national interest, an emphasis which is quite congruent with the earlier concern for territorial integrity, and which certainly does not run counter to that earlier concern. In this sense, while Fianna Fáil may have substantially reconstructed its political appeal as it shifted from a traditional nationalist politics to a more corporatist emphasis, the party cannot be said to have simply jettisoned its past. Thus, despite a virtual U-turn in practical policies, and despite the shift from protectionism to free trade, the language of corporatism allowed the party to maintain its national-ist credentials and to continue to assert itself as the national party. The national interest may have been recast and redefined, but Fianna Fáil retained its role as the party which could best serve that national interest.

This analysis of the election programmes and of the main dimension of competition has also pointed to what, at the risk of some exaggeration, may be termed an ideological realignment of Irish politics in the 1960s. This can be seen in the common ground discovered by Fine Gael and Labour and in their shared social democratic appeal. As the economy grew in an unprecedented way in the 1960s, and as domestic resources multiplied, the two parties redefined the terrain from which they would compete with Fianna Fáil. Both parties emphasised an appeal for social justice and for the more egalitarian redistribution of national wealth. While Fianna Fáil argued that the expansion of resources would eventually benefit all citizens, the smaller parties insisted that a more immediate redistribution of resources was necessary. Their common ground eventually facilitated an electoral alliance, and the formation of a two-party coalition which was to displace Fianna Fáil from government for the first time in 16 years. Despite subsequent intra-coalition disputes, this two-party alliance persisted until 1987. While the frustrations of opposition and the urge for office alone may have created the incentive for coalition in 1973, this analysis reveals that there was also a substantial policy rationale underlying the alliance which could not but augment any of the more opportunistic incentives.

This analysis has been restricted to the period from 1961 to 1982 and, I feel, accurately reflects the dynamic of party competition in that period. There is a strong case to be made, however, that the terms of reference have changed more recently, and that the combination of economic difficulties and partisan strategic considerations may force a new alignment in the party system. These themes will be addressed in the final chapter.

Notes

1. Earlier and very preliminary versions of this analysis have been reported elsewhere: the chapter on Ireland (Mair 1987b) in the first publication of the ECPR research group on party manifestos reports an analysis applying the original ECPR scheme to election programmes published between 1948 and 1981. It should also be noted that, for some of the cases in this 1948–81 analysis, manifesto surrogates were employed which have since been discarded in favour of more reliable documentation. A more recent analysis of those data which deal solely with economic policy has been reported in Mair (1986a). The original data set, coded into the ECPR categories, is available on request from the ESRC Data Archive in the University of Essex.
2. For details of these modifications, see the notes to Table 4.1.
3. The cut-off point for including categories in the subsequent analysis is that adopted by the ECPR group, which is to exclude categories registering less than 1 per cent when averaging all party programmes taken together,

unless any of the categories averages at least 3 per cent in the case of any one party. The following categories are therefore excluded: *relationship with Britain* (.06% overall average); *decolonisation* (.03%); *peace* (.96%); *internationalism—positive* (.56%); *internationalism—negative* (0%); *EC and Nato—positive* (.50%); *EC and Nato—negative* (.08%); *constitutionalism—positive* (.12%); *constitutionalism—negative* (.10%); *decentralisation—negative* (.05%); *government corruption* (.36%); *protectionism—negative* (.14%); *non-specific economic goals* (.81%); *Keynsian demand management* (.02%); *nationalisation* (.59%); *defence of the Irish way of life—negative* (.37%); *traditional morality—positive* (.06%); *traditional morality—negative* (0%). This leaves just 18 categories (and 22 cases) to be included in the factor analysis.

4. The contest in the constituency of Dublin North-East in 1973 where—appropriately—the leading Labour candidate was Conor Cruise O'Brien and the leading Fianna Fáil candidate was Charles Haughey, afforded an interesting insight into the problem of being seen as 'anti-national'. Given O'Brien's opposition to nationalist politics, and given Haughey's evident republicanism, territorial nationalism inevitably proved a major debating issue at local level, with O'Brien facing persistent accusations of being 'anti-national'. Yet, rather than defend their candidate's opposition to nationalism *per se*, the local Labour party took great pains to fudge the question. Thus, a cyclo-styled 'Notes for Canvassers' issued by the local party quoted John Hume, a leading figure in the major constitutional nationalist party of Northern Ireland, the Social Democratic and Labour Party, as having 'strongly condemned efforts to depict honest critics of this policy [i.e. the policy of calling for Irish unity] like Conor Cruise O'Brien as anti-national'. While restating O'Brien's belief that the call for unity in the circumstances then prevailing was both 'futile and dangerous', the leaflet insisted that 'this does not mean that those concerned reject the aspiration (*sic*) towards eventual unity of all the people of Ireland, peacefully through full consent of both communities'. In the end, perhaps the clearest proof of O'Brien's assertion of the sinfulness of being anti-national is that even those viewed as guilty will strenuously protest their innocence.

5. The analogy of the 'rising tide' and the counterclaim that 'some boats cannot wait' were adopted as recently as February 1982 in the television debate between the party leaders (noted by the author).

6. Indeed, it is also tempting to consider quite a full-scale study of the similarities between Fianna Fáil and Gaullism, particularly given that both parties now sit together in the European Parliament.

7. It is interesting to note that in a 1968 postal ballot, members of Fine Gael rejected by 653 votes to 81 a motion which called for the party name to be changed to Fine Gael—the Social Democratic Party' (Gallagher 1982, p. 85)

5
THE CHANGING IRISH PARTY SYSTEM

Despite the emphasis throughout this study, it is evident that one can only go so far in treating the independent impact of the parties and the party system as explanatory factors. Beyond a certain point, parties no longer enjoy the capacity to control their environment. And while the parties do indeed help to determine the terms of reference of mass politics, and do constrain voter choice, they inevitably do so in circumstances which are not of their own making. In the absence of class conditions, for example, no amount of emphasis on class politics is likely to persuade a class alignment. In a wholly secular society, no amount of emphasis on a politics of religion is likely to persuade a confessional alignment.

In the same vein, albeit in a more general sense, it can be argued that certain ideological appeals achieve a particular resonance in certain social and economic contexts, and that these same appeals may falter in alternative contexts. More specifically, and what is especially relevant to the Irish case, it can be argued that particular appeals may prove functional to certain electoral strategies at a time of economic growth and expansion, and yet prove quite disfunctional to these strategies in a context of recession and retrenchment. Thus, for example, I would argue that the corporatist appeal of Fianna Fáil found particular resonance in the 1960s and early 1970s, and facilitated the party's cross-class electoral strategy, precisely because this was a period of economic expansionism, and that the impetus behind the Fine Gael shift towards social democracy was also favoured by this favourable economic environment. In this sense, both appeals may be considered somewhat contingent, and, in a context of austerity, their increasing vulnerability can be anticipated. The following pages will attempt an elaboration of this view.

The Constraints on Party Strategy

The first point which must be emphasised is that the experience of the 1950s had done little to inspire popular confidence in Ireland's capacity to survive and advance as an independent nation. Within a decade of the declaration of a republic in 1948, Ireland's economic prospects seemed exceptionally bleak. The annual growth in GDP in the 1950s had averaged just 1 per cent; employment in industry had fallen by some 9 per cent, and in agriculture by some 24 per cent; total emigration in the 1950s totalled some 400,000 (Maguire 1985, p. 295; Rottman and O'Connell 1982, p. 67; Blackwell 1982, p. 43). With poor unemployment prospects, a stagnating economy, and with under-developed and poorly financed social programmes, disillusion with government was pervasive. If independence was to prove meaningful, therefore, and if the parties were to prove credible in the eyes of the working class and the disadvantaged, it was necessary to achieve massive economic growth and expansion, and, in particular, it was necessary to build an effective welfare state. Political support could no longer be mobilised simply on the basis that Ireland should control its own destiny; independence now also required the realisation of more tangible benefits.

All three parties responded to these needs with a renewed and vigorous commitment to welfarism, and all three sought to extend or to consolidate their support among working-class voters (see, Chapter 4). But while there emerged a clear consensus on welfarism, the language and ideology within which that commitment was expressed differed markedly across the political spectrum.

In very general terms, the key difference lay in the contrasting emphases on *redistributive issues*. Fianna Fáil laid greater emphasis on overall economic expansion, arguing that the poorer sectors of the community would benefit *in concert with* the more privileged sectors, and that the rising tide would lift *all* boats. To adopt an alternative metaphor, the national pie would expand, and hence the different sections of the pie would also expand, but the larger pie would be sliced no differently than before. This qualification is not intended to detract from the Fianna Fáil commitment. On the contrary, as Bew and Patterson (1982, Chapter 6) show, Lemass evinced a genuine and coherent commitment to welfarism and insisted that the strategy for economic revitalisation be accompanied by the more effective in-corporation of working-class interests and demands through both job creation and social spending. But precisely because these interests would be accommodated in concert with the interests of business and capital, Lemass's own definition of the strategy as 'a shift to the Left' (ibid., p. 160) is misleading. The strategy was a national strategy, the appeal was in no sense socially exclusive, and the ideology was essentially corporatist. In the end, the appeal was also contingent. The gains for the working class could only come in the context of gains for the society as a whole. Welfarism may have been central to the party's corporatist ideology, but given that it was not a primarily redistributive ideology, then the commitment to social progress was inevitably dependent on the realisation of economic progress. Without economic progress, therefore, the emphasis on welfarism would falter, and with it would falter the overall appeal of corporatist ideology itself.

The picture seemed to be different on the other side of the political spectrum, where the commitment to welfarism was distinctly distributive. As far as Labour and Fine Gael were concerned, the working class and the disadvantaged should benefit in relative as well as in absolute terms. The national pie should expand, but it should also be sliced differently than before. Labour's commitment in this regard proved quite unequivocal, as the party evinced a sharp turn to the left in the 1960s and, rhetorically at any rate, articulated an unabashed commitment to socialist policies (cf. Gallagher 1982, Chapter 4). Fine Gael also moved to the left, emphasising social justice and redistribution, and joining with Labour in a generalised social democratic appeal. Emerging from the shambles of the second coalition government in the late 1950s, Fine Gael consciously sought to broaden its appeal beyond its traditionally conservative and largely middle-class constituency.

However, it is also important to recognise that while Fine Gael may have emphasised redistribution, its actual *electoral strategy* was more akin to that of Fianna Fáil than to that of Labour. Labour in the 1960s, to some extent at least, was attempting to persuade a class alignment in Irish politics. The party's appeal was relatively divisive and exclusive, primarily aimed at attracting the support of the working class and the trade unions *rather than* that of other groups in Irish society. Fine Gael, on the other hand, like Fianna Fáil, was concerned to win the support of the working class and trade unions *as well as* that of other groups. Each of the two larger parties sought to extend their appeal to the constituency of the deprived, but both also sought to retain their support among the more privileged sectors of the community.

This catch-all approach is more obviously demonstrable in the case of Fianna Fáil than that of Fine Gael, since the corporatist appeal of the former emphasised benefits for all, whereas the social democratic and redistributive appeal of the latter emphasised relative benefits for the disadvantaged. In other words, since the Fine Gael appeal seems to have been as potentially divisive as that of Labour, it may seem difficult to view it as also contributing to an electoral strategy which was not socially specific. Indeed, there is clear evidence from the 1960s to suggest that sections within Fine Gael were worried that the newly discovered social democratic appeal might indeed alienate the party's traditional middle-class constituency. In the wake of the 1965 election, for instance, when Fine Gael first campaigned on the basis of the *Just Society* proposals, an anonymous internal party report (UCDFG P39/BF17(b)) expressed strong doubts as to the potential divisiveness of the new commitment:

> It is clear from the results in Dublin and Cork that we are to some extent losing the support of a group which has consistently provided our staunchest supporters, the urban middle class . . . For too many years we have taken it for granted that the middle-class voter should vote for Fine Gael without being offered anything in return. The voting figures—and the abstention figures—show that day is passing. The complaint has been made that the published Fine Gael policy does not offer any reason whatever why any middle-class voter should vote for Fine Gael and that there is no place in Fine Gael's 'Just Society' for the middle-class man except as a beast of burden for the rest of the community.

But although the shift to the left may have led to some erosion of the party's traditional middle-class support base, nevertheless Fine Gael did manage to retain a substantial base in that constituency. The 1969 Gallup survey, for example, showed the party winning the endorsement of some 37 per cent of the most privileged social category (the AB group—cf. Table 1.6), and of some 16 per cent of working-class voters.

How was this balance achieved? How did Fine Gael retain a substantial middle-class vote at a time when its policies emphasised the need for redistribution? In the first place, and most obviously, for all the rhetoric involved, social policy in Ireland has not been *pronouncedly* redistributive in practice. To be sure, the income maintenance programme has been expanded considerably, as has expenditure on public housing and health and education. At the same time, however, much of the expansion of spending programmes has also benefited the more privileged sectors, while the emphasis on indirect taxation as a major source of welfare finance is in itself regressive. Thus Maguire's (1985, p. 136) analysis of the Irish case concludes that 'the redistributive process operates unevenly from a social class perspective, treating the property owning classes in a relatively favourable fashion'.

What was arguably of greater significance, however, was that the demand for redistribution had been articulated within a context of *overall* growth and expansion. Thus even if the promise of increased social spending was seen to be of relative benefit to the disadvantaged, the relative costs to the more privileged have to be seen in a context in which the latter were also gaining in absolute terms. Since the national pie was growing, any proposal to slice it in a new fashion did not appear overly costly. In a context of growth, even the more privileged could afford to be altruistic.[1]

In short, economic expansion proved as crucial to the electoral strategy of Fine Gael as it did to that of Fianna Fáil. Continued growth allowed Fianna Fáil to pledge benefits for all, including the disadvantaged, and rendered plausible the party's corporatist appeal. Continued growth also ensured that Fine Gael could emphasise a social democratic appeal and the need for some redistribution, and so allowed it to extend its support into the working class without risking too large an erosion of its traditional middle-class constituency (cf. the data up to 1982 in Table 1.7).

The success of both catch-all strategies was therefore more or less predicated on continued growth, and the resonance which they achieved in the 1960s and 1970s derived precisely from the unprecedented expansionism in that period. The extent of economic growth is unquestionable, and a few indicators will suffice. Between 1957 and 1980, for example, Gross Domestic Product grew in real terms by an annual average of slightly more than 4 per cent (Maguire 1985, p. 295), while real personal disposable income more than doubled (Blackwell 1982, p. 45). Employment in industry increased by some 28 per cent, and in the service sector by more than 33 per cent. Perhaps most telling of all, a century-long trend in emigration was finally reversed, and Ireland experienced net immigration in the 1970s for the first time since the mid-nineteenth century (ibid., pp. 47–8). In relative terms, this was indeed the golden age, and a threat to the catch-all strategies of both major parties could only be anticipated if and when economic progress began to falter.

The potential problems to be posed by economic contraction were obvious. In such a recessionary situation, the corporatist emphasis on benefiting all and hurting none would no longer appear plausible—nobody would benefit and all would hurt. At the same time, as far as the social democratic emphasis on redistribution is concerned, any altruistic incentive would be undermined, and the more privileged sectors would be unwilling to hurt more simply in order that the less privileged would hurt less. In a recessionary context, therefore, a corporatist appeal might achieve little resonance, while a social-democratic appeal might well prove so divisive that it could no longer reap aggregate, cross-class electoral benefits.

Ireland now finds itself in just such a situation. Again, a few indicators will suffice: Between 1980 and 1986, real Gross Domestic Product has grown by an annual average of less than 2 per cent (*Economic Review and Outlook* 1986), while real personal disposable income has fallen by 7 per cent (NESC 1986, p. 182). The number of persons claiming unemployment benefit has more than doubled since 1980 and, on the eve of the 1987 election, totalled some 250,000, or 20 per cent of the labour force. Emigration had also begun to accelerate once more, and totalled some 100,000 between 1982 and 1986. Increased poverty and dependence meant that, by 1985, some 18 per cent of GNP was taken up by transfer payments—mainly in the health and welfare programmes—as against 12.5 per cent in 1977, while social expenditure in general had risen from 28.9 per cent of GNP in 1980 to 35.6 per cent in 1985 (NESC 1986). This was accompanied by a more general increase in current public expenditure from 41.1 per cent of GNP in 1980 to 49.9 per cent in 1985, and by a growth in the budget deficit from 6.1 per cent to 8.4 per cent of GNP in the same period. Together with borrowing for capital expenditure, this has meant a very high Public Sector Borrowing Requirement—17.3 per cent of GNP in 1980 and 16 per cent in 1985; a growth in the total national debt—from 94 per cent of GNP in 1980 to a staggering 133 per cent in 1985; and an increasing expenditure on debt service—from 8.2 per cent of GNP in 1980 to 12.9 per cent in 1985 (all figures from NESC 1986). In short, a slowdown in overall growth has created an extraordinarily severe fiscal crisis and has forced a politics of austerity and retrenchment.

So what have been the effects of this environmental change on the appeals of the parties? One of the most immediate consequences has been to push elements of Fine Gael in a more rightward direction, with significant pressure within the party for a renewal of its traditional stance in favour of fiscal rectitude. Amid accusations of being monetarist and Thatcherite, senior figures within the party began to rail against the excessive tax burden and to insist on cuts in public spending and a general policy of retrenchment. For the first time since 1973, serious rifts emerged within the coalition itself, with the increasingly right-wing statements from the more conservative elements in Fine Gael provoking serious disagreements with Labour, which remained committed to a redistributive programme. While the details of the Fine

Gael shift need not be of concern here, nor the catalogue of intra-coalition wrangling (see O'Leary 1984; Horgan 1986; O'Byrnes 1986), nevertheless it is important to underline that the political fallout from this new recessionary context had driven a wedge between the two parties, and eventually led to the collapse of the coalition in January 1987.[2] Early in 1986, for example, a senior Fine Gael backbencher complained that Fine Gael had been 'contaminated' by the left-wing philosophy of Labour, a view which was effectively endorsed by more than 40 per cent of Fine Gael backbenchers in a survey carried out by *Magill* magazine: 'We have good relationships with Labour in government', remarked one of the backbenchers, 'but they genuinely hold a philosophy which is different from ours' (O'Toole 1986, p. 19).

Precisely because of the party's cross-class electoral appeal, proponents of social democracy within Fine Gael faced evident difficulties. The constituency of the deprived could not be ignored, while at the same time the recessionary environment had acted to undermine any sense of altruism among more privileged voters. Indeed, the problem was already apparent in the late 1970s when, in a revealing interview with *Magill* (January 1978, p. 14), party leader Garrett FitzGerald commented that

> [The redistribution of wealth] cannot conceivably be regarded as completed in the light of the fact that at least 20 per cent of our population lives in poverty. This means that a significant proportion of future increments of wealth must be distributed to alleviate property. But we have to face the reluctance of a majority of the people to accept a reduction of living standards in favour of the minority. This reluctance is most evident in a no-growth period, as during the recent world crisis, whereas when prosperity is increasing, it is easier to win acceptance of redistributive measures.

That said, the social democratic emphases were not going to be easily abandoned. To the extent that Fine Gael was attempting to achieve an overall, single-party majority, it simply could not afford to revert to a distinctively middle-class appeal. In 1979, for example, FitzGerald told a meeting of the party's trade-union conference that 'Fine Gael is now seeking to become the acknowledged party of the working man and woman' (*Irish Times*, 5 February 1979). More recently, in a Dáil speech emphasising the extent of the fiscal crisis, he also insisted that 'more and more we must direct our resources in a discriminating manner towards those most in need' (*Irish Times*, 19 December 1985).

There were repurcussions on the Fianna Fáil side also, where the new recessionary environment appeared to undermine the party's corporatist appeal of Fianna Fáil, dependent as it was on expansionism and growth. In many ways, 1977 had proved the high point of the Fianna Fáil corporatist appeal. This was despite the fact that the beginning of the recession itself can be dated back to the mid-1970s, in the wake of the 1973 oil shock. In 1977, however, the Fianna Fáil appeal remained predicated on an expanding economy and on a capacity to benefit all and to hurt none. The catalogue of the party's 1977 promises has already been noted (see chapter 2), including the pledge to abolish domestic rates, to abolish car tax, and to offer I£1,000 grants to first-time buyers of new houses. Together with its welfarist commitments, the Fianna Fáil programme essentially boiled down to a promise to increase spending while reducing tax revenue, and the popular response was inevitably resounding. Yet precisely because this high point of the corporatist appeal coincided with a deepening recession, the recessionary problems were themselves accentuated, for the equation of high spending and reduced tax revenue could only be squared through increased borrowing. Thus, for example, in the four-year term of Fianna Fáil government, the budget deficit increased from less than 4 per cent of GNP to more than 7 per cent, while the total PSBR increased from some 13 per cent of GNP to some 21 per cent in the same period (*Building on Reality* 1984, Figure 7.1).

It is perhaps coincidence, although I believe this to be unlikely, that it is in the wake of this crisis that Fianna Fáil has rediscovered its traditional nationalist—as opposed to corporatist—appeal. As the recession has deepened, so also has the party's commitment to traditional politics. Since the succession to the leadership of Charles Haughey in an internal party coup in 1979 (Garvin 1981b; Walsh 1986), Fianna Fáil has proclaimed a renewed emphasis on anti-partitionism and on the need for Irish territorial unity. In practical terms, this has led the party to insist on a unitary-state solution as the primary means of resolving the Northern Ireland crisis, and has also led it to oppose the recent Anglo-Irish Agreement which, according to Haughey (Dáil Debates, 361:2586, 19 November 1985), has obliged the Republic to renounce its constitutional claim to unity. This emphasis on territorial nationalism pervaded the Dáil debate on the Agreement (Mair 1987c), with Fianna Fáil clearly distinguishing itself from the other parties by insisting—in deputy leader Brian Lenihan's phrase—that 'we now find ourselves as a lone party with the Nationalist forces' (Dáil Debates 361:3122, 21 November 1985). Haughey himself proved no less equivocal: 'we will stand up for our nationalist ideals that up until recently we believed were shared by all parties. We are not going to abandon the basic reason for our foundation as a political movement ... [W]e are not prepared to surrender by desertion the constitutional nationalist position' (Dáil Debates 361:2600, 19 November 1985).

The details of the nature and extent of this renewed commitment to traditional nationalism, and the degree to which it countered the attitudes which had prevailed in Fianna Fáil under Lemass and Lynch in the 1960s and 1970s, do not need to be rehearsed in this particular context (cf. Cox 1985; Walsh 1986; Mair 1987c). Nor is it necessary to document the party's renewed commitment to traditional morality, as exemplified in the alacrity with which it supported the introduction of a constitutional ban on abortion, in its opposition to the final removal of the remaining prohibitions on contraception, and most recently in its effective opposition to the removal of the constitutional ban on divorce (for details, see Cooney 1986; Girvin 1986; Walsh 1986). What these developments do indicate, however, is that through a rediscovery of its more traditional appeals, Fianna Fáil had begun to move away from, or at least begun to complement, the post-1950s emphasis on corporatist ideology. If the corporatism of Lemass and Lynch could no longer prove an effective binding agent for the party's cross-class coalition, then perhaps the Haughey emphasis on more traditional appeals would offer an effective substitute: as Walsh (1986, p. 157) concludes, the party in the mid-1980s was 'marrying religious and political fundamentalism— the partners of the past—with an eye to electoral opportunity'. And while this may simply be coincidence, it is also important to recognise that this shift occurred precisely when the recessionary environment could have been expected to undermine the plausibility of the corporatist appeal.[3]

Fianna Fáil's renewed emphasis on traditional politics, therefore, can be seen as an attempt to rebuild its mass support base in a period of increasing electoral vulnerability. At the same time, however, it involved the party in a number of specific costs. More specifically, the reversion to the past under the leadership of Charles Haughey provoked a serious split within the party, with the more militant anti-partitionist stance precipitating the departure of a number of key figures and the formation of the Progressive Democrats in early 1986. The new party is committed to supporting a more accommodationist stance towards Northern Ireland, and endorsed both the recent Anglo-Irish Agreement and the attempts to effect a more pluralist culture in the Republic itself, and, as such, owes more to the modernising impulses of Fianna Fáil under Lemass and Lynch than to the more traditional stance which has dominated the party under Haughey (Mair 1987c).

In terms of this present analysis, however, what is even more significant is that the Progressive Democrats also articulate a distinct *class* appeal, urging a reduction of both taxation and public spending, and emphasising the need to place a greater reliance on private enterprise and the market in any anti-recessionary economic strategy. In an approach which strongly echoes the emphases of the British Conservative Party under Margaret Thatcher, the Progressive Democrats' first policy statement in the fields of taxation and public spending (Progressive Democrats 1986, p. 17) proposed

 (i) A radical programme of reform of the tax system leading to a low single income tax rate of 25% and VAT rate of 15%. The widening of the VAT base to include food will require cash compensation to those on low incomes.
 (ii) Commensurate decreases in current public spending.
 (iii) A programme of privatisation or divestment of State assets.
 (iv) A radically new budgetary philosophy which works on the basis of a sustainable tax system rather than an unsustainable level of spending.
 (v) A fundamental shift in the balance of economic power from the State to the people.

Over and above its more accommodating stance on Northern Ireland and church–state issues, the new party is therefore promoting a fiscal policy which aims to win support from the constituency of the more privileged at a time when recession has undermined the appeal of redistributionist programmes. Early opinion polls (e.g., *Irish Times*, 11 February 1986) also indicated that this strategy met with a certain degree of success, and that the party had achieved a particularly favourable response from middle-class voters (see also Table 1.8). And this, in turn, brings us back to the strains within Fine Gael. For, in what might be considered as a conservative attempt to persuade a class alignment, the Progressive Democrats reflect precisely the same impetus which has driven elements of Fine Gael to the right.

While the new recessionary environment therefore has had a differing effect on the two main parties—encouraging a drift from redistributive politics in the case of Fine Gael and inducing a return to traditional politics in the case of Fianna Fáil—it has also clarified a new conservativism which, as encapsulated by the Progressive Democrats, has found a substantial degree of resonance in *both* parties. Thus although it was a division in Fianna Fáil which precipitated the formation of the new party, nevertheless early surveys indicated that some 70 per cent of Fine Gael voters approved the notion of a Fine Gael–Progressive Democrats coalition (*Irish Times*, 11 February 1986; 3 November 1986). In addition, the 1986 survey of Fine Gael backbench opinion also reported a preference for coalition with the new party rather than with Labour; indeed, when asked whether they saw any major policy differences dividing Fine Gael from the Progressive Democrats, only 13 per cent of the backbenchers said yes, while some 53 per cent saw no major differences at all—the remainder were unsure (O'Toole 1986).

The 1987 Election

By 1986, the party system was in flux. The recessionary context had appeared to force Fianna Fáil into a more defensive position in which it attempted to resurrect traditional appeals as a means of cementing its broad cross-class coalition. Fine Gael had been driven away from social democracy, and despite occasional protests from Garret FitzGerald, had begun to evince a more explicitly conservative appeal than had been the case since the late 1950s. This shift to the right had forced a rift with Labour, which eventually withdrew from government in an attempt to forge an independent left strategy. Finally, and perhaps most significantly, the new recessionary context had opened up a space on the right for the new Progressive Democrats. The situation was to crystallise in the 1987 election.

The first and most important development in 1987 was the PD threat to the middle-class heartland of Fine Gael. The new party urged a policy of privatisation, sharp reductions in personal taxation, and severe cuts in government spending. It was an unashamedly middle-class appeal, designed to tap into the frustrations of a relatively privileged community which felt beaten down by punitive rates of taxation and by what was perceived to be the drain of productive resources into an overextended and costly welfare state. It was also a successful appeal. Pre-election polls revealed a marked swing to the new party, and a substantial erosion of Fine Gael popularity. Competition on the right had intensified.

The emergence of the PDs and the proven popularity of their appeal were more or less to destroy the last vestiges of social democracy in Fine Gael. Facing severe competition on the right, and heading towards a major decline in its middle-class support, Fine Gael entered the election with a programme which recalled the high point of its period under John A. Costello in the 1950s. The party spoke of economic orthodoxy and fiscal rectitude and little else. The priority was to balance the government accounts, and this could only be achieved by severe cuts in both current and capital spending and by reducing the borrowing requirement. State assets were to be privatised and growth, if it were to be achieved, could only result from stimulating the market through tax cuts, lower interest rates and, if necessary, through a deregulation of the labour market. The theme of social justice was noticeable only for its absence.

Labour, meanwhile, moved to the left. Accepting the need for a more equitable balance between government revenue and government spending, the party nevertheless argued that any immediate cuts would simply hurt the poor and the less privileged. If balance were to be achieved, then the essential solution lay in an increase in revenue, and this in turn could be achieved through the more effective taxation of farmers, the self-employed, and the wealthy. The principal slogan adopted by Labour in 1987 was 'Stop the Cuts', and the party found itself increasingly aligned with the Workers Party, and increasingly at odds with both the PDs and its former coalition ally, Fine Gael.

A new left–right polarisation therefore emerged in 1987, pitting Labour and the Workers Party against Fine Gael and the Progressive Democrats. 'That's Irish politics', remarked PD leader Des O'Malley in an interview shortly after the formation of the new party. 'There's no great divide between the right and the left, as in Britain, and there never will be' (*Irish Times*, 17 January 1986). Ironically, it was the very success of PD mobilisation which was to belie his optimism.

The key question remained, of course, as to how Fianna Fáil would adapt to this newly polarised situation. In the event, and again perhaps ironically, the sheer process of polarisation enabled the party to recover the centre ground of Irish politics, and to launch a programme which, 30 years on, proved a virtual replay of the appeal articulated by Séan Lemass in 1957. The fragmentation of the non-Fianna Fáil constituency placed Ireland's traditionally dominant party in the position which it found the most congenial of all: once again, Fianna Fáil was the only party which was likely to be in a position to form a stable, single-party government and, as the long campaign wore on, this undeniable electoral asset was flaunted as often and as widely as party resources permitted.

But this was just one of the weapons in the party armoury. In addition, and in contradistinction to Fine Gael and the Progressive

Democrats, Fianna Fáil also renewed its commitment to welfarism, and while accepting the need for some degree of fiscal balance, the leadership proved adamant in its refusal to commit itself to cuts which would fall most heavily on those in need. Second, in concert with the Workers Party and Labour, Fianna Fáil underlined the need for growth as the only real solution to the economic ills. To reduce public spending *per se* was no solution; rather, it was necessary to go for growth, which would mean more employment, more taxation revenue, and a reduction in welfare spending. Third, the party emphasised the need for social solidarity, urging a revitalisation of the social partnership of labour, capital and agriculture, in a concerted drive to build national resources. Indeed, as with Lemass, the incorporation of the unions was seen as a necessary element in a new industrial strategy, and it appears that it was the effort to secure the endorsement of the public sector unions in particular which lay behind the Fianna Fáil refusal to endorse the privatisation proposals of the new right.

Thirty years on, the echoes of Lemass proved remarkably strong: the emphasis on growth and the reassertion of the national interest; the attempt to incorporate the unions and the plea for social solidarity; and, not least, the stress on stable, single-party government, coming, as in 1957, in the wake of the break-up of the non-Fianna Fáil coalition. Notwithstanding the earlier emphasis on traditional nationalism, the 1987 election witnessed a substantial restoration of the corporatist imagery of Fianna Fáil, and in 1987, as before, it was presented as the only viable solution to Ireland's economic ills.

But it is also clear that the circle has not closed completely. Fianna Fáil in 1987 is not the same as Fianna Fáil in 1957, and the society which it seeks to manage has also changed substantially. Thus, while the corporatist appeal was adopted as readily in 1987 as it had been in 1957, the response which it generated has proved quite different.

In 1957, in the wake of a decade of alternating governments, and following the collapse of the anti-Fianna Fáil coalition, Fianna Fáil returned to power with 48 per cent of the popular vote and an overall Dáil majority. In 1987, in the wake of almost 15 years of alternating governments, Fianna Fáil has managed to win just 44 per cent of the popular vote and—for the fourth time in succession—has fallen short of an overall Dáil majority. In 1957 Ireland went for growth in an international context of expanding markets and eager investors, basing its economic strategy on the attraction of foreign capital. In 1987 it is going for growth in a context of stagnant markets and cautious investors, and its most immediate problem is that of halting the flight of capital away from the Irish economy. Finally, Ireland in 1987 is attempting to maintain a massive public sector and a costly and still ineffective welfare state, while at the same time it is attempting to reconcile the demands of increasingly conscious and conflictual class interests.

In the late 1950s and the 1960s, Fianna Fáil held the centre ground while Fine Gael and Labour struggled to find a new political identity. Now, as Fianna Fáil once more tries to hold the centre, it is confronted by a left which, although electorally weaker, is also more articulate and less compromising. In addition, Fianna Fáil confronts the opposition of Fine Gael and the Progressive Democrats, which together reflect quite a fully-mobilised and politically self-conscious middle-class constituency. In one sense, this situation is advantageous for Fianna Fáil—the sharp divisions between left and right suggest that any combination against the centre is unlikely (except perhaps on the pluralism—traditionalism dimension—see below). In another sense, however, the outlook may not be so propitious. To the extent that the clash of class interests becomes exacerbated, then Fianna Fáil's own capacity to retain a broad cross-class coalition must be questionable: as the 1987 election polls indicate (Tables 1.7 and 1.8), Fianna Fáil has already begun to lose its hold among the middle class, and the social profile of the party's constituency is now much more skewed towards the working class than at any stage since 1969.

So where does this leave the ideological mosaic of Irish politics in the late 1980s? What is the pattern of contemporary alignments? One thing is certain: while Fianna Fáil may have resurrected its corporatist appeal, the broadly-based social democratic opposition has been eradicated by the recession, and Fianna Fáil must now compete to the right as well as to the left. Moreover, Fianna Fáil must also take account of one other dimension of competition which has emerged with some force in the mid-1980s, and which may well be the only basis for a combination of right and left against the centre. For want of a better term, this may be defined as a pluralism—traditionalism dimension, positing a secularist, anti-irredentist politics in opposition to traditional nationalism and the espousal of orthodox Catholic values. Such a divide was clearly evident during the abortion and divorce referendum campaigns, as well as during the debate on the 1985 Anglo-Irish Agreement, and offers the only potentially enduring dimension of competition which might lead Labour and the Workers Party to join Fine Gael and the Progressive Democrats in opposition to the traditionalism of Fianna Fáil.

In effect, therefore, the present alignment and its potential alliances are triangular rather than one-dimensional (see Figure 5.1—for a similar treatment of the West German party system, see Pappi, 1984), with Fianna Fáil and the left finding possible common ground in a shared commitment to welfarism and the involvement of the unions in the elaboration of economic and industrial strategy. Meanwhile, Fianna Fáil and the right may also find common ground in a shared commitment to the market and to private enterprise, while left and right may find common ground in a shared opposition to the traditional values espoused by Fianna Fáil. In 1987, however, in the wake of the most volatile election in post-war Irish history, and confronted by a new party of the right which may yet demonstrate a capacity to survive and grow, all must remain in the realm of speculation. Moreover, it must be emphasised that this imputed alignment is based on party positions as elaborated in the 1987 election programmes; in office, Fianna Fáil may well prove as reluctant to maintain welfare spending as was Fine Gael in its final months of office.

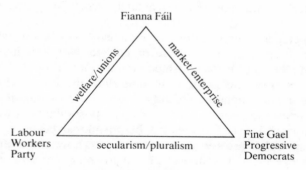

Figure 5.1. Party alignments, 1987

Lessons from Ireland?

One of the most fundamental problems confronted by the contemporary literature on Western European politics is that of determining the extent of party-system persistence and change. More often than not, the problem is addressed in terms of a simple dichotomy: can individual party systems, or even party systems in general, be characterised as persistent or can they be characterised as changing? Are contemporary party systems stable or are they unstable?

As this particular study makes clear, however, such a simple dichotomy is in many senses invalid. An individual party system cannot just be defined as *either* persisting *or* changing, but rather both persists *and* changes at one and the same time. Party systems are complex, multi-dimensional structures, which defy easy and all-embracing characterisations, and while change may be evident along any one dimension, other systemic dimensions may well be characterised by persistence. Indeed, one can go so far as to suggest that these dimensions or levels may sometimes move in opposite directions, such that persistence at one level is *only* made possible through change at other levels. For example, it is easy to conceive of a party system which is characterised by aggregate electoral stability precisely *because* there have been changes at the level of organisation, ideology or strategy. In this case, the parties would have retained their aggregate electoral support because they had proved capable of adaptation, modifying their appeals or their competitive orientations in order to sustain their overall electoral popularity. Conversely, the various levels may change together, in that it is also easy to conceive of cases where organisational, ideological or strategic changes actually *result* in overall electoral change.

The point is, therefore, not to establish 'rules' about when it is possible to speak of persistence or change. Nor is it intended to establish clear causal relationships between one level of change and another. Rather, the point is to underline the complexity of the problem, and to emphasise the difficulties involved in deriving reasonably all-embracing conclusions about a party system 'as a whole'. As was emphasised in the Introduction, before one can begin to talk about party system change as such, it is necessary to know *who* is affected by the change, *what* is the source of change, *when* does change occur and, most importantly, *which* dimensions of change are relevant.

It is also reasonable to suggest that this multi-dimensional perspective can only be achieved through a more *intensive* research strategy (Sartori 1970), one which is capable of offering a more in-depth analysis of a limited number of party systems or, as in this case, of just one party system. In this sense, it is necessary to emphasise once again that this study of the Irish party system is offered as a somewhat cautionary example of the complexities involved in the analysis of party system change and persistence rather than as a case study in the application of some more general phenomenon.

So what can be learned from this study of the Irish party system? There are six elements in particular which stand out. The most obvious point to note is that Ireland shows that an apparently pronounced degree of aggregate electoral continuity may conceal a considerable degree of immediate and/or 'subsystem' fluctuation and change. While the configuration of the party system in the late post-war period bore a striking similarity to that of the early 1930s, this can be more accurately described as a *reconstruction* of the traditional alignment rather than as simple persistence. But while this in itself is a largely uncontentious conclusion, it is important in so far as it allows a specification of precisely what it is that needs to be explained in the Irish case. In other words, rather than explaining persistence as such, which would involve a focus on how the *initial* alignment was frozen into place, and hence would stress the very early and formative years of mass politics, an emphasis on reconstruction or restoration permits a stress on the ongoing dynamic of the party system and on the ideologies, strategies and competitive orientations of the parties *throughout* the history of the state.

Second, this study has also emphasised the extent to which this 'subsystem' fluctuation at the aggregate electoral level has impacted *unevenly* across the party system, affecting primarily the 'non-Fianna Fáil' side of Irish party politics. While the overall Fianna Fáil vote has remained relatively stable since the early 1930s (varying between a low of 41.9 per cent in 1943 and 1948 and a high of 51.9 per cent in 1938), Fine Gael support has fluctuated considerably (from a low of 19.8 per cent in 1948 to a high of 39.2 per cent in November 1982), as has Labour support (from a low of 5.7 per cent in 1933 to a high of 17.0 per cent in 1969). To be sure, Fianna Fáil appears to have suffered considerably from the initial mobilisation of Clann na Talmhan and Clann na Poblachta, but both of these parties quickly aligned themselves with the non-Fianna Fáil side of Irish politics. The same may also prove true of the Progressive Democrats. In this sense they can also be seen as symptomatic of the instability of the non-Fianna Fáil side, even if they eventually also proved to be a sort of half-way house facilitating a crude two-stage transition from Fianna Fáil to Fine Gael. Since the 1987 election, however, the division between left and right may make it no longer possible to speak of a relatively undifferentiated anti-Fianna Fáilism.

Third, this uneven distribution of aggregate electoral change in the Irish party system also has some bearing on the notion of the *freezing of party systems* (Lipset and Rokkan 1967), for it can be suggested that the freezing process itself may be uneven, and that one part of a system may be more frozen than another. This, in turn, emphasises the sheer contingency of the freezing process, for if one side 'persists' while another proves more volatile, this underlines the need to examine the intra-systemic conditions which create this imbalance. In other words, it is not enough to impute a freezing process *per se*; rather, it is necessary to understand why some 'parts' of a party system may freeze while others may not. The Irish case suggests two tentative explanations. The first of these concerns ideology and comes from Sinnott (1978; see also Chapter 2), who emphasises Fianna Fáil's early monopolisation of the more hard and clear-cut symbols of Irish nationalism, and who suggests that such symbolic clarity facilitated the development of more long-standing and deep-rooted affective loyalties. Precisely because the Cumann na nGaedheal/Fine Gael *ideological* position proved more uncertain and ambiguous, he argues, *popular endorsement* of the party also proved more ambiguous and uncertain. The commitment of its supporters proved that much less intense, and those who did vote for Cumann na nGaedheal/Fine Gael also proved more willing to consider other alternatives than did those who voted for Fianna Fáil. In other words, ideological clarity allowed the Fianna Fáil constituency to prove more party-attached than was the case of the constituency of its major opponent.

The second potential explanation for the uneven freezing of alignments concerns *organisation*, with Fianna Fáil maintaining a greater hold over its supporters because of its greater organisational *presence*. The larger party managed to put down better roots in the local communities and, through its extensive and active organisational network, managed to close off the support market. Conversely, in an uneven pattern reminiscent of the left–right imbalance in the French case (see Lipset and Rokkan 1967, p. 50), Fine Gael and the other non-Fianna Fáil parties maintained a relatively ephemeral organisational presence (cf. Chapter 3), and so proved less able to constrain partisan preferences. To the extent that the freezing of party systems is in part a function of the mobilising capacity of parties, and to the extent that this mobilising capacity is itself a function of organisational presence and penetration, then the evident variation at the party organisational level in the Irish case may help to account for the evident asymmetry in the freezing process itself.

Fourth, it has also been suggested that the relationship between voters and parties has changed considerably, in that the system as a whole has become increasingly competitive. This is partly because the persistence of the coalition alternative offered voters a *choice of government* in addition to the traditional *choice of party*, and the overall balance became more finely tuned. Votes count, and the parties have necessarily been obliged to adopt a more competitive stance. In part, however, it is also due to such social, political and demographic changes as are reflected in increasing urbanisation and the gradual shift from West to East, in the growth of government activity, and in the increasing relevance of public policy to the everyday lives of the citizens (see Chapter 2). The result is that the parties, and particularly Fianna Fáil, can no longer take their support for granted. Rather, the parties are obliged actively to woo support and, in the context of an increasingly *available electorate*, they are obliged to try to win over those voters who are in competition. The arguments need not be rehearsed again. What is important, however, is that at least until 1987 this change had occurred without any evidence of substantially increased aggregate electoral volatility. Thus the 'same' parties could win more or less the same aggregate vote even though their relationship with these voters may have changed considerably. What I am suggesting, therefore, is that despite relative stability, the aggregate vote was characterised by an ever smaller proportion of supporters and adherents, and an ever increasing proportion of plain voters. While the overall vote may have remained reasonably stable, it was therefore more contingent. In short, the electorate is now less party-attached (as evidenced in the declining intensity of party identification—see Figure 2.2), and has a considerably greater *potential* for change and volatility. That such volatility was not really evident until 1987 did not indicate the maintenance of the parties' 'hold' as such; on the contrary, I would suggest that it was largely a tribute to their campaigning and competitive skills—skills which were also to be developed to major effect by the Progressive Democrats in 1987.

It is tempting to suggest that a similar type of change characterises other Western European polities. The evidence is difficult to consolidate, however, since it is necessary to probe not just the incidence but also the intensity of affective attitudes. Relevant Eurobarometer data from the late 1970s and early 1980s certainly do suggest a distancing from party and a decline in affective attitudes (Mair 1984). The recent collection of studies edited by Crewe and Denver (1985) also offers some supportive evidence, with relevant data from Britain between 1964 and 1983 (ibid., p. 124) and from Austria between 1972 and 1981 (ibid., p. 283), where in both cases the intensity of identification registers a clear decline. But whether Western European polities are characterised by a widespread distancing from party is not really relevant in this particular context. What does matter, however, and what is clearly evident from the Irish case, is that such distancing—such *change*—may occur *without* necessarily being immediately reflected at the aggregate electoral level. The parties may win the same amount of support as before, but they may do so for different reasons.

Fifth, most crucially, the Irish case also points to the importance of analysing *ideological* change. The parties of the present are not the parties of the past, for they have been characterised by substantial ideological shifts. In the late 1950s, Fianna Fáil moved away from a traditional nationalist appeal and attempted to reconstruct its dominance through an emphasis on corporatist ideology. To be sure, this was not a wholesale transformation, in that the stress on the national interest which was so central to its corporatist appeal gelled neatly with its traditional espousal of territorial and cultural nationalism. Thus the centrality of a national appeal continued, even if its terms of reference had been altered. The policy implications were also radically different, for the earlier position involved a commitment to isolation and self-sufficiency, while the latter stance allowed a more outward-looking approach. Fine Gael also changed during the post-war period, moving away from its traditional conservative and market-orientated stance towards a more social democratic appeal, an appeal which found echoes in that of Labour and which facilitated their coalition alliance in the early 1970s (Chapter 4). Again, the argument does not need to be rehearsed once more; rather, the key point here is that the Irish case shows how a continuity of the party alternatives may nevertheless be quite compatible with a fundamental shift in ideological appeals and in the patterning of ideological competition.

Finally, taking all these points together, and notwithstanding the constraints on party strategy discussed earlier in this chapter, the Irish case clearly emphasises the importance of the independent impact of party in any putative explanation of persistence or change (Sartori 1969; 1976). The parties are relevant, and what they do and say will help to constrain voter choice and partisan preference. In this sense, the parties are at least partially responsible for determining the terms of reference of mass politics, and cannot be reduced to a simply reflective role. This emphasis on the independent impact of party also helps to explain some of the more evident long-term—and possibly now dated?—puzzles of Irish politics such as, for instance, the essential irrelevance of social class to partisan choice (e.g. Whyte 1974). While social structural factors, that is class conditions (Sartori 1969), obviously go some way towards explaining this irrelevance, it must also be explained by reference to the manner in which the parties have mobilised. In the wider Western European context, for example, it can be argued that sectors of electorates are not 'naturally' or 'automatically' socialist, Christian democratic, agrarian, or whatever. Rather, electorates align as they do at least partly because of parties and other organisations which mobilise on class, religious, or agrarian appeals. Thus, despite the obvious relevance of class conditions in contemporary Ireland, it can also be argued that the reason why class is not (yet) a major issue in politics is that no party—including Labour—has (yet) made a serious attempt to persuade a class alignment.

How the parties interact is also of crucial importance, not least in that the strategic credibility of actual alternatives will also affect the predispositions of those voters in competition. While the STV system theoretically prevents vote wastage, and in this sense allows all parties or candidates to compete on an equal footing, none the less, a voter may feel it of more strategic importance to register a preference for one of the alternatives rather than another. The sudden polarisation of the electorate between Fianna Fáil and Cumann na nGaedheal in September 1927, offers a clear example of such a process, with voters seeming to feel the need to come down on one side or the other of the Treaty divide, and no longer being able to afford the luxury of supporting the 'less relevant' parties. Indeed, throughout its development, the Irish case emphasises the importance of such strategic constraints in explaining aggregate electoral fluctuations. The erosion of Clann na Talmhan and Clann na Poblachta support is relevant here, in so far as it can be argued that their failure derived in part from their allegiance strategy. Strategic constraints may also partially explain the more recent erosion of Labour support, in that it was difficult for the smaller party to stress its own independent appeal as long as it remained committed to coalition with Fine Gael. Given Fianna Fáil's traditional eschewal of coalition, Labour's only option for office involved an alliance with Fine Gael and, inevitably, involved an acceptance of Fine Gael dominance within that alliance. From this it follows that for those voters concerned with the implementation of public policy, that is for those voters who choose on the basis of what the parties can actually do (the partisan pragmatists identified in Chapter 2), it may not have been rational to choose Labour *rather than* Fine Gael. Hence, one could have anticipated a gradual drift from the smaller party to the larger, and indeed their respective aggregate electoral results between 1969 and 1982 suggest that this did occur. Survey evidence also suggests that this has been the case. In the three pre-election polls carried out by Irish

Marketing Surveys in May–June 1981, for example, some 20 per cent of those claiming to have voted for Labour in 1977 indicated a preference for Fine Gael in 1981, whereas less than 2 per cent of those claiming to have voted for Fine Gael in 1977 indicated a preference for Labour. The contrast is striking, and serves to emphasise that parties are not simply chosen in a vacuum, but rather are also seen in the context of the prevailing strategic alternatives.

The Irish party system is changing. But, as this study makes clear, the process of change not simply a recent phenomenon. The strategic alternatives and the strategic constraints of the party system have been transformed since its foundation. The manner in which the parties compete and the means by which they mobilise support have also changed with time. Ideologically, they are now different parties, and they now attempt to woo different voters. In the end, the most compelling picture is one of increasingly precarious parties competing for an increasingly pragmatic and instrumental electorate, with their most striking characteristic being their sheer vulnerability. The Irish party system may not have been thrown into disarray until 1987, but the potential for such a convulsion had been established years before.

Notes

1. It should be noted that a climate of altruism was also facilitated by a shift in the attitude of the Catholic Church towards welfare spending. Emphasising the impact of Vatican II, Whyte (1980, p. 352) notes that while the church in the 1950s was wont to warn against excessive state intervention, by the 1960s it was more likely to criticise the state for doing too little. See also Maguire (1985, pp. 173–6).

2. Of course, ideological incompatibility is not the only source of Labour disillusion with the coalition experience. As was noted above (p. 55), the smaller party has also witnessed a substantial erosion of its share of the overall vote and its share of the coaltion vote. For Labour's most recent statement on the coalition question see the report of the party's electoral commission (Labour Party 1986).

3. Other factors have also contributed to Fianna Fáil's change of approach. The recrudescence of violence in Northern Ireland since the late 1960s, and the increasing political instability in the province have undoubtedly acted to stimulate anti-partitionist sentiment in Fianna Fáil. At the same time, however, it is also necessary to emphasise that the extensive vocalisation of such anti-partitionist sentiment is a phenomenon of the 1980s and of Fianna Fáil under Charles Haughey, and that for much of the 1970s a more conciliatory approach held sway. More significantly, perhaps, it is also in the

1980s that Sinn Fein has begun to flex its electoral muscles—both North and South—intervening in the 1981 election in the Republic under the banner of the Anti-H-Block Committee, and running under its own party name in February 1982 and in 1987—in the latter case having for the first time abandoned its abstentionist strategy. This also undoubtedly places immense pressure on Fianna Fáil, and in this sense the party has recently been obliged to compete along the traditional nationalist dimension (see Mair 1987c).

BIBLIOGRAPHY

Election Programmes

Fianna Fáil

1948: 'Party Leaders on Their Programmes, No. 1: Fianna Fáil', *Irish Independent*, 23 January.

1951: Election Leaflet, Galway West Constituency.

1954: 'Radio Broadcast by An Tánaiste, Mr Seán Lemass, on Thursday, 11 May (Dublin: Fianna Fáil, mimeo).

1957: *Let's Go Ahead Again* (Dublin: Fianna Fáil).

1961: 'Taoiseach Foresees Change in Population Trend', *Irish Times*, 12 September.

1965: 'People Will Back Us All The Way Again: Taoiseach', *Irish Press*, 17 March.

1969: 'Taoiseach Opens F.F. Election Campaign', *Irish Times*, 28 May.

1973: 'The Issues of the Election' (Dublin: Fianna Fáil, mimeo).

1977: *Manifesto: Action Plan for National Reconstruction* (Dublin: Fianna Fáil).

1981: *Our Programme for the '80s* (Dublin: Fianna Fáil).

1982 (i): 'Text of Fianna Fáil Election Programme', *Irish Times*, 3 February.

1982 (ii): 'Charles J. Haughey: The Issues', *Irish Times*, 18 November.

Fine Gael

1948: 'Party Leaders on Their Programmes, No. 3: Fine Gael', *Irish Independent*, 26 January.

1951: Election Leaflet, Dun Laoighaire-Rathdown Constituency.

1954: 'Costello Gives 13 Principles', *Irish Press*, 3 May.

1957: 'Taoiseach Gives 16 Reasons for Supporting F.G.', *Irish Times*, 1 March.

1961: *What Fine Gael Stands For* (Dublin: Fine Gael).

1965: *Fine Gael Policy 1965: 'Towards a Just Society'* (Dublin: Fine Gael).

1969: *Winning Through to a Just Society* (Dublin: Fine Gael).

1981: *A Better Future: Let the Country Win* (Dublin: Fine Gael).

1982 (i): 'Speech by the Taoiseach, Dr Garrett FitzGerald, to Galway Chamber of Commerce, 30 January 1982' (Dublin: Government Information Service, mimeo).

1982 (ii): *Fine Gael Priorities* (Dublin: Fine Gael).

Labour

1948: 'Party Leaders on Their Programmes, No. 4: Labour', *Irish Independent*, 27 January.
1951: *Labour's Way to Achieve Prosperity and Security* (reprinted in *Labour Party Administrative Council Report for 1950–51 and 1951–52*, pp. 52–4).
1954: 'General Election, 1954: Labour's Programme', *Labour* (monthly journal of the Dublin Regional Council of the Labour Party), May, p. 2.
1957: *Labour Party Election Programme* (reprinted in *Labour Party Administrative Council Report for 1956–57*, pp. 26–8).
1961: 'General Election 1961: Economic and Social Programme of the Labour Party' (Dublin: Labour Party, mimeo).
1965: 'Labour Election Manifesto', *Irish Times*, 24 March.
1969: *1969 General Election* (reprinted in *Labour Party Annual Report*, 1969, pp. 68–83).
1981: *Election Programme* (Dublin: Labour Party).
1982 (i): 'Text of O'Leary's Statement', *Irish Times*, 30 January.
1982 (ii): *Where Labour Stands* (Dublin: Labour Party).

Fine Gael–Labour Coalition

1973: 'Statement of Intent' (Dublin: Fine Gael and Labour Party, mimeo).
1977: *The National Coalition Government: Achievements, Programme for Progress* (Dublin: Fine Gael and Labour Party).

Cited Texts

Alford, R. R. (1963), *Party and Society: the Anglo–American Democracies* (Chicago: Rand McNally).
Barnes, S. H. (1984), 'The "New Citizen" and the Future of Political Mobilisation', paper presented to the Workshop on Political Mobilisation, European University Institute, Florence.
Bax, Mart (1976), *Harpstrings and Confessions: Machine-Style Politics in the Irish Republic* (Assen: Van Gorcum).
Bell, J. Bowyer (1979), *The Secret Army: the IRA 1916–1979* (Dublin: Academy Press).
Bew, Paul and Henry Patterson (1982), *Séan Lemass and the Making of Modern Ireland, 1945–66* (Dublin: Gill and Macmillan).
Blackwell, John (1982), 'Government, Economy and Society' in Frank Litton (ed.), *Unequal Achievement: the Irish Experience, 1957–1982* (Dublin: Institute of Public Administration), 43–60.
Borre, Ole and Daniel Katz (1973), 'Party Identification and Its Motivational Base in a Multi-Party System: a Study of the Danish General Election of 1973', *Scandinavian Political Studies, 8*, 69–111.
Brady, Conor (1978), 'The Party: an Analysis of Fianna Fáil' (4-part series), *Irish Times*, 17–20 July.

Browne, Vincent (ed.) (1981), *The Magill Book of Irish Politics* (Dublin: Magill Publications).

Browne, Vincent (ed.) (1982), *The Magill Book of Irish Politics 1982* (Dublin: Magill Publications).

Budge, Ian, Derek Hearl and David Robertson (eds) (1987), *Ideology, Strategy, and Party Movement* (Cambridge: Cambridge University Press).

Building on Reality (1984), (Dublin: Stationery Office).

Busteed, M. A. and Hugh Mason (1970), 'Irish Labour in the 1969 Election', *Political Studies, 18*(3), 373–9.

Carty, R. K. (1981), *Party and Parish Pump: Electoral Politics in Ireland* (Ontario: Wilfrid Laurier Press).

Chubb, Basil (1963), '"Going About Persecuting Civil Servants": the Role of the Irish Parliamentary Representative', *Political Studies, 11*(3), 272–86.

Chubb, Basil (1970), *The Government and Politics of Ireland* (London: Oxford University Press).

Chubb, Basil (1974), *Cabinet Government in Ireland* (Dublin: Institute of Public Administration).

Chubb, Basil (1982), *The Government and Politics of Ireland*, 2nd edn (London: Longman).

Clann na Poblachta (1948), 'Our Policy' (mimeo).

Clann na Talmhan (1944), *The Book of Clann na Talmhan* (published by the party).

Coakley, John (1983), 'Minority Parties in Ireland' (NIHE, Limerick: mimeo).

Cohan, A. S. (1977), 'The Question of a United Ireland: Perspectives of the Irish Political Elite', *International Affairs, 53*(2), 232–54.

Cohan, A. S. (1979), 'The Open Coalition in a Closed Society: the Strange Case of Government Formation in Ireland', *Comparative Politics, 11*(3), 319–38.

Cohan, A. S. (1982), 'Ireland: Coalitions Making a Virtue of Necessity' in Eric C. Browne and John Dreijmanis (eds), *Government Coalitions in Western Democracies* (London: Longman), 260–82.

Converse, Philip E. (1969), 'Of Time and Partisan Stability', *Comparative Political Studies, 2*(2), 139–71.

Converse, Philip E. (1976), *The Dynamics of Party Support: Cohort-Analysing Party Identification* (London and Beverly Hills: Sage).

Coogan, Tim Pat (1966), *Ireland Since the Rising* (London: Pall Mall Press).

Cooney, John (1986), *The Crozier and the Dáil: Church and State, 1922–86* (Cork: Mercier Press).

Corish, Brendan (1968), *The New Republic* (Dublin: Labour Party).

Coughlan, Anthony (1984), 'Ireland's Welfare State in Time of Crisis', *Administration, 32*(1), 37–54.

Cox, W. Harvey (1985), 'The Politics of Unification in the Irish Republic', *Parliamentary Affairs, 38*(4), 437–54.

Crewe, Ivor and David Denver (eds) (1985), *Electoral Change in Western" Democracies: Patterns and Sources of Electoral Volatility* (London: Croom Helm).

Crick, Michael (1986), *The March of Militant* (London: Faber).

Crowley, Des (1983), 'Who Pays for the Party . . .', *Success*, April, 28–32.

Daalder, Hans (1983), 'The Comparative Study of European Parties and Party Systems: an Overview' in Hans Daalder and Peter Mair (eds), *Western European Party Systems: Continuity and Change* (London and Beverly Hills: Sage), 1–28.

Daalder, Hans (1986), 'Parties and Political Mobilisation: an Initial Mapping', in Werner Maihofer (ed.), *Noi Si Mura: Selected Working Papers of the European University Institute* (Florence: European University Institute) 49–78.

Dalton, Russell J., Scott C. Flanagan and Paul Allen Beck (eds) (1985), *Electoral Change in Advanced Industrial Democracies: Realignment or Dealignment?* (Princeton: Princeton University Press).

Desmond, Barry (1966), 'Submission to the Administrative Council's Sub-Committee Set Up in March 1966 To Report on Party Administration' (mimeo).

Dittrich, Karl (1983), 'Testing the Catch-All Thesis: Limits and Possibilities' in Hans Daalder and Peter Mair (eds), *Western European Party Systems: Continuity and Change* (London and Beverly Hills: Sage), 257–66.

Economic Review and Outlook (1986) (Dublin: Stationery Office).

Fanning, Ronan (1983), *Independent Ireland* (Dublin: Helicon).

Fanning, Ronan (1984), 'The British Dimension', *The Crane Bag, 8*(1), 41–52.

Farrell, Brian (1970), 'Labour and the Irish Political Party System: a Suggested Approach to Analysis', *Economic and Social Review, 1*(4), 477–502.

Farrell, Brian (1971), *The Founding of Dáil Éireann* (Dublin: Gill and Macmillan).

Farrell, Brian (1985), 'Ireland: From Friends and Neighbours to Clients and Partisans' in Vernon Bogdanor (ed.), *Representatives of the People?* (Aldershot: Gower), 237–64.

Farrell, Brian and Maurice Manning (1978), 'The Election' in Howard R. Penniman (ed.), *Ireland At The Polls: the Dáil Election of 1977* (Washington D.C.: American Enterprise Institute), 133–64.

Farrell, David (1986), 'The Strategy to Market Fine Gael', *Irish Political Studies 1*, 1–14.

Farrell, Michael (1983), 'The Life and Extraordinary Times of Séan Mac-Bride—Part Two', *Magill*, January, 25–37.

FitzGerald, Garret (1977), *The Role of Fine Gael* (Dublin: Fine Gael).

Flanagan, Scott C. and Russell J. Dalton (1983), 'Parties Under Stress: Realignment and Dealignment in Advanced Industrial Societies', *West European Politics 7*(1), 7–23.

Franklin, Mark N. and Thomas T. Mackie (1983), 'Familiarity and Inertia in the Formation of Governing Coalitions in Parliamentary Democracies', *British Journal of Political Science, 13*(3), 275–98.

Gallagher, Michael (1976), *Electoral Support for Irish Political Parties, 1927–1973* (London and Beverly Hills: Sage).

Gallagher, Michael (1978), 'Party Solidarity, Exclusivity and Inter-Party

Relationships in Ireland, 1922–1977: the Evidence of Transfers', *Economic and Social Review, 10*(1), 1–22.

Gallagher, Michael (1979), 'The Pact General Election of 1922', *Irish Historical Studies, 21*(84), 404–21.

Gallagher, Michael (1981), 'Social Change and Party Adaptation in the Republic of Ireland', *European Journal of Political Research, 9*(3), 269–85.

Gallagher, Michael (1982), *The Irish Labour Party in Transition, 1957–1982* (Manchester: Manchester University Press).

Gallagher, Michael (1985), *Political Parties in the Republic of Ireland* (Manchester: Manchester University Press).

Garvin, Tom (1969), *The Irish Senate* (Dublin: Institute of Public Administration).

Garvin, Tom (1974), 'Political Cleavages, Party Politics and Urbanisation in Ireland: the Case of the Periphery-Dominated Centre', *European Journal of Political Research, 2*(4), 307–27.

Garvin, Tom (1977a), 'National Elites, Irish Voters and Irish Political Development: a Comparative Perspective', *Economic and Social Review, 8*(4), 161–86.

Garvin, Tom (1977b), 'Belief Systems, Ideological Perspectives and Political Activism: Some Dublin Evidence', *Social Studies, 6*(1), 39–56.

Garvin, Tom (1981a), *The Evolution of Irish Nationalist Politics* (Dublin: Gill and Macmillan).

Garvin, Tom (1981b), 'The Growth of Faction in the Fianna Fáil Party', *Parliamentary Affairs, 34*(1), 110–23.

Girvin, Brian (1986), 'Social Change and Moral Politics: the Irish Constitutional Referendum 1983', *Political Studies, 34*(1), 61–81.

Hardiman, Niamh and Stephen Lalor (1984), 'Corporatism in Ireland: an Exchange of Views', *Administration, 32*(1), 76–89.

Harkness, David W. (1969), *The Restless Dominion: The Irish Free State and the Commonwealth of Nations, 1921–1931* (London: Macmillan).

Haughey, Charles J. (1981), *Presidential Address to the 50th Fianna Fáil Árd Fheis* (Dublin: Fianna Fáil).

Haughey, Charles J. (1983), *Presidential Address to the 51st Fianna Fáil Árd Fheis* (Dublin: Fianna Fáil).

Higgins, Michael D. (1982), 'The Limits of Clientelism: Towards an Assessment of Irish Politics' in Christopher Clapham (ed.), *Private Patronage and Public Power* (London: Frances Pinter), 114–41.

Hildebrandt, Kai and Russell J. Dalton (1978), 'The New Politics: Political Change or Sunshine Politics?' in Max Kaase and Klaus von Beyme (eds), *Elections and Parties: German Political Studies, Vol 3* (London and Beverly Hills: Sage), 69–96.

Horgan, John (1986), *Labour: the Price of Power* (Dublin: Gill and Macmillan).

Inglehart, Ronald (1977), *The Silent Revolution: Changing Values and Political Styles Among Western Publics* (Princeton: Princeton University Press).

Inglehart, Ronald and Hans D. Klingemann (1976), 'Party Identification,

Ideological Preferences and the Left–Right Dimension in Western Mass Publics' in Ian Budge, Ivor Crewe and Dennis Farlie (eds), *Party Identification and Beyond* (London: Wiley), 243–73.

IMS (1976), *RTE 'Survey'—Politics* (Dublin: Irish Marketing Surveys).

Joyce, Joe and Peter Murtagh (1983), *The Boss: Charles J. Haughey in Power* (Dublin: Poolbeg Press).

Kennedy, Geraldine (1982), 'The Men in Room 547 of the Burlington', *Sunday Tribune*, 9 May.

Kenny, Kathleen Joan (1972), 'The Political System of the Irish Republic: Two and a Half Parties in a Developing Nation' (Syracuse University: PhD thesis).

Kirchheimer, Otto (1966), 'The Transformation of the Western European Party Systems' in Joseph LaPalombara and Myron Weiner (eds), *Political Parties and Political Development* (Princeton: Princeton University Press), 177–200.

Komito, Lee (1984), 'Irish Clientelism: a Reappraisal', *Economic and Social Review, 15*(3), 173–94.

Labour Party (1986), *Report of the Commission on Electoral Strategy* (Dublin: Labour Party).

Lee, Joseph (1979), 'Aspects of Corporatist Thought in Ireland: The Commission on Vocational Organisation, 1939–43' in Art Cosgrave and Donal McCartney (eds), *Studies in Irish History* (Dublin: University College Dublin), 324–46.

Lee, Joseph (1982), 'Society and Culture' in Frank Litton (ed.), *Unequal Achievement: the Irish Experience, 1957–1982* (Dublin: Institute of Public Administration), 1–18.

Lipset, S. M. (1964), 'The Changing Class Structure in Contemporary European Politics', *Daedalus, 93*, 271–303.

Lipset, S. M. and Stein Rokkan (1967), 'Cleavage Structures, Party Systems and Voter Alignments: an Introduction', in S. M. Lipset and Stein Rokkan (eds), *Party Systems and Voter Alignments* (New York: Free Press), 1–64.

Litton, Frank (ed.) (1982), *Unequal Achievement: the Irish Experience, 1957–1982* (Dublin: Institute of Public Administration).

Logan, Bruce M. (1978), 'Parliamentary Democracy in Ireland' (University of Chicago: PhD thesis).

Lynch, Jack (1969), *Presidential Address to the Fianna Fáil Árd Fheis* (Dublin: Fianna Fáil).

Lyons, F. S. L. (1973), *Ireland Since the Famine*, revised edn (Glasgow: Fontana).

Lysaght, D. R. O'Connor (1970), *The Republic of Ireland* (Cork: Mercier Press).

MacKenna, Gene (1976), '"Mind the Organisation", said Dev' in 'Fianna Fáil 1926–1976', special supplement to the *Irish Press*, 26 May.

Mackie, T. T. and Richard Rose (1982), *The International Almanac of Electoral History*, 2nd edn (London: Macmillan).

Maguire, Maria (1983), 'Is There Still Persistence? Electoral Change in Western Europe, 1948–1979' in Hans Daalder and Peter Mair (eds), *Western European Party Systems: Continuity and Change* (London and Beverly Hills: Sage), 67–94.

Maguire, Maria (1985), 'The Development of the Irish Welfare State in the Postwar Period' (European University Institute, Florence: PhD thesis).

Mair, Peter (1978), 'The Break-Up of the United Kingdom: The Irish Experience of Regime Change, 1918–1948', *Journal of Commonwealth and Comparative Politics, 16*(3), 288–302.

Mair, Peter (1979), 'The Autonomy of the Political: The Development of the Irish Party System', *Comparative Politics, 11*(4), 445–65.

Mair, Peter (1981), 'Analysis of the Results' in Ted Nealon and Seamus Brennan, *Nealon's Guide to the 22nd Dáil and Seanad* (Dublin: Platform Press), 150–4.

Mair, Peter (1983), 'Adaptation and Control: Towards an Understanding of Party and Party System Change' in Hans Daalder and Peter Mair (eds), *Western European Party Systems: Continuity and Change* (London: Sage), 405–29.

Mair, Peter (1984), 'Party Politics in Contemporary Western Europe: A Challenge to Party?', *West European Politics, 7*(4), 170–84.

Mair, Peter (1986a), 'Locating Irish parties on a Left–Right Scale', *Political Studies, 34*(3), 456–65.

Mair, Peter, (1986b), 'Districting choices under the Single Transferable Vote' in Bernard Grofman and Arend Lijphart (eds), *Electoral Laws and Their Political Consequences* (New York: Agathon Press), 289–307.

Mair, Peter (1987a), 'Party Organisation: Vote Management and Candidate Selection: Towards the Nationalisation of Electoral Strategy in Ireland', in Howard R. Penniman and Brian Farrell (eds), *Ireland At The Polls, 1981–82* (Washington D.C.: American Enterprise Institute, forthcoming).

Mair, Peter (1987b), 'Ireland: Parties, Issues, Strategies', in Ian Budge *et al.* (eds), *Ideology, Strategy, and Party Movement* (Cambridge: Cambridge University Press, forthcoming).

Mair, Peter (1987c), 'Breaking the Nationalist Mould: The Irish Republic and the Anglo-Irish Agreement' in Paul Teague (ed.), *Beyond the Rhetoric: Politics, Economics and Social Policy in Northern Ireland* (London: Lawrence and Wishart, forthcoming).

Malloy, James M. (1974), 'Authoritarianism, Corporatism and Mobilization in Peru', *Review of Politics, 36*(1), 52–84.

Malloy, James M. (1977), 'Authoritarianism and Corporatism in Latin America: the Modal Pattern' in James M. Malloy (ed.), *Authoritarianism and Corporatism in Latin America* (Pittsburg: University of Pittsburg Press), 3–19.

Malone, Andrew E. (1929), 'Party Government in the Irish Free State', *Political Science Quarterly, 44*(3), 363–78.

Manning, Maurice (1970), *The Blueshirts* (Dublin: Gill and Macmillan).

Manning, Maurice (1972), *Irish Political Parties: an Introduction* (Dublin: Gill and Macmillan).

Marsh, Michael (1981), 'Localism, Candidate Selection and Electoral Preferences in Ireland: the General Election of 1977', *Economic and Social Review, 12*(4), 267–86,

Marsh, Michael (1985), 'Ireland' in Ivor Crewe and David Denver (eds), *Electoral Change in Western Democracies: Patterns and Sources of Electoral Volatility* (London: Croom Helm), 173–201.

McAllister, Ian (1981), 'Party Organisation and Minority Nationalism: a Comparative Study in the United Kingdom', *European Journal of Political Research, 9*(3), 237–55.

McHale, Vincent E. and Sandra Shaber (1976), 'From Aggressive to Defensive Gaullism: the Electoral Dynamics of a "Catch-All Party', *Comparative Politics, 8*(2), 291–306.

McIerny, Michael (1975), 'Portrait of a Fine Gael Liberal (interview with James Dooge)', *Irish Times*, 2 December.

McInery, Michael (1976), 'The Name and the Game' in 'Fifty Years of Fianna Fáil', special supplement to the *Irish Times*, 19 May.

McKee, Paul (1983), 'The Republic of Ireland' in Vernon Bogdanor and David Butler (eds), *Democracy and Elections* (Cambridge: Cambridge University Press), 167–89.

Meenan, James (1967), 'From Free Trade to Self-Sufficiency' in Francis MacManus (ed.), *The Years of the Great Test, 1926–39* (Cork: Mercier Press), 69–79.

Mishler, William, Allan Kornberg, David P. Lindquist and Joel Smith (1974), 'Patterns of Political Socialisation: Stimulating the Development of Party Identification in Two Political Elites', *Comparative Political Studies, 6*(4), 399–430.

Mitchell, Arthur (1974), *Labour in Irish Politics, 1890–1930* (Dublin: Irish University Press).

Moynihan, Maurice (ed.) (1980), *Speeches and Statements by Éamon de Valera* (Dublin: Gill and Macmillan).

Murphy, Christina (1967), 'The Organisational Structure of the Labour Party', *Leargas*, no. 11, November, 10–13.

Murphy, Christina (1968a), 'Party Organisation: Fianna Fáil', *Leargas*, no. 12, January–February, 10–13.

Murphy, Christina (1968b), 'Party Organisation (3): Fine Gael', *Leargas*, no. 14, May–June, 5–7.

NESC (1986), *A Strategy for Development 1986–1990* (Dublin: National Economic and Social Council).

Nealon, Ted and Seamus Brennan (1981), *Nealon's Guide to the 22nd Dáil and Seanad* (Dublin: Platform Press).

Nevin, Donal (1967), 'Labour and the Political Revolution', in Francis MacManus (ed.), *The Years of the Great Test, 1926–39* (Cork: Mercier Press), 55–68.

Nevin, Donal (1969), 'Industry and Labour' in Kevin B. Nowlan and T. Desmond Williams (eds), *Ireland in the War Years and After, 1939–51* (Dublin: Gill and Macmillan), 94–108.

O'Brien, Conor Cruise (1972), *States of Ireland* (London: Hutchinson).

O'Byrnes, Stephen (1986), *Hiding Behind a Face: Fine Gael Under Garret FitzGerald* (Dublin: Gill and Macmillan).

O'Higgins, Michael (1987), 'One Man's Campaign', *Magill*, February, 13–17.

O'Leary, Cornelius (1961), *The Irish Republic and Its Experiment With Proportional Representation* (Notre Dame: University of Notre Dame Press).

O'Leary, Cornelius (1979), *Irish Elections, 1918–1977* (Dublin: Gill and Macmillan).

O'Leary, Olivia (1984), 'The Coalition at Mid-Term', *Magill*, 15 November, 8–17.

O'Reilly, Emily (1987), 'A Hi-Tech Sale That Packs Its Punch', *Sunday Tribune*, 15 February.

Orridge, Andrew (1983), 'The Blueshirts and the "Economic War": a Study of Ireland in the Context of Dependency Theory', *Political Studies, 31* (3), 351–69.

O'Sullivan, Donal (1940), *The Irish Free State and Its Senate* (London: Faber).

O'Toole, Fintan (1986), 'The New Coalition?', *Magill*, February.

Pappi, Franz Urban (1984), 'The West German Party System', *West European Politics*, 7(4), 7–26.

Parker, A. J. (1982), 'The "Friends and Neighbours" Voting Effect in the Galway West Constituency', *Political Geography Quarterly*, 1(3), 243–62.

Pedersen, Mogens N. (1979), 'The Dynamics of European Party Systems: Changing Patterns of Electoral Volatility', *European Journal of Political Research,* 7(1), 1–26.

Pedersen, Mogens N. (1983), 'Changing Patterns of Electoral Volatility in European Party Systems: Explorations in Explanation' in Hans Daalder and Peter Mair (eds), *Western European Party Systems: Continuity and Change* (London and Beverly Hills: Sage), 29–66.

Prager, Jeffrey (1986), *Building Democracy in Ireland: Political Order and Cultural Integration in a Newly Independent Nation* (Cambridge: Cambridge University Press).

Progressive Democrats (1986), *Policy Discussion Papers: First National Conference* (Dublin: Progressive Democrats).

Rae, D. W. (1971), *The Political Consequences of Electoral Laws*, revised edn (New Haven: Yale University Press).

Robertson, David (1976), *A Theory of Party Competition* (London: Wiley).

Roche, Bill (1982), 'Social Partnership and Political Control: State Strategy and Industrial Relations in Ireland' in Mary Kelly *et al*. (eds), *Power, Conflict and Inequality* (Dublin: Turoe Press), 44–67.

Rokkan, Stein (1977), 'Towards a Generalised Concept of *Verzuiling*', *Political Studies, 25*(4), 563–70.

Rooney, Eddie (1984), 'From Republican Movement to Workers' Party: an

Ideological Analysis' in Chris Curtin, Mary Kelly and Liam O'Dowd (eds), *Culture and Ideology in Ireland* (Galway: Officina Typographica), 79–98.

Rose, Richard (1974), 'Comparability in Electoral Studies' in Richard Rose (ed.), *Electoral Behaviour: a Comparative Handbook* (New York: Free Press), 3–25.

Rose, Richard (1980), *Challenge to Governance: Studies in Overloaded Polities* (London: Sage).

Rose, Richard, Ian McAllister and Peter Mair (1978), 'Is There a Concurring Majority About Northern Ireland?' (University of Strathclyde, Glasgow: Centre for the Study of Public Policy, paper no. 22).

Rose, Richard and Derek Urwin (1970), 'Persistence and Change in Western Party Systems Since 1945', *Political Studies, 18*(3), 287–319.

Ross, Michael (1986), 'Employment in the Public Domain in Recent Decades' (Dublin: Economic and Social Research Institute, paper 127).

Rottman, David and Philip O'Connell (1982), 'The Changing Social Structure of Ireland' in Frank Litton (ed.), *Unequal Achievement: the Irish Experience, 1957–1982* (Dublin: Institute of Public Administration), 63–88.

Rumpf, Erhard and A. C. Hepburn (1977), *Nationalism and Socialism in Twentieth Century Ireland* (Liverpool: Liverpool University Press).

Sacks, Paul M. (1976), *The Donegal Mafia* (New Haven: Yale University Press).

Sani, Giacomo and Giovanni Sartori (1983), 'Polarization, Fragmentation and Competition in Western Democracies' in Hans Daalder and Peter Mair (eds), *Western European Party Systems: Continuity and Change* (London and Beverly Hills: Sage), 307–40.

Sartori, Giovanni (1969), 'From the Sociology of Politics to Political Sociology', in S. M. Lipset (ed.), *Politics and the Social Sciences* (London: Oxford University Press), 65–100.

Sartori, Giovanni (1970), 'Concept Misformation in Comparative Politics', *American Political Science Review, 64*(4), 1033–53.

Sartori, Giovanni (1976), *Parties and Party Systems: a Framework for Analysis, Vol. 1* (Cambridge: Cambridge University Press).

Schattschneider, E. E. (1960), *The Semi-Sovereign People* (New York: Holt, Rinehart and Winston).

Schmitter, Phillippe C. (1974), 'Still the Century of Corporatism?', *Review of Politics, 36*(1), 85–131.

Schmitter, Phillippe C. and Gerhard Lehmbruch (eds) (1979), *Trends Towards Corporatist Intermediation* (London: Sage).

Sinnott, Richard (1978), 'The Electorate' in Howard R. Penniman (ed.), *Ireland At The Polls: the Dáil Election of 1977* (Washington D.C.: American Enterprise Institute), 35–67.

Sinnott, Richard (1984), 'Interpretations of the Irish Party System', *European Journal of Political Research, 12*(3), 289–307.

Trench, Brian (ed.) (1983), *The Magill Book of Irish Politics, 1983* (Dublin: Magill Publications).

Valen, Henry (1976), 'National Conflict Structure and Foreign Politics: the

Impact of the EEC Issue on Perceived Cleavages in Norwegian Politics', *European Journal of Political Research*, 4 (1), 47–82.

Walsh, Dick (1976), 'After Lemass: Deluge or Desert' in 'Fifty Years of Fianna Fáil', special supplement to the *Irish Times*, 19 May.

Walsh, Dick (1986), *The Party: Inside Fianna Fáil* (Dublin: Gill and Mac-Millan).

Whyte, John H. (1974), 'Ireland: Politics without Social Bases' in Richard Rose (ed.), *Electoral Behaviour: A Comparative Handbook* (New York: Free Press), 619–51.

Whyte, John H. (1980), *Church and State in Modern Ireland, 1923–1979* (Dublin: Gill and Macmillan).

Williams, T. Desmond (1967), 'De Valera in Power' in Francis MacManus (ed.), *The Years of the Great Test, 1926–39* (Cork: Mercier Press), 30–41.

Winkler, J. T. (1976), 'Corporatism', *Archives Européennes de Sociologie*, *17*(1), 100–36.

INDEX

abortion 215
Administrative Council 99, 101, 126, 130
affective partisanship 74–85
affiliate organisations 99–102
Agricultural Advisory Council 100
Amalgamated Transport and General
    Workers Union 101
An Poblacht 21
ancillary organisations 99–102
Anglo-Irish Agreement 146, 214
Anglo-Irish Treaty (1921) 13

ballot papers 61
Bew, P. 55, 140, 187, 208
Blaney, Neil 34, 129
Blueshirt movement 22, 50
branch organisation 95, 96, 98, 102–6
Brennan, Seamus 73, 119
Browne, Noel 28, 34
Budge, I. 5, 170
Bunreacht na hÉireann 19
Business Election Committee 112

Carlow-Kilkenny 69
Carty, R. K. 63, 84
Catholic Church 28, 220
Cawley, P. J. 72, 73
Centre Party 22, 24, 48, 88
Christian and National Social Order 25
Chubb, Basil 91, 139
Clann na Poblachta 26–9, 31, 34, 47, 52–
    4, 58, 60, 80, 88, 146, 163, 225, 227
Clann na Talmhan 24–7, 29, 31, 52, 53,
    80, 88, 146, 163, 225, 227
class structure 3
clientelistic non-partisans 85
clientelistic partisans 85
Coakley, J. 27
coalition formation 197–202
coalition programmes 194–5
Cohan, A. S. 139, 198
Cómhairle áth Cliath 112
Commission on Vocational Representa-
    tion 177
competition in Irish elections 67
conflict of conflicts 16
Connaught-Ulster 24, 25, 27, 79, 80, 118

consensual issues 166–9
constituency council 95
contraception 215
controlled economy 156, 165, 166, 169,
    170, 174, 175, 184
Cork City 128, 210
corporatist ideology 177–84, 215
    versus social democratic ideology
    184–9
Cosgrave, Liam 122
Cosgrave, Liam T. 122
Cosgrave, William T. 122
Costello, Declan 122, 185
Costello, John A. 122, 185, 186, 192, 218
Council of Local Representatives 101
County Clare 120
County Leitrim 120
County Mayo 117
Crew, I. 6, 226
Cumann na nGaedheal 2, 14–17, 19, 21–
    3, 25, 36, 47, 48, 50, 51, 87, 114, 115,
    120, 122, 134, 224

Daalder, Hans 8
Dáil 13–16, 19, 20, 24, 26, 28, 32, 34, 38,
    53, 56, 79, 91, 108, 113, 117
Dalton, R. J. 1
de Valera, Éamon 14, 15, 17–19, 21, 51,
    167, 178, 188
decentralisation 171
defence of Irish way of life 156, 166, 167,
    174, 192, 193
democracy 156, 165, 169, 173, 195, 196
Democratic Socialist Party 34
Denver, D. 6, 226
Desmond, B. 125
Dittrich, K. 4
divorce 215
Donegal 69, 118, 119
Dooge, James 122
Dublin 27, 83, 90, 103, 106, 108, 117,
    118, 120, 121, 125, 128, 130, 133,
    210
Dun Laoghaire 119

economic contraction 211
economic development 164

economic expansion 164
economic orthodoxy 165–7, 169, 170, 173, 195, 196
economic prospects 208
election issues 217–21
electoral engineering 90
electoral strategy 209–10
enterprise 156, 165, 167, 170, 171, 173
European Community 76
European Consortium for Political Research (ECPR) 141
European Parliament 96

Fanning, R. 162
Farmers Party 16, 22, 47, 88
Farrell, B. 137
Fianna Fáil 1, 2, 8–10, 13–19, 21–9, 34, 36, 38, 40, 42, 44–8, 50–7, 59, 60, 62, 65, 69, 70, 72, 80–3, 86–91, 94–7, 99, 100, 104, 106–11, 114–19, 121, 122, 127, 129, 132–45, 156, 157, 163, 164, 166, 167, 169, 174, 175, 177–84, 186, 187, 189–91, 193, 194, 196, 209, 214, 217, 219–27
    ancillary and affiliate organisations 99–102
    and coalition formation 197–202
    birth of 13
    competition 61–93
    corporatist ideology 177–89
    distribution of Dail seats 1948–87 32
    domains of identification 144–7
    election issues 1987 217–21
    finance and staffing 106–13
    historical overview 13–43
    ideological characteristics 138–206
    income and fund-raising 109–13
    index of class voting 1969–87 43
    indices of proportionality 1948–87 35
    inter-party distances 200
    involvement in government 1948–87 37
    mean scores and level of polarisation 176
    membership and branches 102–6
    organisation 94–137
    organisational style 114–27
    party emphases 1948–57 and 1961–82 157–69
    party movement 1961–82 189–92
    party programme 1961–82 147–56
    post-war trends 29–43
    revitalisation 127–37
    share of electoral vote 1948–87 30

share of electoral vote and Dáil seats 1923–44 20
share of electorate 1927–33 49
social class and party support 1969 39; 1977–87 41–2
strategy constraints 207–17
structures 95–9
voting percentages 1927–33 49
finance 106–13
Fine Gael 1, 2, 8–10, 13, 14, 19, 22–4, 26, 29, 34, 36, 38, 44–7, 51–60, 62, 65, 69, 70, 72, 73, 80, 82, 83, 86–9, 91, 94–7, 100, 103, 104, 106, 107, 109, 111–14, 118, 119–25, 127, 129, 131–6, 138, 139–42, 144, 157, 162–7, 169, 173, 175, 177, 183, 185, 186, 189–91, 193, 194, 196, 197, 209, 216–18, 221, 223–8
    ancillary and affiliate organisations 99–102
    birth of 13
    competition 61–93
    corporatist ideology 177–89
    distribution of Dáil seats 1948–87 32
    domains of identification 144–7
    election issues 1987 217–21
    finance and staffing 106–13
    historical overview 13–43
    ideological characteristics 138–206
    income and fund-raising 109–13
    index of class voting 1969–87 43
    indices of proportionality 1948–87 35
    inter-party distances 200
    involvement in government 1948–87 37
    mean scores and level of polarisation 176
    membership and branches 102–6
    organisation 94–137
    organisational style 114–27
    party emphases 1948–57 and 1961–82 157–69
    party movement 1961–82 189–92
    party programme 1961–82 147–56
    post-war trends 29–43
    revitalisation 127–37
    share of electoral vote 1948–87 30
    share of electoral vote and Dáil seats 1923–44 20
    share of electorate 1927–33 49
    social class and party support 1969 39; 1977–87 41–2
    strategy constraints 207–17
    structures 95–9

voting percentages 1927–33 49
FitzGerald, Desmond 122
FitzGerald, Garret 112, 122, 127, 186, 192, 213, 217
freedom 156, 165, 169, 173, 195, 196
fund-raising 109–13

Gallagher, M. 31, 94, 118, 120, 124
Galway West 69, 133
Garvin, T. 12, 22, 52, 115, 117
Gaullism 188–9
government authority 156, 157, 163, 164, 167, 173, 174, 180, 183, 193
government corruption 156
government efficiency 156, 164, 167, 173, 174
government formation patterns 37
Governor General 19
Gross Domestic Product (GDP) 75, 187, 208, 211, 212
Gross National Product (GNP) 181, 212

Haughey, Charles 143–4, 163, 178, 179, 214–16
Hepburn, A. C. 88

income 109–13
index of class voting 43
index of fractionalisation 29, 30, 32, 33
index of party identification 78
index of volatility 30, 81
indices of proportionality 35
infrastructure 156, 173
Inglehart, R. 76
instrumental partisanship 74–85
interventionism 195
intra-party competition 67
Irish Free State 12, 13, 18, 19, 46
Irish language 156
Irish Nationalism 174
Irish Parliamentary Party 16, 45–6
Irish party system
    development of 12–60
    historical overview 13–43
    post-war trends 29–43
    principal elements of 222–8
Irish Republic 12
Irish Republican Army (IRA) 13, 21, 22, 50
Irish Unity 147, 167, 180, 192, 193

Just Society 184–6, 210

Kemmy, Jimmy 34

Kenny, K. J. 121
Kirchheimer, Otto 4, 5
Klingemann, H. D. 76

Labour Party 1, 2, 8, 10, 13, 14–17, 19, 23–5, 29, 31, 34, 36, 40, 44–7, 52, 53, 55–60, 65, 72, 82, 84, 87–9, 91, 95, 98, 101, 103, 104, 106–9, 111, 113, 114, 124–7, 129, 130, 132, 133, 135, 136, 139–42, 144, 157, 163, 165, 167, 169, 173, 175, 177, 186, 187, 189–91, 193, 194, 196, 209, 217, 219, 225, 228
    ancillary and affiliate organisations 99–102
    and coalition formation 197–202
    birth of 13
    competition 61–93
    corporatist ideology 177–89
    distribution of Dáil seats 1948–87 32
    domains of identification 144–7
    election issues 1987 217–21
    finance and staffing 106–13
    historical overview 13–43
    ideological characteristics 138–206
    income and fund-raising 109–13
    index of class voting 1969–87 43
    indices of proportionality 1948–87 35
    inter-party distances 200
    involvement in government 1948–87 37
    mean scores and level of polarisation 176
    membership and branches 102–6
    organisation 94–137
    organisational style 114–27
    party emphases 1948–57 and 1961–82 157–69
    party movement 1961–82 189–92
    party programme 1961–82 147–56
    post-war trends 29–43
    revitalisation 127–37
    share of electoral vote 1948–87 30
    share of electoral vote and Dáil seats 1923–44 20
    share of electorate 1927–33 49
    social class and party support 1969 39; 1977–87 41–2
    strategy constraints 207–17
    structures 95–9
    voting percentages 1927–33 49
Labour Youth 102
Land Acts 21
land annuities 19

Latin America 177
law and order 156, 167, 174, 192, 193
Leinster 24,25
Leitrim 69, 70
Lemass, Séan 18, 55, 162, 183, 187, 188, 208, 215, 219
Lenihan, Brian 214
Lipset, S. M. 44, 45, 59, 135
Louth 70
Lynch, Jack 89, 178, 180, 215

MacBride, Séan 27, 28
McHale, V. E. 188, 189
Magill 213
Maguire, M. 210
Mair, P. 6
Malloy, J. M. 177, 181
Manoilesco 186
Marsh, M. 78, 89
Mayo East 119
Militant Tendency 102
Mother and Child Scheme 60
Munster 24, 25, 125
Murphy, C. 94

National Agriculture Party 24
National Committee of Labour Youth 102
National Conference 95, 98–9
National Council 96–8
National Delegate Conference 100
national effort 156, 167, 173, 174, 178, 180, 183, 195, 196
National Executive 95, 96, 99, 118
National Fund-Raising Collection 115
National Labour Party 23–4, 29, 53, 146
National League 16, 48, 88
National Progressive Democrats 31, 34
National Women's Conference 100
National Women's Council 99
National Youth Conference 96, 99, 102
nationalism 182
neo-corporatism 178
New Ireland Forum 146
new politics 171
non-nationalist parties 47
non-party voting 67
North Tipperary 112
Northern Ireland 14, 19, 28, 143, 183, 214, 216

O'Brien, Conor Cruise 180
Official Sinn Fein 31
Ógra Fianna Fáil 100, 129
Oireachtas 95, 97–9, 108, 109, 112, 183

O'Malley, Des 218

Parker, A. J. 69
partisan loyalists 85
partisan pragmatists 85
Partition 27–8
Party affiliation 68
    competition 47–55, 59–93, 142–4, 170–202, 224–5
    confidence 86
    dissidents 68
    divisions 138–206
    emphases 157–69
    identification 144–7
    ideological change 226
    loyalty 63
    membership 102–6
    movements 189–92
    organisation 94–137, 134–7, 224
    organisational style 114–27
    orientation 63
    programmes 147–56
    revitalisation 127–34
    -specific issues 166–9
    -system persistence and change 221
    strategy, constraints on 207–17
    structures 95–9
    systems, freezing of 223–4
    voting 67
Patterson, H. 55, 140, 187, 208
per capita income 21
Post Office Workers Union 101
productivity 156, 166, 167, 174, 180, 183
Progressive Democrats 1, 29, 31, 43, 80, 88, 137, 147, 163, 189, 215–18, 220, 225
protectionism 171, 173, 196
public employment 75
public policy 165
Public Sector Borrowing Requirement 212

Quadragesimo Anno 177
quality of life 156, 169, 171

redistributive issues 208–9
redistributive programme 212–13
Robertson, D. 141
Rokkan, S. 3, 44, 45, 59, 135
Rumpf, E. 88
Ryan, James 188

Sacks, P. M. 69, 121–2, 129
Sani, Giacomo 64, 141, 144, 145

Sartori, Giovanni 18, 59, 64, 141, 144, 145, 187
Schattschneider, E. E. 16
Shaber, S. 188, 189
Single Transferable Vote (STV) 61, 65, 227
Sinn Fein 13–16, 21, 29, 31, 42, 45, 46, 48, 50, 60, 134
Sinnott, R. 17, 87, 224
Sligo-Leitrim 69, 71
social citizenship 187
social class and party support 39–42
social-democratic ideology 184–9
social group interests 166, 167, 174, 192, 193
social harmony 156, 167, 173, 174, 178, 180, 183, 195
social justice 156, 165, 169, 170, 174, 175, 184
social services 156, 165, 167, 174, 192, 193
Socialist Labour Party 34, 58
Spirit of the Nation 179
staffing 106–13
system of channelment 59

Taoiseach 75
tariffs 19, 21
technology 156, 173
Trade Union movement 100, 101, 116
traditional morality 156, 215
traditional nationalism 193
Transport and General Workers Union 101

Ulster Unionists 45–6, 143

VAT 216
voter typology 85–6

Walsh, D. 215
welfarism 208, 209
Whyte, J. H. 8, 9, 39
Winkler, J. T. 177, 181, 186
Women's Advisory Council 102
Women's Group 101
Women's National Council 102
Workers Party 29, 31, 42, 58, 218–20
Workers Union 101

Young Fine Gael 100